Judaism Transcends Catastrophe
God, Torah, and Israel Beyond the Holocaust

Volume V

Faith Seeking Understanding
The Tasks of Twenty-first Century Judaism

Judaism Transcends Catastrophe
God, Torah, and Israel Beyond the Holocaust

Volume V

Faith Seeking Understanding
The Tasks of Twenty-first Century Judaism

Jacob Neusner
Editor

Mercer University Press
Macon, Georgia

ISBN 0-86554-519-7

Faith Seeking Understanding: The Tasks of Twenty-first Century Judaism

Edited and Introduced by
Jacob Neusner

Copyright 1996
Mercer University Press
Macon, Georgia

Library of Congress Cataloging-in-Publication Data

Judaism transcends catastrophe: God, Torah, and Israel beyond the Holocaust/
    Jacob Neusner, editor.
    x + 196 pp.   6 x 9" (15 x 23 cm.)
    Includes bibliographical references.
    Contents:
    v. 1. Faith renewed: the Judaic affirmation beyond the Holocaust
    v. 2. God commands.
    v. 3. The torah teaches.
    v. 4. Eternal Israel endures.
    v. 5. Faith seeking understanding : the tasks of twenty-first century Judaism.
    1. Holocaust (Jewish theology). 2. Holocaust, Jewish (1939–1945)—Influence.
    BM645.H6J83v.5   1994–1996   296.3'11   94-38718
        ISBN 0-86554-460-3 (v. 1)
        ISBN 0-86554-461-1 (v. 2)
        ISBN 0-86554-492-1 (v. 3)
        ISBN 0-86554-495-6 (v. 4)
        ISBN 0-86554-519-7 (v. 5)

Contents

Part One—Doing Theology in Judaism

Part Two—Three Long Perspectives on the Theology of Judaism beyond the Holocaust

Part Three—A Closing Affirmation

Preface

The polemic of this anthology, which is meant to be a highly crafted statement and not merely a collection of this and that, a political portrait of ephemerally important folk, is simply stated: "God after Auschwitz" endures as of old, and that is the God of Sinai, known to us through the Torah. Eternal Israel after Auschwitz has not only survived but remained faithful to its election, loyal to its covenant, and true to its vocation of exploring what it means to form a kingdom of priests and a holy people. To be born that eternal Israel, or to find a place in that Israel, for those who are there, abides God's ultimate act of grace: so eternal Israel has always affirmed, and so, whether in or after Auschwitz, eternal Israel today confesses. That confession and affirmation adumbrate not intellectual problems but spiritual mysteries; it is how life is defined and lived for me, and for all of us who embody in our time and place the remnant of that eternal Israel.

In this anthology, I mean to offer the reader the occasion to take up enduring issues of theology as Judaic theologians in our own day have framed those issues. For Christianity, as much as Judaism, formulates its religious experience in the theological categories represented here: (I) the encounter with God in history; (II) finding God in the world, or how we meet God in the here and now (here: God); (III) responding to revelation, or God's self-manifestation (here: Torah); (IV) forming the community of the faithful, in Christian language, the body of Christ (here: eternal Israel), as well as (V) theological thinking about theology. So far as the two religious traditions, Christianity and Judaism, are conceived within a single, shared structure, what Judaic thinkers define as their discipline and task bears relevance to Christian thinking about the same category, and the contrary also is the case. These are the issues of the five volumes:

(1) for the Holocaust in particular, how a religious reading of the massacre of millions of Jewish children, women and men has defined the issues of the last half of the twentieth century, the bases for the affirmation of God beyond the Holocaust (thus: "Judaism transcends catastrophe");

(2) for God, how we know God, where we meet God, the meaning of prayer, other forms of religious encounter and experience;

(3) for the Torah, the definition of the Torah as God's self-manifestation; the issues of how we mediate between the form of that manifestation, which is to say, writing of a particular age, and eternal truths that are made manifest;

(4) for Israel, we want to know how people have thought about the vocation and election of Israel, not only in the aftermath of the Holocaust and the foundation of the state of Israel, but in more enduring categories as well; and how these categories that endure—this is the way of life that God has given us for our service to God, this is the life of faith that we lead in the Torah—have formed a system for the interpretation of what happens in the here and now.

(5) for theology, the account of how theologians have defined their work, the program they have defined for their heirs, the philosophically-minded religious intellectuals of the coming century.

My purpose is to afford access for faithful Christian and Judaic readers to a kind of religious thinking and writing, profoundly Judaic in character, that is possessed of acute relevance but at the same time subjected to wasteful neglect. As I explain in the Introduction, people suppose that "after Auschwitz theology," or "post-Holocaust theology," must deal with only one question, which is, the problem of evil. But that supposition is only partly right, therefore entirely wrong. In fact, Judaic theology from 1945, all of its in one way or another a response to the catastrophe of the German murder of millions of Jews by reason of nothing they ever did but only what they were, which is, born of one Jewish grandparent.

No thinker whom we read in these pages wrote a single line in the oblivion of forgetting or ignoring the revelation of absolute evil that has taken place in our time. But the important thinkers, those whose writing will instruct the coming century, brought to the Holocaust the issues of transcendence, the classical categories and enduring doctrines of the Torah the world calls "Judaism." That is why I think it important to afford access here to moments of theological reflection that form in a variety of idioms and voices a single cogent work sustained, rigorous thought. In post-Holocaust writings I aim to show coherence, cogency, consistency; proportion and balance; authority and commanding mastery; in all, the classical tradition of Judaic theology as it has come to expression in diverse, authentic formulations in our time. I do so in the conviction that first-rate minds provide the rest of us with a model and a standard for our own religious thought, and much first-rate work is encompassed in these pages.

I address Christian as well as Judaic readers because the issues of Christian theology, framed in their own idiom to be sure, run along the same lines as those facing eternal Israel. We want to know what the world can reveal about God, so do they. We explore the responsibilities of the covenant with God that defines our being, so do they. We want to understand what it means to be "Israel," meaning, the people of God assembled before Sinai and children of Abraham, Isaac, and Jacob, and so, by their own word, do they. The dilemmas of faith and temptations of unbelief—how can an all-powerful God have made the world to be what it now is, for instance—confront us both. Judaism and Christianity share a common heritage of revelation, Judaism's written Torah (a term explained in the Introduction), and Christianity's Old Testament. Whatever one of us learns about God in the here and now and in revelation is going to lay claim upon the attention of the other, since by our own word both of us maintain that each party worships and loves the same, one and unique God (along with Islam).

That explains why I choose as my publisher a press conducted by academic colleagues who without apology stand for a clear and explicit religious position, and my publisher has chosen my work because of its comparable recognition that I here make an uncompromisingly religious statement. I take pride in presenting this anthology through the medium of this Southern Baptist university press; valuing the written Torah ("the Old Testament") as the word of God, just as eternal Israel does, that university and its press form an appropriate medium for an account of how God speaks in our place and time. And through theologians' intellect, as much as through saints' deeds and prayers, in responding, we answer the call that comes first and provokes response. Our response may not be the one God wants, but it is an authentic response to a call that, in the end, we maintain, comes to us from God.

Religious faith begins with God, not with us, for the world does not witness to God, but, more often than not, against Him. For me it follows that revelation, in the Scripture we share, the Torah/Bible, forms the beginning of our diverse religious thought. Theology for each of us follows rules of disciplined and rigorous reflection that God in the Torah/Bible has exemplified and that the words of God in the Torah/Bible embody. It is not for us to know why God has made the world the way it is, or to understand the reason why ancient Israel endures through the three great faiths that identify with it, rather than only through us, Israel after the flesh and (we think) the spirit too. But that is how it is, and how it has been for long enough, now, as to defy easy explanation. None of us conceives that theological negotiation is possible; each party believes its torah is the Torah, and that is how God has made us. That Baptists can find in an anthology of Judaic theology a work worthy of their publication forms a tribute to both the Baptists and the intellectual achievement of the theology of Judaism portrayed here. I do not know why God chooses to be heard in one way by Baptists in the Bible, in another way by Holy Israel in the Torah, but I do know that the faith of the Baptists and the steadfastness of holy Israel attest to the glory of one and the same God, and I honor their service as they mine.

This is no history of Judaism either, nor do I promise a thumb-nail account of how nearly two thousand years of thought took place prior to the last half of this century. Right at the outset, I lay out the issues of the Holocaust and then turn to the classical categories. But in each volume, I mean to offer perspective on the issues at hand. That is why I begin with a brief account of how, in the formative age of Judaism and its canon, catastrophe has elicited rational reflection, and, for volumes two through four, how the categories find definition: God, Torah, and Israel in the definitive documents of Judaism. In volume five, the counterpart is my own position on the next task in the theology of Judaism. In these opening statements I offer perspective on what is to follow.

Then I turn to the repertoire of writings on these same topics in our own time, not a survey of popular opinion, which is irrelevant to theology, but a re-presentation of informed thought, which embodies the theological voice. Each speaker is given a brief introduction, in which I explain what I find important in what is to be said.

Readers here take up not individual thinkers' whole systems, but specimens of thought of a number of thinkers on classical problems.

Since I have placed this anthology into the categorical context of Christian theology, I call attention to four other books co-authored by Bruce D. Chilton and myself, on the problem of comparative theology, the first three on the comparison of theological structures, the fourth on the comparison of theological systems, of Judaism and Christianity. These are as follows:

Christianity and Judaism: The Formative Categories. I. Revelation. The Torah and the Bible. Philadelphia: Trinity Press International, 1995.

Christianity and Judaism: The Formative Categories. II. The Body of Faith: Israel and Church. Philadelphia: Trinity Press International, 1996.

Christianity and Judaism: The Formative Categories. III. God in the World. Philadelphia: Trinity Press International, 1997.

Judaeo-Christian Debates. Communion with God, the Kingdom of God, the Mystery of the Messiah. Minneapolis: Fortress Press, 1997.

These works are free-standing but may prove of interest to Judaic and Christian readers interested in the comparison and contrast of the two great traditions of Scripture.

No work of mine can omit reference to the exceptionally favorable circumstances in which I conduct my research. I edited these three volumes as part of my labor of research scholarship, expressed through both publication and teaching at the University of South Florida, which has afforded me an ideal situation in which to conduct a scholarly life. I express my thanks for not only the advantage of a Distinguished Research Professorship, which must be the best job in the world for a scholar, but also of a substantial research expense fund, ample research time, and some stimulating and cordial colleagues. In the prior chapters of my career, I never knew a university that prized professors' scholarship and publication and treated with respect those professors who actively and methodically pursue research.

The University of South Florida, and all ten universities that comprise the Florida State University System as a whole, exemplify the high standards of professionalism that prevail in publicly-sponsored higher education in the U.S.A. and provide the model that privately-sponsored universities would do well to emulate. Here there are rules, achievement counts, and presidents, provosts, and deans honor and respect the University's principal mission: scholarship, scholarship alone—both in the class room and in publication. Here at last I find integrity, governing in the lives of people true to their vocation and their mission.

Jacob Neusner
Distinguished Research Professor of Religious Studies
University of South Florida, Tampa

Introduction

This five-volume anthology systematically presents how the enduring issues of the Judaic faith have transcended catastrophe and shaped the mind of the age beyond. The occasion—a half-century after the liberation of the remnant of suffering Israel, God's holy people, from the German death factories—invites the question, how has the faith, Judaism, recovered its voice? Or has that faith fallen silent, unable to speak beyond the abyss? We know the answer and here celebrate the fact of the renewal of holy Israel, God's people, in the faith of the Torah. That is what this set of theological anthologies proposes to spell out.

Now, had Israel then cast off its covenant with God and thrown its lot in with Satan, the rest of humanity would have deplored but understood its tragic end. But that is not what has happened. With the turning of the century and the daily passing of the generation that accomplished the physical feat of surviving, the time has come to take note of what has taken place among us all. An entire people, overcoming despair and renewing hope, embodied the faith of Job: even though He has slain so great a part of us, yet shall we all trust in Him. It is on that foundation, and only on that foundation, that holy Israel has surpassed death and tasted resurrection. Every faithful Jew who practices Judaism takes part in that resurrection—beyond the shadow of the valley of death, where, in ways we cannot understand, God was with us.

The Torah—the faith's own name for itself—governs holy Israel in God's compelling voice. Nothing has changed. The commanding voice of Sinai has overwhelmed the cacophony of death. For it is now clear that from 1945 to today we have witnessed one of the remarkable moments in the history of theology in the West, Judaic and Christian alike: the power of rigorous thought to think about events that in advance none could even have imagined. The theological minds of eternal Israel in our own day have met a challenge of which few in prior generations can have taken the measure. The Torah (or "Judaism") has triumphed, transcending radical evil, in classical terms, meeting Satan and through holy Israel affirming the living God made manifest in the Torah.

That is not to be taken for granted. Surveying the ruins of the ancient civilization of European Judaism, few imagined that the faith would renew itself, large parts of the Jewish people reaffirming despite and against it all that God rules, God loves. The past half-century has witnessed the unfolding of one of the great religious dramas of all time: how people survived evil beyond imagining and affirmed their heritage of faith. When Israel, the Jewish people, looked outward, around and backward, from 1945, so far as the eye could say lay ruins: villages and towns where the Torah had been proclaimed for a thousand years, now bereft of the presence of holy Israel; great cities, once vital with the vivid affairs of eternal Israel, now in ruins. With everything that flourished in 1939, homes, families, entire societies, now a mass of ashes and an empire of death, who can then have predicted what in fact took place? For it was not the mass-apostasy that the failure of faith would have provoked, but the determination, among religious Jews (Judaists) and secular ones alike, to reaffirm, renew, rebuild. What happened then was not to have been predicted at all: the rebirth of eternal Israel, the reaffirmation of its loyalty to God's word in the Torah, the renewal of faith in the one and only God of all ages. For not only did the remnants of the people, Israel, emerge from death factories where Satan ruled, they renewed their lives by forming a new political entity, the State of Israel, and by rebuilding throughout the world beyond the religious community of Israel that embodies Judaism, that is, the Torah, in the here and now.

Many find in the creation of the State of Israel the response of the people, Israel, to the Holocaust. And they surely find good reason for their view. But the challenge of the Holocaust to faith vastly outweighed the political crisis in which the Jewish people in Europe found itself. And it is here, in particular, that the remarkable renaissance of love for God and obedience to the Torah (variously construed to be sure) formed a response equal in power, but greater in weight and meaning, even to the political one involved in state-building. Israel, the holy people, did more than found the State of Israel. It also found its way to Sinai, once more taking up in these times, in this place, the yoke of the Kingdom of Heaven. Having emerged from the kingdom of Hell, this entire religious community now bears witness to the presence of the living God.

They affirmed the enduring covenant with God. They resumed the holy life of the faith. By word and deed they proclaimed the hope for the salvation of Israel and humanity through the Messiah. So the people Scripture sets forth as God's first love renewed its sustained, and sustaining, life of loving loyalty and obedience to God's Torah. Satan was vanquished by Israel's faith beyond the Holocaust. So, a calamity in many ways unique in history survived, Israel's remarkable rebirth marked the transcendence of catastrophe such as the world has seen only seldom. Why turn to theology to call attention to the renewal of religion? It is because in the profound reflections of the intellectuals of this religion the order, rationality, and coherence of events and faith emerge. Here we find not a narrow theodicy—beyond dogged faith, what theodicy is necessary, and facing the Holocaust, what theodicy is possible?—but a broad and nourishing theology of renewal.

To that religious experience of affirmation and rebirth, theology devotes its best intellectual energies in the pages of these five volumes. Here we see how the first-rate thinkers of the people, Israel, addressed the crisis of the day, on the one side, but also took up the disciplines and tasks of the classical theological heritage of the Torah, on the other. If no generation in the history of Judaism has confronted so critical a catastrophe, none was better served by its thinkers. Even our sages of blessed memory, who carried the Torah beyond the ruins of the Temple and reconstructed the kingdom of priests and the holy people through the Mishnah and the Talmud, accomplished no more towering achievement, nor did they face more intimidating obstacles to faith, than have the theologians of our own half-century.

The anthology shows the ways in which the important Judaic theologians writing in English have thought about the five issues that could not be avoided and had to be met head on: the defining hour of the Holocaust, then the three principal categories of the theological structure of Judaism: God, Torah, and Israel, meaning the eternal people to whom God spoke at Sinai, and then the challenge of the coming century. We here encounter not descriptions of opinion or historical accounts of what various people have thought about the Holocaust, God, Torah, and eternal Israel, and the tasks of theology for generations to come. Rather we read in their own words the theologians' propositions, arguments, passionate advocacy of particular positions. This is theology not recorded but lived in vivid intellects, how thoughtful, rigorous, demanding and restless minds have taken up the critical, anguished issues of a living faith at its time of crisis. The writers assembled here show diverse capacities of learning, acumen, perspicacity, and wit; some write one way, some another. But all of them do precisely what theologians in the traditions of Islam, Christianity, and Judaism are expected to achieve. That is the formulation in well-crafted prose of faith seeking understanding through processes of rationality; sustained and vigorous argument concerning the solution of conceptual problems of a religious character. More than mere philosophers of religion speaking about matters in general, mediating commanding revelation (for Judaism: the Torah) and rigorous, worldly reason, these writers reshape conviction and conscience into intellectually compelling statements of an entirely rational order.

A generation of theologians of Judaism, the one from World War II to the end of the Cold War, which faced the enormous intellectual challenges of the Holocaust, the founding of the State of Israel, now completes its work. The earlier figures, represented by the names of Berkowitz, Herberg and Heschel, have gone to their rest, and the later ones, represented by Borowitz, Fackenheim, and Vogel, now bring their thought to fruition and wisely undertake their valedictory statements. The next generation has yet to coalesce; we simply cannot at this time predict the shape and structure of thought; Judaic theology out of the most recent generation proves still ephemeral and has yet to find either its voice or its agenda. But in the moment of ebb tide, as the waters eddy and seek their new force, a backward perspective illuminates; we can at least take the measure of the high tide that has flowed out. So it is time to inquire into how rigorous religious intellectuals asked themselves the urgent questions precipitated by the greatest catastrophe Israel, the eternal people, has ever faced.

This anthology of five volumes about theological thinking about the Holocaust, God, Torah, and eternal Israel and Judaic theology of the second half of the twentieth century and beyond allows us to take stock of what has happened in the Judaic intellect. The anthology demonstrates that the classic and enduring—chronic in a healthy sense—issues of religious truth, not solely the critical and painful—acute—issue of evil and theodicy, elicited intelligent and profound thought over the past half-century. Not only so, but much that has been written endures as a legacy and a heritage for the thoughtful among the faithful in the century that is now dawning. It is meant to showcase important discussions on the principal categories of the theology of Judaism in the period from World War II to the end of the Cold War.

What makes such an anthology urgent is not only the passing of a generation. It is also that, in general, Jews present themselves as a wholly secular social entity, and the media of religious expression common among their Christian neighbors do not define how Jews make their religious statement. It is the simple fact that while the Jews are a social entity of a single religion, Judaism, or no religion at all (acceptance of any religion other than Judaism marks a person, in functional terms, as no longer part of the Jewish people), the proportion of Jews who also are Judaists, that is, practitioners of Judaism, varies but hardly encompasses the entire community. Not only so, but even among Judaists, serious encounter with the intellectual heritage of Israel takes place only in modest proportion. Faith without learning (an oxymoron in Judaic piety) is very common; faith surpassing understanding, which two generations from 1945 to the present in fact embodied, is not fully grasped.

God

It follows that, because of the prevailing secularity of the Jews' public discourse (and not merely its mediocrity), the modest place accorded to Judaists in the scheme of the Jews' ethnic existence, and the uncomprehending disdain for the reality of God's presence in and through eternal Israel, many, Jewish and gentile, have missed the astonishing intellectual events of our time. If attentive to the better publicized theological discourse, the more discerning will have judged the theological response to the Holocaust shallow and predictable. If God is all-powerful, then what does the Holocaust tell us about God? And if God is not all-powerful, then the Holocaust "proves" there is no God. So the issue of theodicy has exacted, and not only from theologians by any means, many sleepless nights. Many people now suppose that the only theological issue important in Judaism is theodicy, which is to say, theologies that focus upon "God after Auschwitz."

All Judaic theology from 1945 and onward, I think, for centuries to come, will have to qualify as "after-Auschwitz"-theology, not only for chronological reasons, but for substantive ones. We have learned facts about this world that, before the rule of Satan, we could never have conceived. A central religious task of rigorous thinking will always require confrontation with these facts, as much as, for the prophets, the demise of Northern Israel and the destruction of Jerusalem in 586 precipitated deep thought on how God acts in history. But what the catastrophe teaches, how eternal Israel has responded, the commanding voice of Sinai, the renewed encounter with the living God in prayer and acts of service—these all together form that theology in the shadow of the Holocaust. The reason is that, beyond the shadows, there has been much illumination: eternal Israel, responding to the living God, renewed its covenant in the Torah. That is the story of the rebirth of Judaism throughout the world, on the one side, and the message, too, of the theologians whom we meet in these five books. In an exact sense, for all who mourn for Israel's millions, murdered by the Germans from 1933 through 1945, every breath is an act of affirmation: we, Israel, choose to live, despite it all, because of the call of the One to whom we respond.

That is why all Judaic theology is a "Holocaust-theology." But few presently understand that every piece of religious expression, encompassing the entirety of Judaic theological writing, forms a response to the issue of the Holocaust; there is no other fact of transcendent religious character that compares in our time, or, many would maintain, in all time. Here I show a different picture. It encompasses not only the reaffirmation of God beyond the gates of Hell. It extends also to how thinkers have worked on a wide front, all of them under the shadow of the catastrophe of the Holocaust, but all of them engaged by classic issues and the revealed Torah. True, that statement contradicts how people presently assess the condition of eternal Israel and of Judaism. Any observer, following public life, would have supposed there has been paralysis in the encounter with the classic challenges to systematic thought.

I here make manifest that that is not the case. I show how thought has taken place in the main lines of theology of Judaism not despite the Holocaust nor solely in response to the Holocaust but in the renewal of the religious life of reflection in the aftermath of the Holocaust: how people mediated between new experience and received truth. The enduring categories of thought—God, Torah, Israel—continue to form the definitive outline of truth. For that forms the challenge to thought, which is to say, the religious mind transcends events and transforms them into enduring truth, making occasion into eternity. For the secular Jews, these questions come to formulation in secular speech: fiction, poetry, film, music; and they are given a secular articulation in politics and social thought. For the religious Jews there is yet another response. It takes two forms, the inchoate, profound expression of live as it is lived under the covenant with the Almighty: the life of faith and trust, hope, patience, and service, which the Torah teaches. And, it takes the second form of reflection on the meaning and truth of that life, reflection in the form of not only prayer or poetry or artful gesture, but sustained and rigorous thought, lucidly set forth in crafted prose. Secular Jews dominate the public square. But religious ones—Judaists, not only Jews—have also found voices, and in this anthology, these voices gain their hearing.

Israel

In this same context—the distinction between the secular and the religious in the life of the Jews—a further complication must be introduced. When in the theology of Judaism we speak of "Israel," we do not mean the State of Israel in particular but the eternal, holy people. That people, of whom Scripture speaks, to whom God gives the

Torah, of course encompasses the Jewish part of the population of the State of Israel, but it is not limited to that one sector of the Jewish people, not at all. In fact, the name, "Israel," bears a variety of meanings. In the Torah, "Israel" always speaks not of a place nor yet of a state but only, invariably, of the people Israel, the extended family of Abraham and Sarah, Isaac and Rebecca, Jacob and Leah and Rachel; the kingdom of priests and the holy people. In all Judaic theology, and in all Jewish ethnic writing, before 1948, when people spoke of "Israel" they meant the Jewish people. All other usages in which "Israel" appeared referred to the same sense, e.g., in Hebrew, "land of Israel," did not mean, "the land, Israel," but "the Land that belongs in particular to Israel, the people." In the liturgy of Judaic prayer, "Israel" refers to the elect people of Israel, to whom God gave the Torah, wherever they live; it does not refer to a particular place or to a particular group of Jews as distinct from all others.

The confusion between the received, theological meaning carried by the word "Israel" began in 1948, when the Jewish State, founded by the Zionist movement, to which, as a matter of fact, most of the Jews in the world and in the Land of Israel subscribed, called itself "the State of Israel." Now that formulation, "the State of Israel" by contrast quite properly speaks of the Jewish state, located in the Land of Israel (as the Jewish people have always known that place). When the Psalmist speaks of "The guardian of Israel does not slumber nor sleep," he means, of course, "the guardian of the holy people," and not "the guardian of the Land of Israel," or obviously of "the political entity, the State of Israel." "Israel" as the holy people to whom God revealed the Torah, identified in the here and now as Israel the Jewish people, obviously should not to be confused with the contemporary State of Israel, a this-worldly fact, to be sure bearing profound religious meaning to Judaism. Since people refer to the State of Israel simply as "Israel," I distinguish the State of Israel from the holy people of Israel of whom the Torah speaks by referring to the latter as "eternal Israel." That will sidestep the difficulties in sense and meaning brought about by calling a secular state by a name that bears its own, distinct theological referent.[1]

So it is time to distinguish the ethnic from the religious, the secular from the theological, out of the voices of a half-century of pained and anguished reflection upon, not merely response to, the catastrophe of the ages that took place between 1933 and 1945. For those who see Israel not as an ethnic group alone but as God's people, those who interpret the world not in its own terms alone, but as testimony to the Almighty, those who distinguish this world's facts from eternal truths, those who view humanity "in our image, after our likeness," the issues surpass ethnic testimony about sound social policy or political action. Judaists, without apology, without shame, see the world under the aspect of God's rule, find in the Torah surpassing truth, appreciate the Israel of this world in its transcendent setting.

Torah

The profoundly secular character of the Jews' public life and therefore shared discourse in the USA and Europe obscures the equally deep, rooted religious faith of Judaists' inner life. This book and its companions give testimony to the living faith, Judaism—which calls itself "the Torah," which sees itself as the "Israel" of which the Torah speaks and which identifies itself as the statement of the eternal God, creator of heaven and earth, ruler of all worlds, and ultimate redeemer of humanity. Specifically, they show how Judaic thinkers, rooted in the absolute and unshakable givenness of God's presence in history and rule over Israel, responded in rigorous, rational, theological ways to the defining moments of our day.

Theology in this context refers to systematic and rigorous reflection on religious questions; faith seeking understanding through processes of rationality; sustained and vigorous argument concerning the solution of conceptual problems of a religious character. In Judaism, theology has taken a variety of forms, important ideas expressing themselves through patterns of behavior as much as through propositions of belief. But in times past, and in our own day, rigorous and systematic religious thought has yielded a harvest of sustained, proportioned, coherent theological writing. This anthology means to portray how Judaic theology in the past half-century has conducted its work of making sense of the world measured by the dimensions of

(1) the Holocaust events themselves
(2) the revealed Torah
(3) the one, unique, and only God who is made manifest in the Torah at Sinai
(4) the eternal, holy nation, Israel, God's first love
(5) the presence, in eternal Israel, of rigorous, philosophically-insistent intellects and their theological program for time to come.

Knowing what we have learned in this awful century, how do we read the Torah, think about the power and mercy of God, make sense of the mystery of Israel? And what tasks face us in the coming generation?

The Holocaust: What makes the theological adventure of Judaic religious thought compelling and of broad interest to a wide audience of religious faithful, Christian and Judaic alike, over the past fifty years? The gates of the death factories, built by the Germans in World War II, closed finally in 1945. No event in the history of humanity bears more profound implications for our understanding of Torah, Israel, and God, not the fall of Man and Woman, not the Golden Calf, not the exile of the lost tribes, not the destruction of the Temple in 586 B.C.E., nor again in 70, not the massacre of Rhineland Jewries in the First Crusade, nor the expulsion of the Jews from Spain, nor the advent of Communism, nor the empowerment of Fascism and Nazism. Seen by themselves or all together, these turnings in time made sense on the received cartography of the known ways, God's and humanity's. But the received solutions to the problem of evil—Job's or Jeremiah's for instance—for many proved insufficient, incommensurate to what now has happened. Consequently, Judaic thinkers writing in the American language faced a challenge of reflection, critical thought, and sustained, rigorous intellection. Some directed their attention to the problem of evil and the issue of theodicy.

God, Torah, Israel

But others took up the ancient discipline of rationality in quest of religious truth and broadened the discussion. The Holocaust for them presented the occasion, even the provocation. But it did not define the issues. These, for eternal Israel, had been determined at Sinai, when, God having made the world and brought Israel into being and assembled the holy people before the mountain, completed the trilogy by giving the Torah. Creation, revelation, redemption defining the workings of the unfolding system that Sinai set forth, God, Torah, and Israel constituted the structure by which all reality, here and above, natural and supernatural, would be ordered. So for those who surpassed the occasion, the Holocaust stood for a new beginning in the unending encounter, in intellect, with the living God of Sinai's Torah.

Now, a half-century later, it is time to take stock of the work of a generation that has run its course. Clearly, two distinct kinds of theology require attention, "Holocaust-theology," and "theology that takes account of the Holocaust." The former, as is clear, rightly insist that all thought within the Torah find its defining program in the catastrophe of 1933–1945 (whether or not completed by the miracle of 1948 to the present day represented by the creation of the State of Israel, the Jewish state, in the Land of Israel). The latter carry forward the classical program of Judaic theological thought—how to live the holy life that God has commanded to covenanted Israel, how to reflect intelligently on the defining categories of that sanctified community's existence, God, Torah, Israel. Among these latter thinkers, the Holocaust found full recognition; but those events were not permitted to silence thought or impose upon the full and transcendent program of intellectual reflection constraints of what are, ultimately, an adventitious character. For they did not permit episodes to define eternal issues, but only to contribute new facts to the contemplation of those issues. So far as the Holocaust contained defining moments on the character of humanity and the holiness of Israel, it was to make, and it did make, its full, ample, and necessary contribution. But the Holocaust for this second set of writers, the more classical ones in education and sensibility, was to be faced within the received and eternal framework of the Torah.

The Theological Adventure in Contemporary Judaism

Ample evidence, part of which is laid out in these five anthologies, demonstrates that, transcending catastrophe, great intellects of Judaism accomplished two remarkable tasks of an intellectual character, and they did so forthrightly and courageously.

First, they faced head-on what came to be called "the Holocaust." A formidable corpus of writing by systematic thinkers of Judaism took up the problems of religious belief presented by the events of 1933–1945, when millions of Jews, men and women and upwards of a million children, were murdered by reason of not their faith but the mere fate of having been born into a Jewish family. In fiction, poetry, film, music, as well as in the media of sustained and rigorous thought in the form of ideas carefully crafted and persuasively set forth, the issue of the catastrophe was framed. Certainly, no generation has ever confronted a more insistent or formidable challenge than finding ways to think theologically about the unthinkable.

The faithful of Christianity and Judaism alike have found in the results not only important religious ideas, commensurate to the enormous dimensions of the challenge, but also the occasion for the renewal of faith. That is why the religious response to the Holocaust has rightly won for itself so rich a response of public appreciation. These anthologies do not have to provide a reprise of that protracted chapter in post-Holocaust theology of Judaism. But within the demanding discipline of reasoned thought about religious questions that theology comprises, a specific, theological formulation of matters was set forth. And that has to be appreciated to make sense of everything else. The achievement of the theologians—as distinct from philosophers, poets, film makers, composers, novelists, moralists, and publicists—was to insist that the Holocaust ask not a thin question of theodicy, but a thick question of encounter: God was there, the Torah was there, with eternal Israel in Auschwitz.

Second, some of these same thinkers and others as well in the same period, under the shadow of the same tremendous events, furthermore took up the received agenda of Judaic theology, that is, the program of mediating between revelation, the Torah, and the present hour that defines the work of theology in that religious tradition. From the formation of the classical and authoritative writings of Judaism, called all together "the Torah," to our own day, each generation has taken up the labor of making its own what the ages had handed on, the fundament of faith for which the Torah stands. The past half-century has witnessed a remarkable display of how enduring and historically-rooted intellectual traditions have taken over and made their own the newest of humanity's, and eternal Israel's, discoveries. When thinking about God, Torah, and Israel, the three generative categories of thought, the Judaic theologians took up an age-old discipline of continuous reflection, always aware of the catastrophe in Europe, but never struck dumb by it. This corpus of religious thinking of a rigorous character in Judaism shows us how Judaism not only faced the Holocaust but also, through appeal to enduring theological disciplines, transcended it as well. And it is to that labor of intellectual transcendence that these three anthologies are devoted.

What justifies the work in the proportions that characterize these anthologies—the Holocaust forming only part of the portrayal of the encounter with God in our time —is simple. While ready access to the first of the two massive enterprises of Judaic theology, both in its conventional form and in the unconventional formulations of the second half of the twentieth century, is easily gained in numerous and widely-appreciated works, to the second labor, the more classical, few have afforded an opening. That is to say, we may readily find anthologies of Judaic theological and Jewish ethnic responses to the Holocaust, and many of these have rightly enjoyed a massive hearing. But the paramount status rightly accorded to the theological challenge of the Holocaust has tended to obscure this other kind of theology that the generation beyond the Holocaust has formulated.

That is the theology that has continued the ages-old discussion of the enduring issues of Judaic faith to which the greater part of these volumes is devoted. Theologians of mighty power met the challenge, only to find their work neglected in favor of other kinds of expression, because of the paramount secularity characteristic of the Jewish world. For the secular taste, the Holocaust validated atheism; God could not stop those events, so is not God; or God could stop them but did not, so is evil. For the religious perception, God is always, everywhere, eternally God, without qualification, condition, or apology. In the context of the iron, incorruptible faith of eternal Israel since its origins, silence before the unknowable hardly defined a task beyond accomplishment. So the secular reading of the Holocaust prevailed in public life.

But of course for those of us who find our being in God's Israel and the purpose of our being in God's Torah, the Holocaust is reduced in its dimensions when treated as an event only in this world's terms. So reading the Holocaust in the narrowly political, secular, and ethnic reading of the catastrophe—or in terms essentially secular people assume pertain to theology impoverishes. More happened at Auschwitz and the other capitals of evil embodied than this world contains. And we have known the reality of pure evil from of old; for our paradigm, if there is no ultimate evil, there also is no meaning to the ultimate redemption. And God is diminished. But in the structure of a this-worldly reading of existence that predominates in Israel, the Jewish people, as distinct from eternal Israel in the here and now, how the received, enduring dimensions of the Torah are to be measured has scarcely attracted attention.

Theodicy

The issues of religious encounter with the living God that religious Jews—practitioners of Judaism, called Judaists—find urgent but secular, ethnic Jews scarcely acknowledge are not addressed in theodicy alone, or in declarations that there was a God but he died in Auschwitz and similar formulations. Consequently, when people take up the examination of the theology of Judaism in the generation now completing its work, they take for granted one issue defines discourse. That issue is the one of theodicy, framed as "God after Auschwitz." People have taken for granted that, when we turn to theology, all we shall discuss is what we can know about God in light of the revelations of systematic murder of the people, Israel, in Europe. That is a legitimate issue; it is not the only one.

It is a broadly held impression that, in the aftermath of the murder of nearly six million Jews in Europe in world war II and also the creation of the State of Israel, the theology of Judaism has given itself over to the enormous problem of theodicy presented by the former, and the political concerns defined in response to the creation and maintenance of the latter. So God is no longer God in creation, revelation, and redemption, as Judaism has always encountered God. God is now subject to human judgment, requiring explanation and defense. But we in holy and eternal Israel have known more about God than the works of this day's history. We have defined our existence in more dimensions than the political and the empowered. Not only so, but theologians, who undertake in each generation to mediate the Torah to the acutely-present moment, have set forth rigorously argued systems, or components of systems, that provide rational and philosophically-defensible re-presentations of the received and revealed Torah of Sinai.

It is time to right the balance. That is not by an opposite and equal distortion, namely, re-presenting the theology of Judaism in the last half-century under the aspect of Sinai but not of Auschwitz. No theologian of Judaism has imagined such a vision; it were folly. All theologians of Judaism from 1945 onward have written in full consciousness of the events of 1933 to 1945, and every one of them in every line acknowledged those events. No religious thinking in Judaism has aimed at obscuring or diminishing the dreadful power of the ultimate revelation of evil—the counterpart and opposite of Sinai. But all of those represented in these pages have conducted the theology of Judaism in a different way.

The Holocaust-theologians start where they finish: at Auschwitz, The theologians who transcend catastrophe and move, as time moves, beyond the Holocaust, conduct their thought in a different realm. They surpass calamity and transcend the Holocaust by continuing the ancient and lasting conversation with the Torah, speaking of this morning's headlines in the language of eternity. Specifically, theologians who carry on beyond the Holocaust do so by placing that theology of Judaism in its own, enduring context, under the aspect of Sinai that of course illuminates all life, all time, all being, even unto death. What some have called "the commanding voice of Auschwitz" then is taken in to the commanding voice of Sinai. In this setting, one immense event casts its shadow over all that has come before and over all that will follow; but it is not the whole of time, nor does it set forth the entirety of truth.

Theology

I have throughout used a term not defined at all, "theology." An entire volume in this anthology, the final one, is devoted to the Judaic definition of theology. But to begin with, we turn to the definition of the particular kind of thinking that is represented in these anthologies: theological thinking, not philosophy, not "Jewish thought" (which rarely is defined but generally means, Jews thinking about Jewish things), and not history, literature, or anything else but itself.

To state matters simply: theology philosophically sets forth religion. That statement paraphrases the definition of Ingolf U. Dalferth,

> Theology is not philosophy, and philosophy is not a substitute for religious convictions. But whereas religion can exist without philosophy, and philosophy without religion, theology cannot exist without recourse to each of the other two. It rationally reflects on questions arising in pre-theological religious experience and the discourse of faith; and it is the rationality of its reflective labor in the process of faith seeking understanding which inseparably links it with philosophy. For philosophy is essentially concerned with argument and the attempt to solve conceptual problems, and conceptual problems face theology in all areas of its reflective labors.[2]

Accordingly, by the definition of theology that is before us, what we here examine is contemporary Judaic theologians' systematic and rigorous reflection on religious questions; faith seeking understanding through processes of rationality; sustained and vigorous argument concerning the solution of conceptual problems of a religious character.

To understand the claim of this anthology, a clear definition of theology is required at the very outset. For that purpose I reverse the elements of the definition provided by Dalferth. The predicate becomes the subject in this way:

> (1) *where* we have rational reflection on questions arising in religious experience and the discourse of faith,
> (2) *there* we have theology.

When we find reflective labor on the rationality—the cogency, harmony, proposition, coherence, balance, order, and proper composition—of statements of religious truth, *e.g.*, truth revealed by God, then we have identified a theological writing. In these pages I present numerous, sustained examples of reflective labor on the rationality of statements of religious truth and consequence:

> God commands.
> The Torah teaches.
> Eternal Israel endures.

Those three theologoumena encompass the entire theology that Judaism has maintained and today sustains as God's truth. They form Judaism in its theological manifestation.

Concern with argument, the attempt to solve conceptual problems—these characterize that writing. By themselves, of course, they do not mark a writing as theological. Argument concerning conceptual problems yields theology when the argument deals with religion, the conceptual problems derive from revelation. Only the source of the givens of the writing—revelation, not merely reasoned analysis of this world's givens—distinguishes theology from philosophy, including, as a matter of fact, philosophy of religion. But that suffices.

To make this point clear, let me refer to the canonical documents and how they make their points. Take for example that splendid formulation of religion as philosophy, the Mishnah. The Mishnah states its principles through method of natural history, sifting the traits of this-worldly things, demonstrating philosophical truth—the unity of one and unique God at the apex of the natural world—by showing on the basis of the evidence of this world, universally accessible, the hierarchical classification of being. That is a philosophical demonstration of religious truth. The Talmud of Babylonia states its principles through right reasoning about revealed truth, the Torah. The Torah (written, or oral) properly read teaches the theological truth that God is one, at the apex of the hierarchy of all being. That is a theological re-presentation of (the same) religious truth. But that re-presentation in the two Talmuds (and in the Midrash-compilations, not treated here) also exhibits the traits of philosophical thinking: rigor, concern for harmonies, unities, consistencies, points of cogency, sustained argument and counter-argument, appeal to persuasion through reason, not coercion through revelation. In our time, as through the past centuries, in Judaism, the methods of philosophy applied to the data of religious belief and behavior produced theology. The method of philosophy shapes the message of religion into a re-statement characterized by rationality and entire integrity.

Since I have made reference to the received and classical documents of Judaism, a very brief account of the sources out of which all authentic Judaism thought proceeds is here required. That is important for the understanding of the opening chapter of each of these volumes, which provides the starting point of all Judaic theological thought, which is, the canonical definition of the several categories that form Judaism. A brief account of that authoritative canon must start with the end-product, which is, the Torah as defined at the end of the formation of Judaism.[3] For many people, both Christian and Jewish, take for granted that "Judaism" is pretty much the same thing as "the Old Testament," and if they know the word "Torah" at all, they mean by it "the Pentateuch," the Five Books of Moses, Genesis, Exodus, Leviticus, Numbers, and Deuteronomy.

But Judaism is no more the religion of the Old Testament alone than Christianity is the religion of the New Testament alone. "Torah" for Judaism is the counterpart to "Bible" for Christianity. Just as Christianity reads the Old Testament in the light of the New, so Judaism reads what it knows as "the written Torah" in the complementary and fulfilling setting of "the oral Torah." So to understand the enduring conversations about religious truth that theologian of Judaism conducts, we have to acquire a very exact knowledge of the sources of religious truth that the Torah comprises. What then is this "Torah" that forms "the Bible" for Judaism?

It is the Torah in two media, written and oral. That Torah, called in due course "the one whole Torah of Moses, our rabbi," was formulated and transmitted by God to Moses in two media, each defining one of the components, written and oral. The written is Scripture as we know it, encompassing the Pentateuch, Prophets, and Writings. The oral part of the Torah came to be written down in a variety of works, beginning with the Mishnah, ca. 200 C.E. The canon of the Judaism the theology of which is described here is made up of extensions and amplifications of these two parts of the Torah. The written part is carried forward through collections of readings of verses of Scripture called Midrash-compilations. The oral part is extended through two sustained, selective commentaries and expansions, called talmuds, the Talmud of the Land of Israel, a.k.a. the Yerushalmi (ca. 400 C.E.), and the Talmud of Babylonia, a.k.a., the Bavli (ca. 600 C.E.).

In literary terms, then, the formation of Judaism reached its fruition in extensions of the oral Torah and the written Torah. For the oral Torah, the formative age came to its conclusion when the Talmud of Babylonia set forth the theological statement of Judaism by expressing the religious convictions of the Talmud of the Land of Israel in accord with a profound reconsideration of the philosophical norms of the Mishnah, ca. 200. C.E. Joining the method of the Mishnah to the messages of the prior Talmud, the framers of the second Talmud thereby defined the theological, including the legal, norms of Judaism. For the written Torah, the Midrash-compilations of the successive ages, corresponding to the two Talmuds and associated with them, carry forward the same modes of discourse and express in their ways the same hermeneutics.

The Talmuds' distinctive hermeneutics, which contains within itself the theology of the Judaism of the dual Torah, is exposed not in so many words but in page-by-page repetition; it is not articulated but constantly (even tediously) instantiated; we are then supposed to draw our own conclusions. The unique voice of the second of the two Talmuds, the Talmud of Babylonia, which bears that hermeneutic, speaks with full confidence of being heard and understood; and that voice is right; we never can miss the point. For the hermeneutic itself—insistence on the presence of philosophy behind jurisprudence, law behind laws, total harmony among premises of discrete and diverse cases pointing to the unique and harmonious character of all existence, social and natural—properly understood, bears the theological message: the unity of intellect, the integrity of truth.

As the Mishnah had demonstrated the hierarchical classification of all natural being, pointing at the apex to the One above, so the second Talmud demonstrated the unity of the principles of being set forth in the Torah. The upshot is that Judaism would set forth the religion that defined how humanity was formed "in our image, after our likeness," not to begin with but day by day: in the rules of intellect, the character of mind. We can be like God because we can think the way God thinks, and the natural powers of reason carry us upward to the supernatural origin of the integrity of truth—that sentence sums up what I conceive to be the theological consequence of the Talmud's hermeneutics.

The Talmud of Babylonia therefore forms the pinnacle and the summa—what we mean when we speak of "Judaism"—because from the time of its closure to the present day it defined not only Judaic dogma and its theological formulation but also Judaic discourse that carried that dogma through to formulation in compelling form. Not only so, but the entire documentary heritage of the first six centuries of the Common Era was recast in that Talmud. And that body of writing was itself a recapitulation of important elements of the Hebrew Scriptures and in its basic views indistinguishable in theological and legal character from elements of the Pentateuch's and Prophets' convictions and requirements. Scripture itself ("the written Torah") would reach coming generations not only as read in the synagogue on the Sabbath and festivals, but also, and especially, as recast and expounded in the Talmud in the school houses and courts of the community of Judaism.

Other received documents that had reached closure during that long period of time—the Mishnah, the Tosefta, the Talmud of the Land of Israel itself, the score of Midrash-compilations—furthermore flowed into the Talmud of Babylonia. So each prior writing found its proper position, in due proportion, within the composite of the Bavli. And the Bavli made of the entire heritage of the revealed Torah, oral and written, not a composite but a composition, whole, proportioned, coherent. That is what I mean by, "the Talmudic re-presentation," that is, the second Talmud's re-presentation of the Torah given by God to our rabbi, Moses, at Mount Sinai.

That re-presentation was accomplished through one medium: a governing, definitive hermeneutics, the result of applied logic and practical reason when framed in terms of the rules of reading a received and holy book. I need not hide my conviction that the persuasive power of the Talmud's hermeneutics explains the Talmud's success in taking the primary position in the canon of Judaism. That conviction admittedly is subjective, resting as it does on the unprovable premise that ideas and attitudes account of conduct and social policy. But it is the indubitable fact that the second Talmud effected the re-presentation of all that had gone before. Given the Talmud's priority of place among all Judaic writings, before and since for all time, I set forth an objective fact when I maintain that the Talmud also stated in its distinctive way, through its particular hermeneutics, the authoritative theology of the Judaism for which it formed the summa. Religious belief and right behavior to express that belief

—both would find definition in its pages, exposition and exegesis in accord with its modes of analytical thought. With the Bavli, the theological text had been inscribed; all the rest was commentary.[4] The commentary would flourish from then to now; the exegesis of that exegesis would define the future history of Judaism.

For the later history of Judaism, from late antiquity to the present day, theology would take a distinctive, and I think, unique form. It provoked rigorous argument, rather than merely laying out well-defined propositions. In this way it guided the conduct of theological thought, rather than merely defining its propositions and syllogistic goals. When the sages of Judaism chose to make their statements of norms, they began in the Talmud, worked within its categories, framed their ideas in accord with its intellectual discipline, and spoke in its language about its problems. They did so in the (descriptively-valid) conviction that the Talmud had made the full and authoritative statement of the Torah of Sinai, oral, covering the Mishnah and Midrash-compilations, and written, covering Scripture, as well. That is why everything to come would validate itself as a commentary to the text set forth by the Talmud out of all the prior texts that all together comprised the Torah.

It remains to explain that a well-known Judaism is not treated here. Specifically, In this setting, I do not address "the Judaism of Holocaust and Redemption," which from 1967 to the very recent past enjoyed enormous power in the life of American Jews. It was the Judaic religious system formed around the events of the Holocaust in Europe and the creation of the State of Israel, and held that the principal task of the Jews (not "eternal Israel") is to remain Jewish (without a supernatural definition of what that meant, that is, without a Judaism) and to support through political and philanthropic activity the State of Israel. It was enormously influential among American Jews, accounting to them why they should remain different from gentiles, but defining the difference in this-worldly terms, with no bearing on the conduct of everyday life and affairs. Profoundly secular in every way, that Judaism elicited the kind of devotion that, under other circumstances, religions ordinarily do.

But as a matter of fact, by any definition of religion and theology, that Judaism was no religion and had no theology. It was, and in its surviving pockets still is a chapter of the politics and sociology of Jewish Americans, itself an element in the politics and sociology of Americans in general. "Holocaust and Redemption" writing has no place in the theology of Judaism, except as rigorous theologians have transformed the issues, as they have, into the occasion for profound theological reflection. "The Judaism of Holocaust and Redemption" formed a Judaic system—an account of the way of life, world view, and definition of the social entity of a particular version of "Israel," but even though powerful in Reform and Conservative Judaisms, it was not a Judaic religious system, lacking as it did a serious confrontation with God and with issues of transcendence and holiness.[5]

Clearly, my focus is on issues of faith seeking understanding, the rational, philosophical construction of religious belief. It is not on the facts of who said what; I do not describe what pretty much everybody has thought, and I entirely ignore the institutional embodiments of the faith in the partisan seminaries and organizations of synagogues, e.g., Reconstructionist, Orthodox, Reform, Conservative, humanistic, and the like. In these pages the sects of contemporary Judaism play no role at all, because the issues that divide them are trivial and personal. Not only so, but locally-important theologians are not surveyed, since the criteria of selection emphasize the excellence of thought, not the ephemeral influence of the thinker. None of the worldly facts of episodic popularity bears theological consequence; all form mere accidents of local politics and sociology.

Episodically-famous personalities, joined to such institutions and occasions of ritual celebration by them, mean nothing. Mediocrity lays no claim upon the future. We are not here to celebrate platitudes and banalities. Conventional thinking fails the challenges of classical faith, and routine and full minds do not require a hearing that is not compelled by politics. Writers in the English language, and those whose works translated into English, that are not treated here are not neglected; they are rejected. Nor do I choose to pay attention to what by the standards of the Torah are simply heresies, on the one side, or rationalizations for apostasy, on the other. That is why I ignore some local icons, whose writing I find merely homiletical, on the one side, and theologians whose theology consists of the announcement that there is no God, on the other. For different reasons, neither class of theologians of Judaism deserves a hearing when the faithful come together rigorously to analyze the faith.

At stake here are issues alone. And I should maintain the catholic character of the writing, coming as it does from theologians identified with Orthodox, Reform, Conservative, and other Judaisms, resident in the English-speaking world or overseas, justifies that decision. Here are no party platforms nor partisan voices, celebrated here but unknown there, but rather, sober efforts at purveying truth—God's truth, so far as, in this world, we gain access to it. That is why this anthology presents not a historical-biographical repertoire covering everybody who was around at that time, but a sampler of vivid thinking and provocative, engaged writing. I bear sole responsibility for the judgments represented by inclusion and exclusion; nothing is tacit.

I have chosen writing that means to persuade, not merely inform; writing from heart to heart; writing that sets forth in the medium of words a deeply-felt religious sentiment, attitude, emotion, or conviction. In these pages readers meet embodiments of faith, hope, love for God, in the words of exemplary figures. That is why readers may expect to be not merely informed as to information but invited to participate in the thought and argument of interesting minds on important questions. When people go to a museum formed as a storehouse, they acquire information; they are left inert and unchanged. But when they go to a museum designed to teach, instruct, and engage, they enter into the experience of what is placed on display. They are affected and changed. Here they describe in vigorous advocacy of propositions, fully analyzed, amply documented, the encounter with God that has brought regeneration and renewal after the unparalleled catastrophe of our century.

Endnotes

[1] I have spelled out the many meanings imputed to "Israel" in various Judaic religious systems in my *Judaism and its Social Metaphors. Israel in the History of Jewish Thought* (New York: Cambridge University Press, 1988).

[2] Ingolf U. Dalferth, *Theology and Philosophy* (Oxford: Basil Blackwell Ltd., 1988) vii.

[3] By "Judaism" throughout these pages I mean one Judaic system in particular, the Judaism of the dual Torah, oral and written. The canon of that Judaism in particular is what is described in this and following paragraphs. Other Judaic systems have flourished and do today. Here the focus is upon the system that predominated and now continues, in a variety of modulations, to define Judaism for most practitioners of (a) Judaism, and to provide a principal source for all the others. That operative definition is descriptive, of course. All of the Judaic theologians represented in this anthology appeal to that one canonical literature and acknowledge its authority and authenticity as represented of God's revelation to eternal Israel.

[4] We of course should not ignore the fact that the labor of extension, amplification, application, and commentary in the richest sense went forward, and now goes forward, in a variety of directions. But no contemporary Judaic system begins elsewhere than in the Talmud and the oral part of the Torah represented by it. In the seminaries of all Judaic systems, and in the synagogues of all contemporary Judaisms, the Torah is presented in both the written and the oral components, though, I hasten to add, different Judaisms take up, each its own position on what fits into that entire Torah and how the Torah ia to be received and re-presented.

[5] Reading that Judaism in its correct, secular framework, I have dealt with that matter at some length in *Stranger at Home. Zionism, "The Holocaust," and American Judaism* (Chicago: University of Chicago Press, 1980).

Chapter 1

The Tasks of Theology in Judaism

Jacob Neusner

The principal task of theology in Judaism is to draw out and make explicit the normative statements of the acknowledged sources of Judaism and to learn how to renew discourse in accord with these norms. Theology's task, specifically, is to delineate the worldview shaped within the experience and aspirations of the community of Judaism and to perceive the world within that view. The goal is that, in time to come, the sight of ages to come may be yet more perspicacious too. (1) Vision received, (2) vision reformed, (3) vision transmitted—these are the tasks of theology in Judaism.[1]

1. Vision Received

The beginning of the work is to state what it is that Judaism teaches, to define both its principal concerns and its methods of expressing its ideas. The work of definition is to discover what it is that theology to begin with wishes to say. This descriptive task—the perception of the vision received—is theological in its purpose. But it requires the disciplines of hermeneutics, history of religions, and history. The tasks of theology in Judaism will be carried out at the intersecting frontiers among these useful disciplines, even though, as I shall explain, merely working along lines laid out by them will not yield a significant theological result.

Let us start with hermeneutics. The reason to begin here is that, when we wish to define Judaism, we first have to locate and encompass the whole range of texts that find a place in the canon of Judaism. For to define a religion is to state the substance of its canon, that is, to spell out the canonical ideas found in the canonical literature. And, second, the work of coming to grips with that range of canonical texts with which the theologian of Judaism must reckon is an exercise in the exegesis of exegesis. The theologian has to explain how these texts have been so read as to be received as everywhere pertinent. For Judaism is a religion of great age and diversity. To uncover the fundament of ultimate conviction everywhere present, and to do so with full reverence for diversity in the history of Judaism, we have to look for what is ubiquitous. And that, I think, is the process and the method: how things are made to happen ubiquitously and consistently. Discernment of process yields the rules that we may extract from the happening and the substantive convictions that lie behind the rules. For when we ask about process and method, our interest is not simply in formal, but also in substantive traits. Axiomatic to the "how" of process and method is the "what" of substance, the elements of worldview that generate both the process and the method.

At this stage in the work, the theologian's task is not to declare the truth. The truth, Judaism everywhere holds, is revealed in Torah. Truth, therefore, is to be discovered in Torah. The theologian has to locate that point, within the intellectual structure of the faith, at which discovery may take place. The work is to lay out the lines of the truth, the frontiers of Torah. Now if, in the present age, we take seriously the commonplace proposition that Judaism is a way of life, we are not going to find it easy to choose those people whose way of life defines Judaism and reveals Torah. The diversity among the Jews as a group is too great. Some Jews do not see themselves as engaged in an essentially religious mode of being at all. Others, whom we shall have to call by a separate name, Judaists, do see themselves as participants in a religious mode of being, Judaism. These religious Jews are themselves diverse. The way of life of all those who are Judaists is not uniform. In this regard, therefore, the sustained effort to uncover the fundament of the true faith by description of the way of life of the Judaists is fruitless. The status quo does not contain within itself the fundament of the true faith. To turn the way of life into a statement of theology or a source for deeper meaning is hopeless. All we should gain is a statement—at best— of culture. Once we admit that fact, we no longer have the choice of speaking of Judaism as a way of life in a this-worldly and merely descriptive sense. If, on the other hand, we turn to historical descriptions of the "authentic" way of life of Judaism, for instance, the *Shul ḥ an ʿArukh,* we no longer speak of the way of life of all of the living at all, but of a holy book that is part of a holy canon. We might, therefore, just as well turn forthwith to the canon. Or, to state matters more bluntly, Judaism is not going to be described by sociology. But Judaism must be described and interpreted.[2]

And yet, how the holy books are to be read for the work of theology is not clear. They already have been read for a very long time, and remarkably little theology has come forth. The work of definition remains primitive. So, clearly, the canon has to be read in some way other than the way in which, under the current auspices, it presently is read. The established hermeneutics of *yeshivot* and Talmud departments, and of philosophers of Judaism and ideologists as well, proves arid and productive mainly of contention when, to begin with, this hermeneutics is of any intellectual weight at all. The exercise in repeating the holy words without understanding much, if anything, of what they say and mean cannot in this context be taken seriously. Such repetition is not reading or learning at all. Pretense and ritual are not the same thing, and ritual learning must include learning. So we have to find a way of reading the holy books congruent to both their character and our interest in them.

It seems to me that that requirement is met with two questions. First, *how* do these texts convey their message? What is it that we learn from the way they say things and the way in which people have learned and are taught to hear what they say? Second, *what* do they say that is pertinent to living as a Judaist today? That is, once the text comes into being, leaving its own particular moment of history and undertaking a journey beyond its concrete and specific context, the canonical text has to discover new life in other contexts. And the way that happens is through the urgent work of exegesis. The task is the comparison of the words of one text to the ways of another world and the finding of modes of harmonization and mediation between the one and the other.

Now when the theologian comes along, it is not to do the work of descriptive hermeneutics, of explaining solely how the diverse texts have been made to speak. What the theologian requires, for the much more complex work of generalization, is information about commonalities amid the diversities of exegesis, the exegesis of exegesis, so to speak. The theologian, first, has to uncover the processes and modes of thought. To know how a given text has been received is interesting. To know how the methods of reception, transmission, interpretation, and application of that text correspond to methods to be located in the reading of other texts is to know something important; the deeper structure of the processes of hermeneutics, the method within the diverse methods of the received exegesis. The work of generalization must come. What is available for generalization, it is clear, is what is common among exegetical techniques of diverse and discrete documents. That is, as I have said, how all of them are read, through all times, and in all places.

When, of course, we speak of times and places, second, we arouse the interest of the historian of religions. For what do we know about the exegesis of a text if we cannot describe the contexts of ideas and circumstances of visions in which that exegesis is done, that is, the particular choices that have been made among a broad range of possibilities? Surely the impulse and motivation of the exegete have to enter into the account of the results of exegesis: What was the question that had to be answered in those times and for those groups of people? It is not enough to wonder what it is that we learn from hermeneutics, that is, *how* people say things about the commonalities of faith. We have also to know what it is that, under diverse circumstances, they wish to say: The *substance* matters as much as the method. Here is the point at which comparative and historical studies in religions come to the fore.

When it comes to the work of description not only does context have its part to play; so too does consideration of choice, that is to say, comparison. What things people *might* have said we must know in order to understand the choices that they *have* made and the things they *do* choose to say. So these two go together: the consideration of formal language, mode of interpreting and applying the canon that, all together, I hope we may call hermeneutics, and attention to the range of the choices selected for serious attention, the work of comparison of diverse contexts and expressions of a given continuum of religion or of diverse religions to, for analysis of which we generally call upon the historian of religions.

There is yet a third kind of thinking about religions that is to be invoked—an interest in the larger concrete, social, and historical framework in which Judaism comes to particular expression and definition, an interest characteristic of historians.

When we have some clear picture of the procedures and methods of exegesis of the texts and of the choices available and made, we have yet to link out results, our conception of the dynamics of Judaism and of its processes, to that world of the Jewish people that took shape in these processes and out of these dynamics.

There is, I mean, an ecology of Judaism: a natural framework in which all elements interact with all other elements to form a stable, coherent, and whole system. For if Judaism is to be described as it has endured, it has to be described where it has endured: in the political-social and imaginative life of the Jewish people, in its mind and emotions. And that part of the task of description and interpretation is best done by historians of the Jewish people, those who (in the present context) take on the work of relating the social and historical framework of the group to its inner life of feeling, fantasy, and imagination. The question to be asked in this setting is how it is that the distinctive myths and rites of Judaism—its way of shaping life and its way of living—continued to possess the power to form, and to make sense of, an enduring world in diverse and changing contexts. When we consider that Judaism continued in a single, remarkably persistent system for nearly 2,000 years, from the second century to the nineteenth and even the twentieth, we must ask what has so persisted, amid time and change, to have continued to make sense of the world to the Jews, and of the Jews to their world. That perennial and enduring congruence between myth and circumstance, context and system, surely will enter into our definition of Judaism alongside the elements of process described and choice explained.

My main point is that the defining of the received vision of Judaism is through processes of exegesis, which govern feeling and imagination, make sense of context and situation, and persist with remarkable stability for a very long time. The discovery and statement of these rules of process permit us to speak of Judaism. The received vision of Judaism is to be defined as those distinctive processes of exegesis of the canon that yield coherent choices, made time and again through the ages, repeated in one circumstance after another. The work of description is to be done through the disciplines of hermeneutics, history of religions, and history. But in the end, these through their combination do not constitute theology. They only define the parameters within which theology is to be done.[3]

2. Vision Reformed

Our three-part assignment, then, is to work out the hermeneutics of texts, to uncover the choices before the ones who wrote the texts and the many who received them and so to understand what the religious community selected against the background of what it thereby rejected, and, finally, to analyze the concrete contexts in which the processes of exegesis and selection took place.

First,· we must determine what is the text, or the kind of text, upon which theological work is to be done.

It seems self-evident that, in nineteenth- and twentieth-century theological discourse, a wrong choice has been made. For when we ask about the canon upon which theologians of Judaism draw in modern and contemporary times, the answer is twofold: modern philosophy of religion, on the one side, and the Hebrew Scriptures, the Written Torah, on the other. A few particularly learned theologians cite talmudic sayings too. Proof of this proposition is through a simple mental experiment. When you read the work of nearly all modern and contemporary voices of Judaism, what books must you know to understand their thought? And what do you *not* need to know? It is commonplace that you must know Kant and will do well to know Hegel. You also should know some stories and sayings of the Hebrew Scriptures, the Written Torah, and some tales of the Talmud and midrashim, the Oral Torah. Except for Abraham J. Heschel and Joseph B. Soloveichik there is not a single important theologian of the present or past century who cannot be fully and exhaustively understood within the limits just now stated—modern philosophy of religion, Written Torah, and a few pithy rabbinic maxims—because none draws systematically and routinely upon the other resources of the canon of Judaism. But the entire range of the holy books of Judaism speaks, in particular, through Heschel.

In my judgment Judaism cannot draw for definition solely upon the Written Torah and episodic citations of rabbinic *aggadah.* This is for two reasons. First, it has been the whole of the Dual Torah, written and oral, of Moses, "our Rabbi," which has defined Judaism through the ages and which must therefore serve today to supply the principal sources of Judaism. Second, the whole (Dual) Torah in fact is many, for the canon of Judaism—Torah—has received new documents in every age down to our own.[4] If, therefore, we conclude that the correct sources of Judaic theology are formed of the one whole Torah of Moses, our Rabbi, we once more find ourselves at that point at which we began, with the question of canon and hermeneutics of canon—how it is delineated and interpreted.

The canon of Judaism defines the sources of theology of Judaism and sets forth the field within which theological inquiry must be undertaken. One part of that canon is well known to, and shared by, others: the Written Torah. That part is not to be neglected because it is not unique to Judaism. Heschel, for his part, understood that, despite all that has been done to make the Written Torah alien to Judaism, the "Old Testament" remains the *Tanakh,* the Written Torah of Judaism. He deemed his most important book to be the *Prophets.* The second half of the Torah, the oral part, *aggadah* and *halakhah,* however, is not to be neglected—just as Heschel, for his part, understood it: the Mishnah, the Talmud, and the great corpus continuous with the Mishnah and the Talmud. Here, too, Heschel undertook work of surpassing intellectual ambition—in his *Torah min hashshamayim beaspaqlaria shel haddorot,* an essay in the conceptions of revelation of the authorities of Mishnah, and, in a still larger framework, in the character of religious epistemology in Judaism.[5]

Thus far I mean to stress two points. First of all, the sources of theology of Judaism are the whole and complete canon of Torah. That canon is defined for us by the shelves of books deemed by the consensus of the faithful to be holy and to warrant study in religious circumstances, that is, to be part of Torah. The canon of Torah is sufficiently open so that the words of even living men may be received in faith and recorded in piety. Torah is an open canon: *The processes by which books find their way into that canon define the convictions of Judaism about the character and meaning of revelation.*

Second, I am able to point even in our own day to a theologian whose *ouevres* do conform to the criterion of breadth and rigorous learning as the Judaic canon by which all theology is to be measured, and by which most theologians, alas, are found shallow and ignorant.

Having indicated through the corpus of Heschel's work the character of the canon of theology in Judaism, I may now come to a further point. Even the most productive and by far the best theological mind in modern and contemporary Judaism missed the principal theological canon of Judaism. For Heschel neglected the chief source of Judaism as *halakhah.*

3. Vision Reformed, Vision Transmitted

The center of Judaism is its way of life. No accurate and careful description of Judaism omits that obvious point. We already have noted that merely describing how Jews now live is not to define the way of life of Judaism. That is a sociological fact. But it is now to be balanced against a theological conviction everywhere affirmed in the history of Judaism from the second century to the nineteenth and twentieth centuries. Judaism expresses its theology through the pattern of deeds performed by the practitioner of Judaism. We are what we do. Judaism is what Judaists are supposed to do. I cannot think of a proposition more widely held in ages past and in our own time than that the theology of Judaism *is* its *halakhah,* its way of living. If, therefore, we want to describe what Judaism teaches, we have to make sense of what Judaism requires the practitioner of Judaism to practice.[6] But what is the meaning of the practice, and how is that meaning to be uncovered?

Under some circumstances Judaism borders upon orthopraxy (eat *kosher* and think *teraif* [unkosher]) and, under others, upon what Heschel called "religious behaviorism." That is, we find robots of the law, who will do everything required by the law and think nothing on account of the law—religious behaviorists. And we also find nihilists of the law, who do everything by the law and think the law allows thinking anything we like—ortho-practitioners. These corruptions of the faith are revealing. What seems to me worth noticing in them is that orthopraxy is deemed an acceptable option, while religious behaviorism is rarely recognized, let alone condemned. Surprisingly, little effort (Soloveichik here is definitely the exception)—and no wide-ranging, systematic, and *sustained* effort whatsoever (with no exception) —exists to state the theology of Judaism principally out of the sources of the *halakhah*.[7]

The fact is, however, that so far as Judaism today is a living religion it continues its life though *halakhah*. One authentic monument to the destruction of European Jewry likely to endure beyond the present fad is contained in the response literature of the ghettos and the concentration camps.[8] That is where Judaism is lived, defined in the crucible of life and death. There is a theology of Judaism emergent from and triumphant over the "Holocaust." But we have yet to hear its message, because we scarcely know how to listen to Judaism when Judaism speaks idiomatically, as it always has spoken, in accord with the methods and procedures of *its* canon, in obedience to *its* rules, and, above all, in the natural course of the unfolding of *its* consistent and cogent processes of thought and expression. The *halakhah* endured in the crucible of Warsaw and Lodi when *aggadah* and theology fell dumb.

The coming task of theology in Judaism is to define Judaism through the theological study of the now-neglected canon of the *halakhah*. To begin with, the canon must be allowed to define its literary frame for theological expression. One of the chief reasons for the persistent failure of the philosophers of *halakhah* down to the present time to accomplish what they set out to do is the confusion of their categories. They work through the whole of *halakhah* on a given subject. They therefore present results entirely divorced from context, on the one side, and from dynamic processes of exegesis, on the other. So they tell us things, mere facts. That is, they end up with a description of merely what "the *halakhah*" has to say, without analysis or explanation of meaning—a clear account of the context in which, and setting to which, *halakhah* framed the message, and how the message was framed. They therefore tell us about *halakhah*. They do not, however, convey a shred of wisdom or insight into the processes and methods of *halakhah* relevant to any given age of Judaism, past or present. But the *halakhah* did not and does not take shape in a timeless world. It is meant to *create* a world beyond time—a different thing. Its genius was to take shape in a very specific and concrete moment yet to transcend that moment and to address ages to come as well. We shall not know how that was done if we persist in ignoring the diversity of the context and canon of the *halakhah*. We have to confront the specificities of its books and their diverse messages and methods of all, the historicity and religiosity of the *halakhah*.[9]

Once the canon is suitably defined in its diversity and specificity, what is it that we wish to know *about* these documents? The first thing is to grasp the processes of their unfolding: the hermeneutics generative of the exegetical processes that occupy the *halakhic* thinkers of the ages. One significant issue must be how the *halakhic* process expanded its range and so was able to encompass and make its own each and every circumstance confronted by the Jewish people. For Judaism is a world-creating and world-explaining system. The system, as is obvious, works through law. The law, moreover, functions through processes of argument and discussion. These make intelligible and bring under control of rules of all of those fresh data of the world that, together, at a given point, constitute time and change. The system persists because it makes sense of all data and draws within its framework the newest facts of life. When it can no longer deal credibly with the new world within its vast, harmonious framework of rational inquiry and reasoned dispute, of exegesis of the canon in light of the newest concerns of the age, and of the newest concerns of the age in the light of the canon, the system collapses. That is to say, faced by two facts that could not be brought within the intelligible framework of the system of Judaism, Emancipation and modern, political anti-Semitism, Judaism has considerable difficulty. Specifically, it did not succeed in shaping meaningful issues for argument in accord with its established methods and its rational agendum for reasoned debate. So the theologian will want to reflect upon both how the system works and how it does not work. There is a clear frontier delineated by the end of inner plausibility. There is a border defined by the cessation of self-evidence.[10]

4. Vision Transmitted

At the outset I specified the first two principal tasks of the theologian in Judaism as those of definition and correlation: definition of Judaism—vision received; correlation of Judaism with the life of Jewish people—vision reformed. At the end let me point out that these tasks are not to be done in isolation from one another, because the sources of definition of Judaism, the *halakhic* sources, address themselves to the life of the Jewish people and propose to reshape that life in accord with the paradigm of the holy: *You shall be holy, because I am holy.* In this context, there are two sources for theology in Judaism: first, Torah, whole, unending, a never-to-be-closed canon; and, second, the human experience of the Jewish people raised to the level of Torah through *halakhah.*[11] Theology in Judaism makes sense of life already lived. But theology in Judaism has to reflect upon a particular mode of life already lived: the life lived in accord with Torah, therefore with *halakhah.* What is to be defined and explained is the correlation between the (ideal, normative) human images of the *halakhah* and the actual shape of life lived in accord with the *halakhah.* What is this particular kind of humanity that is shaped within the disciplines and critical tensions of the law? What are the larger human meanings to be adduced in interpretation of this particular kind of humanity?

To answer these questions the texts that constitute the sources of theology in Judaism have first to be reread, systematically, thoroughly and, at the outset, historically, one by one. A fresh set of questions has to be devised—questions about, first, the inner issues addressed by the *halakhic* texts, second, the human meaning of those issues, when interpreted, third, against the particular times and settings in which the texts are framed, and, fourth, also against the continuing and enduring social and historical realities of the Jewish people. These are the four criteria of meaning yielded by correct interpretation.

To start at the end, we have to know about those ongoing considerations that must be taken into account by all normative statements on behavior and belief, those traits of society and imagination that characterize every context in which Judaism comes to expression and which, therefore, define the other limits of Judaism.

Next, we need to discern those particular and distinctive concerns of a given situation and to isolate what is fresh and unanticipated therein.

For once we have uncovered the concrete and specific context in which a major conceptual initiative is given shape in *halakhah,* third, we are able to enter into the human circumstance that will help us to understand the question—the existential problem—dealt with by a given initiative.

And, finally, it is at that point that we may bring to full articulation the inner issues addressed by the *halakhic* text. Then we do not reduce them to accidents of a given context. We confront them in their ultimate and whole claim to speak in the name of Torah and to talk of holy things, of God and humanity in God's image.

It is principally in the great *halakhic* texts that the humanistic concerns of theology in Judaism are encapsulated and awaiting discovery. So far as Judaism proposes to express itself through the deeds of the Jewish people and the society that they construct together, we require access to two things. First is philosophical reflection upon the meanings present in common human experience, and second is the language prescribed and expressed within Torah. That common human experience, so far as it is accessible to Torah, is shaped by *halakhah*—when *halakhah* is understood for what it is. So at the end let us state what it is and is not.

Halakhah is Judaism's principal expression, too long set aside since the splendid philosophical-*halakhic* accomplishment of Maimonides, is to express the theology of *halakhah* in its fullness and complexity. If we take *halakhah* as the crucial category for the worldview and methods defined as Judaism, in contrast to the other definitions of the principal sources of Judaism, then we want to know the range and perspectives of the vision of the *halakhah.* What the worldview is that shapes, and is shaped by, the ethos of the *halakhah,* the conceptions of humanity and of the potentialities of human society—these things await definition. But, I wish now to suggest, theology is something more than merely the making explicit of what is implicit and constitutive.

The work of the theologian—as distinct from that of the scholar of history or hermeneutics—must be constructive and creative. For we must grant to theologians what we do not want for scholars: the freedom as constructive religious thinkers to propose fresh perspectives on, and even alterations in the worldview and ethos of, the law. This freedom, we know, has been assumed and vigorously exercised by the great thinkers of the *halakhah* who understood the deep paradox of the famous play on words, *heru'al halluh h ot*—"freedom [is] incised upon the tablets of the law." If, as we tell ourselves, in discipline there is freedom, then to the theologians we cannot deny the greatest freedom of all: to speak in fresh and original ways within the *ha-lakhic* frame, as they do within the frame of biblical and aggadic materials all the time. For, it is self-evident, affirming a *halakhic* definition of Judaism is a theological decision, in the rich sense of the term: the doing of normative and constructive theology.

Having specified the historical and hermeneutical work to be done, we therefore turn to adumbrate the constructive task. For, as I implied, theology is not solely the description of theology, the evocation of worlds past and remembered. If theology also is not the invocation of worlds here now and coming in time, it is hardly needed. The first task of the theologian is to describe and interpret that world of meaning. But the second, and still more important, task is to carry forward the exegesis of the worldview of Judaism by continuing *halakhic* reflection upon the world. That is, theologians have the work of viewing the world and shaping a vision of what we are and can be.

For in its way *halakhah* in the end lays before us a conception of who the community of Israel is and what the community of Israel can be. *Halakhah* speaks of the holiness of the community of Israel within the holiness of God. Its themes and issues then focus upon the way of life of the community of Israel, to the end that the community of Israel may fulfill its promise and potential as the people of the Lord, the kingdom of priests, and the holy people. Now when theologians look at the world today and see the world within the disciplines of *halakhah* and the perspectives of the holiness *halakhah* means to nurture, their creative and constructive work begins. This work is to lay down statements of continuing norms for a new context and to renew the ancient norms through the lessons of a new age. What, after all, do we deal with, if not an exploration of human nature and of the divine image impressed within human nature? And what is at the heart and soul of Judaism if not the inquiry into the image of God in which we are made, therefore into the potential sanctity of us and of the world we make?

We cannot, therefore, concede that the theological work is done for all time in the pages of Maimonides' *Mishneh Torah* or *Shul h an 'Arukh*. We insist that the work is to be done in our own days, when decisions are made that bespeak a vision of who we are and what we can be, of what it means to be in God's image and to live in a community meant to express God's will. The ancient, medieval, and modern rabbis did and do more than a work of history and hermeneutics. On the basis of what their eyes are trained to see and their minds to perceive, in age succeeding age they forge anew and contemporary understanding of a new and unprecedented world. That was what was original for them: Maimonides does not merely quote the ancient sources, though *Mishneh Torah* is a melange of quotations. Through his reflection and arrangement he says something new through something 1,000 years old. What we have to learn is that the *halakhic* process contains the theological process of Judaism. When we understand how that process works we shall gain access to Judaism. The reason is that the *halakhic* corpus contains such vision as we have, and have to share, about the sacred potentialities of humanity and of the human community. The tasks of theology today begin in the exegesis of exegesis done. But they lead to the doing of the exegesis of this time, the interpretation of our world and of its days. The creation of worlds goes on in world without end. That is what, as Rashi says, it means to be "like God"—to create worlds.

Judaism is a religion about this world and about the human being. Its encompassing conceptions concern the human being, made in God's image and little lower than angels, and the community framed and formed by human beings, the arena for the working out of God's word and will. Distinctive to Judaism is the intensely practical and practiced law. The word is not abstract. The will is for the here and now. But the word is yet a word, the will is not solely about what I eat but how I understand and feel—and what I am. In the end, we always are what we are, that is, we are mortal and die. But before that, we may become something "in our image, according to our likeness," like God—only that we die. And there, in that painful tension between death and living, between our mortality and the promise and vision of the sacred in ourselves, is the sanctuary of life, the arena for our struggles and our anguish. In the pain and the suffering, in the living in the face of the dying, is the sacred. The achievement, the vanquishing and the being vanquished, too, are sacred. Holiness is the pathos, holiness, the triumph.

5. Cui Bono?

It remains briefly to address two questions, usefulness and relevance. At the outset theology in Judaism has a threefold set of tasks: (1) to define Judaism, (2) to discover the human situation to which Judaism responds, and, finally (3) to create those modes of advocacy and apologetics that will permit contemporary Jews to gain renewed access to that Judaism subject to definition. This third task may be captured in the question: To whom is such a theological enterprise as I have described going to be useful? And alongside there is a second question, important to those who will want to study, and even interpret, the theology of Judaism in the setting of universities, therefore in discourse with a diverse and plural intellectual constituency: To whom, outside of Judaism, are the results of this kind of theology going to be relevant?

The obvious fact is that the two questions are one. For Jews seeking to define and understand Judaism and scholars of religions with the same fundamental questions—What is this thing? How does it work?—part company only at the end. Jews have yet a Jewish question not shared by others: How shall I find my way inside, or, if inside, what does it mean to *be,* to live, inside? But these are the same questions once again. The study of religions must encompass attention to the study of theologies, and, given the situation of teacher and student, the study of religions is going to include much effort (perhaps too much) given to the understanding of theologies.

Now I think it is everywhere understood as a datum that in our classrooms there will be no advocacy but the academic kind, and surely no active theologizing. But there must be understanding, an exercise in interpretation, in the framework of the common humanity or the study of religions collapses into the recitation of facts, a rubble of trivial observations. To prevent the ruin of the work, we quite properly turn to anthropology and sociology, philosophy and psychology, drama, poetry, and art —indeed to each and every source of insight available to us in humanistic leaning. But if my proposal is a sound one, then we find yet another source of insight to which to turn: theology itself. If the work is done with a decent respect for the diversity of our students and for the rights of all of them to be what they are without our interference, then surely the insights sought in descriptive theological inquiry and exposition—the human meaning of the law—may turn out to crown the construction of meaning (if not the search for truth) at which we labor.

Notes

[1]It is a commonplace that *halakhic* statements are normative and theological statements represent the private opinion of an individual. This paper is meant to restate the theological task in such a way that it too may be perceived, within the communities of the faithful of Judaism, as part of public discourse, not merely private opinion. At this time, however, I do not wish to enter into issues of Judaic dogmatics. The reason that the work of dogmatics, the restatement of available and required truths for the current age, need not now be done is that it is premature. For a long time we were told that, in any event, Judaism has no theology, and it certainly has no dogmas. While the dogma of dogma-less Judaism has passed away with the generation to whom it seemed an urgent and compelling proposition, it has left discourse about and within Judaism in disarray. There is a poverty of philosophical clarity and decisive expression amid a superfluity of conviction, too much believing, too small perspicacious construction. As one person put it, "There is no God, but Israel is his sole, chosen people." Of still greater weight, dogmatics lays the groundwork for the exercise of advocacy and apologetic. That exercise is a work of mediation between culture and revelation, between where the people are and where Torah wishes them to be. It seems to me self-evident that, until we have a richer and more responsible conception of what it is that awaits both advocacy and mediation, that is, Torah or Judaism, formulation of dogmas for defense is unimportant.

[2]Obviously, I cannot concede that Judaism is practiced today only by those who now carry out the teachings of Jewish law, *e.g.*, as summed up in the *Shul ḥ an 'Arukh*. It does not seem to be descriptively valid since vast numbers of Jews also regard themselves, and are generally regarded as, Judaists who do not live in accord with all of the law of Judaism all the time or ever. The choice then is (1) to declare that Judaism has no *halakhah,* or (2) to declare that all who do not keep the *halakhah* are not Judaists. Both propositions seem to me factually so far from the truth as to have to be set aside. The problem explored here then becomes urgent and unavoidable.

[3]See Parts 4 and 5.

[4]This is the principal point of my conference address at the University of Chicago, April, 1977, printed as "Transcendence and Worship through Learning: The Religious World View of Mishnah," *Journal of Reform Judaism* 25/2 (Spring 1978): 15-29. I was surprised that the Reform theologians

and rabbis at that meeting did not see the congruence between this description of the open-ended canon of Torah and the Reform conception of progressive revelation. Instead I found myself criticized for laying too much stress on the importance of reason, as against emotion, in the processes of the unfolding of revelation. But since when is how we feel today a revelation of God's will and word for the world? Further, a definition of Judaism which draws principally upon the Written Torah read other than through the perspective of the Oral Torah, its full and exhaustive interpretation, is not Judaism either. That is to say, so far as there are rules that permit us to speak of Judaism, these rules must be observed. Otherwise what we do is make things up as we go along and call our invention Judaism. But so far as we claim to communicate with other ages and other people in our own age, we cannot simply make things up as we go along. When there is no shared realm of discourse, past and present, there is that capricious alternation of noise or silence that is, in the life of emotions, the prelude to death and, in the life of the intellect, the symptom of the end of reasoned discourse. Since theology is the work of and for intellectuals pursued through reasoned discourse about, in part, a realm of distinctive and rich emotions and educated feelings, we cannot afford the costs of ignorance and capriciousness.

[5]To complete our definition of the theological canon through our sketch of Heschel's remarkable choices, we have to refer to the entire intellectual range formed of the philosophers of Judaism of the Middle Ages, Maimonides and Judah Halevi being Heschel's particular but not sole choices, the metaphysics of the Zohar, which Heschel fully grasped, and those doctors of the heart and soul who created the Hasidic tales. Into this comprehensive framework of the Judaic canon, Scripture, Oral Torah, Zohar, philosophy, mysticism, prayerbook—rationality and feeling, revelation and reason—which Heschel took into his mind and made his own, Heschel also received the achievements of the Nineteenth- and Twentieth-century theologians of Christianity and philosophers of religion. I once told Heschel I thought the center of his work lay in religious epistemology, the sources of religious truth. He said to me, "No, you are wrong. The center is the question of ontology." This is stated by Fritz A. Rothschild (*Encyclopaedia Judaica,* 8:425) as follows: "Heschel's own work attempts to penetrate and illumine the reality underlying religion, the living and dynamic relationship between God and man, through the objective, yet sympathetic understanding of the documents of Israel's tradition and of the experience of the pious Jew." Note especially Abraham Joshua Heschel, *A Passion for Truth* (New York, 1973), by far his most enduring work—and the most remarkable.

[6]Joseph Dov Soloveichik certainly is to be invoked as a principal exponent of the position outlined here, *e.g.,* in his "Ish hahalakhah," *Talpiyyot* (1944): 651-735, and "The Lonely Man of Faith," *Tradition* 7/2 (1965): 5-67. As Aaron Rothkoff wrote, "The man lives in accordance with the *halakhah,* he becomes master of himself and the currents of his life . . . he ceases to be a mere creature of a habit. His life becomes sanctified, and God and man are drawn into a community of existence, 'a covenantal community,' which brings God and man together in an intimate, person-to-person relationship. It is only through the observance of the *halakhah* that man attains this goal to nearness to God" (*Encyclopaedia Judaica,* 15:132-33). It is no criticism to observe that Soloveichik's observations, while profound, thus far are episodic and not systematic. Despite his formidable insights, the work of interpretation of the *halakhah* as a theological enterprise simply has not yet begun. Nor do I think it can be done by *halakhists* within the intellectually impoverished resources of their training. They are, to begin with, in no way humanists. Perhaps had Rosenzweig lived he might have done this work, just as he—nearly alone—turned to the *Siddur* as a principal source of theology. In any event Soloveitchik never kept the promises of his work, which remained suggestive, rather than definitive, despite the absolutely worshipful reception he received in one circle of Orthodox Judaism in the USA. Heschel described him to me as "a learned

homilitician," and when, for the purpose of this anthology, I examined Soloveitchik's corpus for writing suitable here, I found nothing very interesting or well-crafted. His devotees describe his Torah as "oral," and it may be that, in its oral version, it possessed an intellectual power conspicuously lacking in the written down statements. In any event I see nothing in his legacy from which the coming century will derive a model, or even much instruction.

[7]My description of Heschel's corpus seems to me probative. I can point in his works to systematic and profound reflection upon the theology of the whole of the canon of Judaism except for the *halakhic* part; that is, that part that, speaking descriptively, all concur, forms the center and the core. The fact that Heschel lived wholly and completely in accord with the *halakhah* is beside the point, just as it is beside the point that another great theologian of modern Judaism, Martin Buber, did not. What the two have in common is that through them *halakhah* did and does not speak, and, in the case of Buber, what to begin with is heard from *halakhah* is simply a negative fact, the existence of something *against* which theology will find its definition. What we do have as theology of *halakhah* in Heschel and Soloveichik is sermonic and not sustained; it is episodic and not systematic. I say this of Heschel, however, in full awareness of the unkept promise of his *The Sabbath: Its Meaning for Modern Man,* which comes as close as any essay in contemporary theology of Judaism to take up in a systematic and existentially profound way (as against the intellectual ephemera of sermons), the intellectual premises of *halakhah.* There is in the corpus of Heschel no work that draws upon and responds to the *Shulhan Arukh.* Maimonides' *Mishneh Torah,* the Talmud as Talmud (not merely as a storehouse of interesting sayings and stories), or, above all, and the source of it all, Mishnah and its companion, Tosefta. If it is not in Heschel, then, as I have said, it is nowhere else. I cannot point to a single systematic and sustained work of theology out of the sources of Mishnah and Tosefta, out of the Talmud as a *halakhic* monument or any significant part thereof, out of the monuments formed by the medieval commentaries and codes, down to the present day. For historical study of the social-religious meaning of *halakhah,* see Jacob Katz, *Masoret ummashber* (Tel Aviv, 1958), *Tradition and Crisis* (Oxford, 1961), *Exclusiveness and Tolerance* (Oxford, 1961).

[8]Some of this has been translated into English as *The Holocaust and Halakhah,* by Irving Rosenbaum (New York, 1976).

[9]Just as Heschel could address himself to the issues of religious ontology of the prophets, the rabbis named in Mishnah, Maimonides, and Judah Halevi, the Zohar Hasidic literature, prayerbook, and on down to our own time, so the theologian of *halakhah* will have to allow each and every document of *halakhah* to emerge in all its concrete specificity. But where to begin? Self-evidently, it is to Mishnah and its tractates and divisions that we look for *one* beginning. But if we do not also look to Scripture and its many and diverse codes of law, clearly etched along the lines of the Priestly Code and the Holiness code on the one side, and the earlier thinking of the Deuteronomical schools on the other, we shall miss yet other beginnings. And I think it is obvious that, for theology as Judaism to be compelling in our own time, it will have to contend with the testimonies of documents standing on the threshold of the canon even now; I mean, the Dead Sea Scrolls (see Lawrence H. Schiffman, *The Halakhah of Qumran* [Leiden, 1976]), the Targumim, and the other documents important to our own day and unknown or neglected before now. In outlining the limits of the *halakhic* canon, we want to inquire after the processes of thought and the reaching of concrete conclusions of the masters of *halakhah,* early and late. They who expressed their theology through law and only through law so shaped the norms, social and psychological, of age succeeding age. They surely must define Judaism, not merely the epiphenomena called its "way of life."

[10]Alongside description and interpretation of the processes of exegesis must come a second arena for delineation: the range of choice permitted by the system and prohibited within the system. One may only eat certain few foods, but the problems connected with the eating of those foods are rich and engaging. Stated more broadly, the proposition does not change. There is a given way of life defined by the processes of exegesis of the law and through its diverse literature. That way of life has to be described in the context of humanity and of the humanities: what sort of people, society, and culture emerge when life is lived in this way and not in some other. The *halakhic* literature awaits this kind of mention: description of the life of emotion and of relationship; of the society of home, family, and town; of the choices made, and the alternatives avoided, by the individual and by the group. The whole is best framed by the *halakhic* corpus. Since, moreover, we have access to other great systems of religion expressed through distinctive ways of life—I refer, by one instance, to Islam, with its legal literature, its processes of exegesis, and its way of life, but I do not exclude reference to Buddhism, on the one side, and to Christianity, on the other, both of them profoundly *halakhic* constructions at important points in their history—there is a sizable task of comparison to be worked out. So alongside, and cogent with, the exegesis of exegesis, that is, the description of the processes of Judaism, another task must be done: The comparison of the results, the description of the history of Judaism within the history of religions. Through this work there is a chance to gain that perspective upon which definition must depend. And I need hardly dwell upon the centrality of the work of the historian of the Jews, able to relate the *halakhic* process to the concrete social and historical circumstances of the Jewish people. For the historian and sociologist of the Jews in the end provide the most interesting evidence about the concrete workings of Judaism.

[11]What follows is a response to David Tracy, *Blessed Rage for Order: The New Pluralism in Theology* (New York, 1975) 43 ff. I hasten to clarify that it is the model, not the substance, which I invoke as a clarifying exercise of intellect. Tracy describes the revisionist model as "philosophical reflection upon the meanings present in common human experience and language, and upon the meanings present in the Christian fact." Of acute relevance is Tracy's first thesis, "The two principal sources for theology are Christian texts and common human experience and language." If I may rephrase in this setting the outcome of my earlier propositions, it is that the principal sources for theology in Judaism are, first, the *halakhic* texts as they are lived out in ordinary life and, second, the common human experience and language that will help to make sense of the inner meanings of those lived texts. This is, I hasten to say, not a translation of Tracy's propositions into the setting of Judaism. It is an effort to respond to what seems to me a sound insight, arising on its own, within the context of Judaism.

Part One
Doing Theology in Judaism

Chapter 2

Facing Up to the Options in Modern Jewish Thought

Eugene B. Borowitz

Theology in Judaism mediates between the inherited truth of revelation and the human condition of the acutely-present moment, and that task bears its own legacy of ambiguity and unclarity. Obviously, theology stands for more than a survey of public opinion, whether in books or in today's streets and synagogues. Revealed truth cannot, after all, give way to the ephemeral opinion of the moment, and that simple verity finds its most compelling validation in the past fifty years of Judaic theological thought. For the one thing that has not happened is a surrender to the negative charge of theodicy: God has been affirmed, Israel renewed, Torah regenerated, in the aftermath of the Holocaust. Those who advocated atheism or invented a God-idea appropriate to the mystery of Israel's tragedy found no hearing the went their own way. Here the voice of the half-century for Reform Judaism, speaking also in behalf of the faithful of other Judaic religious systems and their worlds, sorts out the choices facing Judaic theology. With the humility that marks the truly formidable intellects, Borowitz confesses that some of the problems at hand "exceed our present theoretical capabilities." He therefore sets out to clarify the options and explain the choices, and, in summarizing his repertoire of Choices in Modern Jewish Thought, some of which we have considered in this anthology, he also shows the courage to say what he himself confesses. This confession assigns priority to what he calls "tradition" and what we have learned to the "the Torah." He takes up the issues of covenant, insisting that "commitment to the Covenant insists that a relation to God is primary to the life of the Jewish people and the individual Jew." In these and the further affirmations he sets forth, Borowitz takes his stand against the secular, and in favor of the fundamentally religious, interpretation of what it means to be a Jew. In so doing, he opens the issue of the century to come: what in the end does it mean for a human being to form part of "Israel," whether the (supposedly) ethnic group in North American politics and society or the (allegedly) secular State of Israel. In the premise, which sanity requires, that there will be no future Holocaust, the issue as he frames it is not, to be or not to be, but what to be, meaning, what does God want us to be?

***

With Jewish thinkers today differing so widely in their views, how can one hope to get a clear and coherent account of what one believes as a Jew?

The common strategy, compromise, will not work. We cannot simply collect what we find most appealing in the ideas of each thinker and thereby gain a coherent philosophy of our own. Cohen's God, Baeck's mystery, Kaplan's peoplehood, Buber's Covenant and Heschel's prophetic sympathy, will not mesh together. The premises on which they are founded substantially contradict one another. Indeed, the thinkers consciously created their systems out of a desire to take a different approach to Judaism from that which had existed before and which they considered inadequate. (The thinkers included in this book were chosen because they are the best representatives of the divergent streams of thought in contemporary Judaism.)

At the other extreme, some people find that one of the major Jewish thinkers still speaks for them. They see the competing views as so essentially flawed that they do not constitute a serious challenge to the one they espouse. Such problems as they perceive in their own position merely represent the agenda for their Jewish intellectual growth, not a reason for giving up or radically revising it. Thus one not uncommonly meets disciples of Kaplan, Buber or Heschel in the Jewish community today.

Most thoughtful Jews, I find, can follow no one intellectual line. They remain undecided whether God's revelation, or Divine-human encounter, or human reason or experience ought to be the basis for understanding Judaism. Each standpoint has its appeal but each also has its weaknesses. Optimally, we need a fresh philosophical approach which would reshape our concept of Judaism so that we would retain all the gains of previous systems while circumventing their faults. I would like to encourage as many students of Judaism as I can to undertake that creative task. Through their efforts, Jewish theology will carry on in as lively a way in the future as it has done in recent decades.

I myself do not see that any currently suggested system, or any that I may devise, can hope to convince most thinkers that they should accept its transformation of the system and the problems of Jewish philosophy. The complexities of our time simply exceed our present theoretical capabilities. From within, our diverse understandings of Judaism and our clashing methodologies about how best to study it, preclude any easy agreement as to what constitutes authentic Jewish thought. From without, the fragmented and discordant motifs which sound in our culture and social sciences cannot provide a context for a freshly integrated Judaism. We live in a time of intellectual uncertainty, one far greater than that of previously searching and unsure generations. The fundamental premises of every discipline and of thinking itself are continually being challenged and our civilization's high esteem for doubt makes such skepticism difficult to refute. Moreover, education, the widespread diffusion of new ideas and unceasing proposal of radically diverse views keep us keenly aware of the unprecedented intellectual pluralism amidst which our thinking needs to be done.

I do not see then that we can think about Judaism in quite the same relatively self-assured way that modern Jewish philosophers have customarily followed. Each proclaimed his own theories as if they fully constituted Judaism and referred to divergent views only by inference or in passing. Each was so confident that his system settled all the significant problems of his time that he did not undertake a direct confrontation with the theorists who differed from them. I suggest that our unsettled intellectual situation requires a less self-centered approach. It should proceed in two successive steps.

Clarifying the Options, Explaining One's Choices

We would begin studying a topic by utilizing a comparative approach. That means inquiring about the divergent views of thoughtful interpreters of Judaism writing about this issue. (The fateful problem of the proper utilization of non-Jewish thinkers for elucidating the contemporary content of Jewish faith must be faced by the investigator at this point.) A careful contrast and comparison of their positions should clarify the major issues facing the thoughtful Jew. Since taking one intellectual option over another always involves certain gains and losses, exposing the consequences of a given choice—"If, . . . then . . ."—becomes a central task in this method. Furthermore, because we have no agreed standard for evaluating one suggestion over another, knowing the practical consequences of accepting a given position may be decisive for determining which philosophy we can accept. By candidly exposing the various theological alternatives, thinkers can better perceive and clarify their own assumptions while equipping their readers to think for themselves more responsibly. Obviously, my preference for this approach stems from my deep concern for personal autonomy but I believe that less personalistically inclined thinkers should employ it to remain conscious of the variety of questions and proposals facing our community.

On one level, this book is my response to that challenge. But, though it deals with important themes of Jewish faith, one does not need to be a Jew to do this part of the task. Any competent, empathetic student of ideas could produce such an intellectual geography.

Only at a second level does this activity become distinctively Jewish. Thinkers then respond to the intellectual options by indicating what they personally believe. They set forth the reasons—to the extent they are able—for having rejected other positions and accepted just the ones which they affirm. In the process, they ought to demonstrate the interrelationships and internal harmony of their beliefs. They bring their work to a fitting climax by showing the consequence of their ideas for Jewish life and responsibility.

I should therefore like to conclude this book with a small sample of my efforts to make a substantive statement of my Jewish faith. In 1977, the Central Conference of American Rabbis invited me to prepare a paper on God which its members could study in advance of a discussion on this topic at their annual conference. I quickly discovered I could not satisfactorily deal with this central issue unless I also explicated the assumptions on which my treatment was based and the consequences to which it led, at least intellectually. What follows is one of the concluding sections of that lengthy, detailed paper (found in its entirety in their *Yearbook* for 1977) in which I tried to give a brief, positive summary of my views.

My Theology of Judaism: A Provisional Statement

I do not see any way to begin theology afresh, without preconceptions and as if there were no history. The very hope of doing so is itself the result of a Cartesian tradition and marks its proponent as an adherent of the European liberal academic community. The problem of what tradition one finds oneself in, which one proposes to affirm or reject or that one then chooses, is fundamental to the theological or philosophical enterprise and substantially determines the content which will ensue. The modern Jewish theologian faces this problem with special difficulty because of being situated between western culture and Jewish tradition. These partially clash, the former being dominated by Christianity insofar as it is religious and antipathetic to religion insofar as it is secular. As a liberal Jewish theologian I add to this problem my inability to accept the Jewish tradition absolutely and use it as the measure of my involvement with the culture. I necessarily begin from a history of some generations of liberal theology.

In terms of what is perceived as the present agenda, I can try to assess the successes and failures of the old liberalism, and in terms of the contemporary intellectual scene or my creativity, make some determination of where I will take my intellectual stand. Two corrections of classic liberal theology seem to me to be necessary. One, a redirection of its concern with science, might still be accommodated by its usual rationalism. The other, a commitment to substantial particularist consequences, seems incompatible with known rationalisms.

Classic liberal theology was mainly concerned with accommodating religion to science and culture which largely accepted the naturalistic world view. While affirming the continuing importance of science to our sense of things, I do not see it as the dominant challenge to our human self–understanding. Rather, the accomplishments of science have themselves (by their threats to our personhood) raised to primary concern the problem of being a person (socially as well as individually understood). Unfortunately there seems no satisfactory way to bridge the person–science dichotomy. Despite the problems this causes me, I feel I must stand on the person side of the struggle. The notions of self and the concept of relationship (genuine interpersonal involvement) then become my central hermeneutic for the explication of a contemporary pattern of Jewish belief. (On its admitted inadequacies and some remedies for them see my other writings.)

Liberal Jewish thought might have accepted some sort of existentialist personalism as it once was willing to substitute naturalism for Neo-Kantianism (or stands ready to adopt Whiteheadian or phenomenological theologies), as long as this did not disturb its accustomed universalistic focus. Yet for all that classic liberal Jewish theology performed the valuable and necessary task of making ex–ghetto Jews citizens of the world, it did not motivate them to be particularly learned or observant Jews. This lack of motivation was an explicit problem before the Holocaust, the establishment of the State of Israel and the contemporary spiritual emptiness of Western civilization. Today an inability to speak to the particularistic needs of liberal Judaism would be a major intellectual disaster. I believe that instead of validating itself by its universalism, a contemporary liberal Jewish theology must do so by the power of its particularism. The task is complicated by the proper rejection by most liberal Jews of a purely or largely particularistic theology. The contemporary agenda is set by the need to maintain the gains of universalism (by which Jews have their rights in modern society) while giving equal priority to the people of Israel and its distinctive way of life. Having less confidence in Western culture than in Jewish tradition, though taking neither as an absolute, I give Jewish tradition priority in my thought. Tradition makes authoritative but not irresistible claims upon me and I respond to them out of my Western culture situation in a personal, not systematic way, utilizing the notions of self and relationship to clarify what Jewish belief means to me.

Classic Jewish Faith and the Modern Notion of the Self

A possible incoherence already emerges in the linkage of Jewish tradition and selfhood. The former is more concerned with God's objective will, Torah, than with personal self–determination; and the latter makes autonomy, not law, tradition or community, usually not even God, its foundation. Identifying the two (reason–equals–revelation as in the medieval solution of this problem) not being feasible, in my opinion, only a dialectic between self and tradition can be affirmed. Since this cannot be stilled, it produces a dynamic to this position which keeps it necessarily fluid. However, I believe it can be saved from the charge of destructive contradiction. Realistically exposed, the self is not self–evidently worthy of the dignity we assign to it. It therefore requires some sort of meta–existentialism which Jewish tradition, with its teaching of humankind created in God's image, can provide.

More difficult is the assertion that the tradition, in some way, would, on coming in contact with the modern concept of the self, find it an appropriate and valuable insight to assimilate to its teaching. Historically, Jewish selfhood was exercised only within the rigorous limits imposed by law, tradition and community. Practically, today, the leaders of traditional Judaism seem more concerned with the defense of the law and its structures against the self than with incorporating something of the modern sense of the self into the actual operation of their system of authority. Against this it must be noted that the overwhelming majority of modern Jews consider themselves essentially self–legislating (and this despite party label or institutional affiliation). The unprecedented, full–scale abandonment of the *halachic* system is unlikely to be reversed. Insofar as it has a positive intellectual basis (as against social causation) it stems from the acceptance of the autonomy of the individual. Since there are some intuitions of this in Jewish tradition, since it appeals to the Jewish sense of individuality, since it is hoped that an integration of selfhood and tradition, mutually influencing and transforming, can be carried out so as to yield the mixed particularist–universalist theology sought, the marriage of tradition and the modern sense of self seems a valuable option to pursue.

Where mind is the primary model of theology, one speaks of ideas. In naturalism, one prefers forces or processes. If our concern is persons we speak of relationship, the way the self links itself to the world or anything in it. The fundamental relationship in which the Jew stands is the Covenant. However, it was made and is maintained primarily with the people of Israel and not the individual Jew. To be sure, the people of Israel is not an entity outside of its individual members and no claim is made that it possesses some folk–soul or national–will of its own. Nonetheless the individual Jew's direct, personal relationship with God is not begun by that Jew but by the historic experience of the Jewish people into which the contemporary Jew is born. (There is obviously a major difference here between Christian notions of "getting faith" and the Jewish sense of entering the Covenant.) Individual Jews then, are immediately involved in a dialectic not only of self and God (thus setting a limit to the anarchy of atheistic existentialism) but of the self and the Jewish people in relation to that god (thus setting a limit to the exercise of an anarchic because individualistic liberal Jewish sense of autonomous selfhood).

Implications of Existence in Covenant

This sets the agenda for contemporary liberal Jewish apologetic theology. As against all secular interpretations of being a Jew, commitment to the Covenant insists that a relationship to God is primary to the life of the Jewish people and the individual Jew. The first concern of our apologetics, then, needs to be the recapture of the living reality of God in individual Jewish lives and thus in the Jewish community. The major target in this regard is the crypto–agnosticism with which most Jews have evaded this issue for a generation or more. In the face of contemporary nihilism, I am convinced, the old hope of serious values without commitment to God is increasingly untenable. The second concern of our apologetics is to help the individual Jew identify personally with the people of Israel. That is somewhat easier in our present time of high regard for ethnic difference and the search for one's own folk roots. Yet the primary model most people use in their thinking remains the Cartesian one of the detached self seeking truth without preconceptions or commitments. This has particular appeal to Jews since it immediately releases them from Jewish attachment in accord with the social pressures on any minority to assimilate to the majority.

Moreover, if there is no universalism then Jews lose whatever right they have to be part of general society. It thus becomes important to argue that all selfhood, though possessing universal dignity, is historically and particularly situated. Because of its uncommon worth, if for not more theological reason, Jews should will to make the fact of their being born into the Covenant the basis of their existence.

This construction of our situation as Jews overcomes what I take to be the fundamental difficulty with previous theories. Those which were God–centered were reductive of our peoplehood. Yet those which made the Jewish people central so reduced the role of God in our folk life that they effectively secularized us. Furthermore, if peoplehood is the primary factor in Jewish existence what remains of the autonomous self? When the Covenant relationship is the basis of our understanding of Judaism, self, God and people are all intimately and immediately bound up with one another. This does not settle how in any instance the self will respond to God or to the Jewish people, relationship being too fluid for that; yet Covenant sets up a constraining dialectic in place of liberal Jewish anarchy, universalism or secularism.

Covenant Theology: God—and Evil

As to God, a new humility emerges. Persons have relationships which are deeply significant for their lives without fully or nearly understanding those with whom they have such relationships. As against rationalist models, *concepts* of God (clear intellectual envisagements of God) are of subsidiary interest—if not positively discouraged. Making concepts primary tends to make thinking a substitute for relating and implies a thinking humanity is God's equal. In a relationship thought is not abandoned but it must not dominate. It serves as a critic of faith and as explicator of its consequent responsibilities. This is the safeguard against superstition and cultism. At the same time there is openness to many forms of envisaging God. That is, any concept of God which makes relationship possible (or is appropriate to living in Covenant) is acceptable here. This seems closer to the traditional model of *aggadic* thinking than liberal theologies have been as a result of their emphasis on an idea– of–God as the essence of Judaism. And it provides for continuing intellectual growth in our understanding of God, a characteristic of all of Jewish history, particularly in our time.

Specifically, I do not see that thinking in terms of Covenant prohibits after–the–fact explanations of the God with whom one stands in relation, as an impersonal principle, or a process which has certain person–like characteristics (e.g., the conservation of values.) For myself, however, the most appropriate model of thinking about the God with whom I stand in relation is a personal one. That is not to make a detached, metaphysical observation concerning the nature of God but only to say that, when I try to think about God, this is the best basis I have found for drawing an analogy to the God with whom I stand in Covenant. Persons being the most complex things in creation, I find this an intellectually reasonable procedure. Further, my experience of being involved with God being a personal one, this envisagement seems appropriate. Some additional explication of what it means to say that God is person–like might, I think, be given.

The notion of relationship provides an approach to living with the problem of evil and, specifically the Holocaust. Relationships exist not only when there is immediate confirmation of them but also in its absence. To trust means that the relationship is considered still real though no evidence for it is immediately available. One also believes such confirmation will yet be forthcoming. The practice of Judaism, the life of Torah, is an effort to build a strong relationship with God. Within the context of such closeness, Jews have largely been able to live with the evils in the world.

There are special reasons why it has been difficult to continue this approach in modern times, most notably the loss of our belief in personal survival after death. The Holocaust raised our problems in this regard to an unprecedented level of tension, for some to the point of breaking the relationship with God. It remains stupefyingly inexplicable. Yet, perhaps to our surprise, it has not destroyed the Covenant. For most Jews the ties with the people of Israel are far stronger than anything we had anticipated. The absence of God during the Holocaust cannot be absolutized. It should not be used to deny that God has since been present in our lives as individuals and in that of the people of Israel (notably during the victory—rather than the new–Holocaust—of the Six–Day War of 1967).

The perception of a transcendent demand upon us to preserve the people of Israel, the affirmation of a transcendent ground of value in the face of contemporary nihilism, have led some minority of Jews to a restoration of our relationship with the other partner in the Covenant, God. The absence of God and the hurt we have felt are not intellectually explained. Yet it is possible, despite them, to continue the relationship. For the intellectually determined the most satisfactory way of dealing with this issue is to say that God's power is limited. For those to whom this raises more problems than it solves, there is acceptance without understanding. Both positions are compatible with relating to God in Covenant. I find myself constantly tempted to the former through mostly affirming the latter, a dialectic I find appropriate to affirming the Covenant.

Covenant Theology: The People of Israel

As to the people of Israel, a full–scale ethnicity is presumed here, with the understanding that this ethnicity has itself been transformed by the Covenant relationship. In the transition which the Jews have been undergoing since their entrance into modernity, our social situation has tended to lead us into accepting either religious or secular definitions of the Jews. A sense of the Covenant relationship discloses that such interpretations are reductionist of the multiple layers of Jewish existence. With Covenant primarily a social relationship, primary attention must be given to the effort to live it in social form. The people of Israel having its historic–religious roots in the Land of Israel, the creation there of a Jewish society faithful to the Covenant becomes the primary manifestation of fulfilling Jewish existence.

The Jewish society on the Land of Israel, however, is always subject to the special judgment implied in the unique task it has undertaken, building the Covenant–centered society. While it is theoretically conceivable that such a Jewish society might exist without the political apparatus of a state, in our time statehood is the indispensable instrument of social viability in the Land of Israel. The State of Israel, then, as state, is a means to the fulfillment of the Covenant and not its end. Therefore criticism of it from the vantage of the Covenant purposes of the Jewish people may be considered a Jewish duty.

At the same time, since Jews can fulfill the Covenant relationship anywhere, it becomes possible to validate Diaspora existence. Jewish life there, however, will be judged not only in terms of its faithfulness to God but in terms of its creation of the sense of community so fundamental to the Covenant.

Covenant Theology: Torah—Duty as Personal Responsibility

As to Torah, our sense of Jewish duty emerges from standing in relationship to God as part of the people of Israel. Various theories of revelation might be appropriate to accepting relationship as basic to our existence. For me, the personalist teaching of God's presence as commanding permits me to retain my autonomy while setting me in an individual bond with the people of Israel. I find it especially harmonious with Judaism seen as existence in relationship and my experience trying to live it. However, it should be understood, as against strictly antinomian interpretations of such revelation, that I take the Jewish self not to be atomistic, unattached and individual when standing in relationship with God, but as one of the Jewish people. Hence, responding to the Divine presence cannot only be a matter of what is commanded to me personally at this moment (or what was commanded to the people of Israel at some other time) but what is commanded to me as one whose individuality is not to be separated from my being one of the historic Jewish people.

I therefore come to God with a cultivated consciousness of my people's past and its recorded sense of what God demanded of it. But this apperception is not determinative for me. The immediate experience of relationship with God is. I respond to God autonomously. Yet I do so out of a situation, Covenant, in which Jews have been over the ages and which many other Jews now share. While my time and place, while my individuality introduce certain new factors in the determination of what my duties must now be, I am very much like other Jews of the past and today. Hence, what my reactions to God will be are likely to be very much like theirs. Such responses must also include my consciousness of being one of the people of Israel today. Perhaps, in a heuristic spirit, the Kantian corollary may be displaced to give us some guidance: respond to God with such a sense of your duty that you could will that anyone of the Covenant people, being in such a situation, would respond with a similar sense of duty.

This approach does not restore Jewish law to us or the sense of disciplined action connected with law. I do not see how we can do that theoretically or practically. Law and autonomy are incompatible as long as we are not in the Days of the Messiah. We modern Jews therefore stand in a post–*halachic* situation. That is one of the keystones of our liberalism. Yet it is important to overcome the anarchy which autonomous individualism can easily lead to in so pluralistic a time as ours. (Since our Covenant relationship to God is as a people, it implies some common way of Jewish living.)

The older liberal approach of containing autonomy only within the moral law will no longer do. Intellectually it is not clear that every rational person necessarily must be obligated to the sort of ethical responsibility Kant and his followers took for granted. Jewishly it is clear that limiting autonomy by ethics necessarily makes all the rest of Jewish observance instrumental and therefore unessential. Practically this results in an enforcement of the societal pressures to live as universalists and ignore Jewish particularity. If particularity is of greater concern to us today theologically, the old ethics-ritual split must be rejected as conflicting with our intuition of our present Jewish duty. When action is determined by living in the Covenant relationship, no radical distinction can be made between the source of our ethical duties and our more directly "spiritual" ones. They all come from one relationship and therefore cannot be played off hierarchically one against the other. Yet within this I would suggest that something of the old insight of the liberals as to the primary significance of ethics remains. Our sense of how we must respond *to other human beings* comes rather directly from the personal quality of the relationship between us and God, thereby highlighting the personhood of all people and our responsibility to them. Our sense of what we wish to express *to God* directly comes mainly from who we are and what we as a community feel we want to do in response to God's reality.

The former is more closely related to our sense of God, the latter to our response to God—though each involves the other aspect. They are not two disparate realms of commandment but points on a spectrum of relational response.

Obligation Without External Discipline—and Hope

I do not see that law can arise from such a sense of commandment. Yet it is quite conceivable that something like Jewish "law" might yet surface in our community. One referent of the decision–making process by the individual is the community. We could reach a time when a sufficient number of Jews trying to live in Covenant would do things in sufficiently similar a way that their custom could become significant for them and for other Jews to take into account in determining their Jewish duty. In some stable American–Jewish situation, one might then create, on a Covenantally autonomous basis, a communally influential pattern of living. This would be less than law but it would be more than folkways for the primary response would be to God. The creation of such patterns would be the modern substitute for *halachah* and it is thus possible to suggest that we live in a pre–*"halachic"* time, in this Covenantal sense of the term.

The goal for the individual Jew and the Jewish community remains what it has always been, to create lives of such everyday sanctity and societies of such holiness that God's kingdom will become fact among us. Restoring personalism to Judaism makes personal piety again possible, even mandatory. Ethics can no longer displace God's presence in our lives. Our recent tradition had so little confidence in human power that it waited with virtual resignation for God to bring the Messiah. The liberals had such unbounded confidence in human power that they as good as dispensed with God in trusting to themselves and in humankind's progressive enlightenment to bring the Messianic Age. A sense of Covenant makes messianism a partnership between God and the people of Israel. It requires patience on our part as well as continued religious action; yet it gives us courage despite our failures and hope despite an infinite task which laughs at our successes, for God too is bringing the Messiah.

Chapter 3

What Is Jewish Theology?

Arthur Green

The range and vitality of theology of Judaism emerges in this chapter, which like Borowitz's takes its starting point within a particular tradition of the Judaic system of the dual Torah, the Hasidic and Kabbalistic, or mystical one. Green, like Borowitz, undertakes a definition of the theological enterprise in such a way as to identify a source of received truth and to define the problem for theological thought in terms of mediating that truth and the issues of the day. Green formulates the issues, however, in terms that accommodate all Israel, the eternal people: to discover the meaning of human life and Jewish existence, understood as a life of participation in the Judaic faith community. At stake in Judaic theology is knowledge of God. But, Green rightly urges, a theologian of Judaism is one who works with the Jewish people, "not just with the symbolic vocabulary of the Jewish tradition." so while Green shows us yet another theological tradition and its resources, like Borowitz, his is no sectarian venture.

***

The following remarks are offered from a particular theological point of view. I do not present them as an objective description of a historical phenomenon called Jewish Theology. They are, if you will, a theologian's rather than a historian's definition. I see myself as a theologian in the tradition of an Eastern European school of Jewish mystical theology, itself the heir of the Kabbalistic and Hasidic traditions. The chief figures in this school (here identified as such for the first time) in the twentieth century were Judah Loeb Alter of Ger, author of the *Sefat Emet*, Abraham Isaac Kook, Chief Rabbi of the Holy Land, Hillel Zeitlin, teacher and martyr of the Warsaw ghetto, and my own teacher Abraham Joshua Heschel.

This school is defined by a sense that the starting point of theological reflection is the cultivation of inwardness and the opening of the soul to God's presence throughout the world. The members of this group may all be characterized as experientalist mystics. Each of them celebrates inward religious experience, their own as well as that provided by literary or historic example, as the primary datum with which the theologian has to work. Each in one way or another also points toward an ultimately unitive view of religious truth. They are all engaged in a search for Jewish expression of transcendent oneness, such as might "broaden the bounds of the holy"

*Previously published in *Torah and Revelation*, ed. Dan Cohn-Sherbok. Copyright 1992 by the Edwin Mellen press. Used by permission of the Edwin Mellen Press to overcome even such seemingly ultimate distinctions as those between the holy and the profane or between the divine and human realms.

This group of thinkers also has some other key elements in common. All are awed by the constantly renewing presence of God within the natural world; they may in this sense be said to share a "Creation–centered" theological perspective. Their perspective is deeply immanentist: God is to be known by seeing existence through its "innermost point" or by addressing the questions of "depth theology." A certain crucial veil needs to be lifted in order to enable the mind to achieve a more profound (and essentially intuitive) view of reality. Their religion is in this sense universalistic, relating in the first instance to a divine reality that is not limited to the particular Jewish setting. Within the group there is an evolution to be traced on this question, from the *Sefat Emet*, still living within the Hasidic/mythical universe which sees only the Jewish soul as potentially aware of divinity, to the much greater universalism of a Heschel, a full respecter of the spiritual legitimacy of non–Jewish religious life.

These Eastern European spiritual teachers are all thoroughly comfortable with their Judaism, a garment that is completely natural to them. None of them is primarily a "defender" of the tradition, nor is any of them interested in proving his own orthodoxy to others. They all see *halakhah* as a natural part of the way Jews live, but they do not turn primarily to halakhic texts as their source of spiritual nurturance. In this way they are to be distinguished from another group of Eastern European religious figures, the pan–halakhists or the Lithuanian school, who proclaim *halakhah* itself to be the only authentic expression of Judaism.

I begin my remarks with this excursus on spiritual lineage because I want to make it clear that I see theology as a significant undertaking only in a devotionalist context, i.e., a context where prayer (in the broadest sense), a cultivation of interiority, and awareness of divine presence are given primacy. As this may be considered a somewhat odd or off–beat position among contemporary Jews, I begin by emphasizing its historic roots. In a broader sense, the views I articulate may be called neo–Hasidic. I believe that post–modern Jews' recovery of the Kabbalistic/Hasidic tradition is a decisive event in our ongoing spiritual history, one that should have a great impact upon the future of Jewish theology.

Bearing this legacy in mind, I shall attempt that which the tradition in its wisdom so thoroughly avoids: a definition of Jewish theology and its task. *Each Jewish theology is a religious attempt to help the Jewish people understand the meaning of human life and Jewish existence out of the store of texts, symbols, and historical experience that are the shared inheritance of all Jews.*

This definition seeks to emphasize several key points. It begins by understanding theology as a "religious" undertaking. This point is far from obvious, especially in a world where theology too often dresses itself in academic garb and seeks a borrowed legitimacy from philosophy or social science. By "religious" in this context I mean to say that theology emerges from living participation in the life of the faith–community. It seeks to give expression to the essentially ineffable experience of divinity and to articulate a series of beliefs around the relationships of God, world, and person.

In order to do this, theology must have recourse to language. Herein lies the first of many tensions that characterize the theological enterprise. The mystic knows God mostly in silence. Surely the deep well of inner awareness in which God is to be found reaches far beyond the grasp of worlds or concepts. Both personal experience and Kabbalistic tradition confirm this. Knowing full well the inadequacy of words and the mental constructs they embody, the theologian has no choice but to become articulate. In this we are heirs to both the prophet and the mystical teacher who rail against their inability to refrain from speaking.

Our speech is saved from utter inadequacy by our tradition of sacred speech. God speaks the world into being, according to our Torah, an act that is repeated each day, or perhaps even each moment, in the ongoing renewal of creation. We know that such divine speech is not in our human language, nor is this cosmic speech–act anything quite like our own. Nevertheless, the claim that we worship a God of words is of value as we seek to use language to speak about the sacred. Our prayerbook introduces each day's verbal worship by blessing God "who spoke and the world came to be." Prayer is the bridge between the abstract notion of divine language and the use of human words to speak of God. Let us say it in the language of grammar; the divine first person use of speech—God's own "I am"—is usually inaccessible to us, except in rare moments. Our third person voice in theologizing—"God is"—rings hollow and inadequate. These are brought closer by our willingness to use speech in the second person—the saying of "You" in prayer, our response to the divine "you" addressed to us—which redeems speech for us and brings the divine into the world of language.

This clearly means that theology is dependent upon prayer. Prayer is a primary religious activity, a moment of opening the heart either to be filled with God's presence or to cry out at divine absence. Theology comes later, the mind's attempt to articulate and understand something that the heart already knows. In defining theology as a "religious" activity, I mean to say that it grows out of a rich and textured life of prayer. The theologian's prayer–life, which may be as filled with questioning, doubt, and challenge as it is with submission and praise, is the essential nurturer of religious thinking.

In Jewish terms, theologizing is part of the *mitsvah* of knowing God, listed by Maimonides as first among the commandments. Knowledge of God is the basis of both worship and ethics, according to many of the Jewish sages. The term *da'at* or knowledge bears within it a particularly rich legacy of meaning. It is best translated "awareness," the intimate and consciousness–transforming knowledge that all of being, including the human soul, is infused with the presence of the One. This *da'at*, sometimes compared in the sources to the knowledge with which Adam "knew" his wife Eve, is far more than credence to a set of intellectual propositions. It is a knowing whose roots extend back into the Tree of Life, not just to the Tree of Knowledge.

But the language the Jewish theologian speaks is not one of words alone. The traditions of Israel are filled with speech–acts of a trans–verb sort. These are epitomized by the sounding of the *shofar*, described by some sources as a wordless cry that reaches to those places (in the heavens? within the self? in the Self?) where words cannot penetrate. The same may be said of all the sacred and mysterious silent acts of worship: the binding of *tefillin*, the waving of the *lulav*, the eating of *matzot*. All of these belong to the silent heart of the Jewish theological vocabulary.

In defining Jewish theology as an "attempt to help the Jewish people," I mean to say that the theologian has an active and committed relationship to the community. A Jewish theologian is a theologian who works with the Jewish people, not just with the symbolic vocabulary of the Jewish tradition. There is no Judaism without Jews, and that is no mere tautology. To be a Jewish theologian, especially in an age when the very future of our existence is threatened, is to accept the value of Jewish continuity and to direct one's efforts toward the building of a Jewish future. This does not mean that theology is to become the handmaiden of survivalism, or that particular theological ideas are to be judged on their value for Jewish survival. But it does mean that the theologian speaks out of the midst of a living community, and addresses him or herself in the primary sense to that community of Jews. If there are other masters to be served, as there always are (I think of such masters as pluralism, consistency, scholarly objectivity, and so forth), let us remember that the Jewish people should come near the head of the line.

Here again I need refer to the particular tradition out of which I speak. In this tradition, Jewish theology has passed only in the last two generations from the hands of *rebbes* to those of their less–defined modern successors. The legacy of the Hasidic master is not yet forgotten here. He may be characterized as a latter–day descendent of the Platonic philosopher/king. Drawn by his own inclination to dwell exclusively in the upper realms of mystical devotion, he is forced by communal responsibilities to dwell "below," amid his people, and concern himself with their welfare. Cleaving fast to both realms at once, he thus becomes a pole or channel between heaven and earth. While the contemporary theologian should stay far from the pretense and pomposity that often result from such exaggerated claims of self–importance, he or she would do well to imitate the grave sense of communal as well as spiritual responsibility, and the link between these two, that went with the mantle of those who "said Torah."

Jewish theology seeks to understand "the meaning of human life and Jewish existence." The questions faced by theology are universal. It exists in order to address itself to the essential human quest for meaning; while nurtured from the wellsprings of tradition, it grows most vigorously in the soil of personal religious quest. It wants to address itself to issues of life and death, to our origins in Creation and the purpose of existence itself. Its answers will come in Jewish language, to be sure, and hope-fully in rich and undiluted Jewish language. But it takes its place as a part of the hu-man theological enterprise, and is healthily nourished today as in all ages by contact with the best in philosophical, religious, and scientific thinking throughout the world.

Alongside its universal concerns, Jewish theology will also have to turn itself to the particular, seeking out the meaning of distinctive Jewish existence and the special contribution that the Jewish people has to offer. We have just lived through the most terrible age of martyrdom in Jewish history, and ours is a time when being a Jew can still mean the potential sacrificing of one's children's lives so that our people may live. At the same time, our community suffers terrible losses due to assimilation and indifference. In the face of this reality, the would–be theologian in our midst must offer us some reason why the continuation of our existence is religiously vital, even at such a terrible price. To do anything less would betray the trust we as a com-munity place in the theologian.

"Texts, symbols, and historical experiences" are the quarry out of which a con-temporary Jewish theology is hewn. We are a tradition and a community shaped by and devoted to a text. In the primary sense, text refers here to the written Torah, read and completed each year by the Jews in an ever–renewing cycle of commitment. Whatever the origins of that text, the Jewish religious community has accepted it as holy. It may no longer stand as the authoritative word of a commanding God, but it remains the most essential *sanctum* of the Jewish people, a source of guidance, wisdom, and ancient truth. Our relationship to it may at times include protest and rebellion along with love and devotion. But it remains *our* Torah, and we are its Jews. We can no more reject it and spiritually remain Jews than the fish can reject water, to use a classic image, or than the mature adult can reject his/her own legacy of memory, one that inevitably includes both pain and joy.

Many of our most important sources are written in the form of commentaries to this text. These the theologian must study, seeking to add her/his contemporary voice to this tradition. Here the aggadic strand is particularly important. Jewish theology in its most native form is narrative theology. The theologian was originally one who "told the tale"—that of Creation, of Exodus, of Abraham and Isaac, or of Ruth and Naomi—and subtly put it into a distinctive theological framework. This method is ours to study and continue, as is amply demonstrated by the widespread renewal of Midrashic writing in recent decades, a great sign of health within Jewish theological creativity. The contemporary Jewish theologian could do no better than to retell the tale in his or her own way.

Works of ancient *aggadah* were recreated by the Kabbalists within their own systematic framework to create a profound sort of mystic speech. Study of this aggadic/kabbalistic tradition and the search for ways to adapt it to contemporary usage is a key task of Jewish theology. The old aggadic/homiletic tradition is re-opened once again within Hasidism. Study of the creative use made of traditional sources by the Hasidic masters will serve as another important paradigm for contemporary efforts. The vast literature of Hebrew theological and moral treatises, a genre almost completely neglected other than by historical research, should also be important to the theologian. Contemporary Judaism is also enriched by the literary and poetic creations of many writers in Hebrew, Yiddish, and other languages of Jewish expression. These too should be part of "text" in its broadest sense, as should be the artistic and musical creations of many generations and varied Jewish communities throughout the ages.

I have already mentioned symbols as forms of silent religious speech. Here I would like to digress in order to add a reflection on the power of religious symbolism as constituted int he language of the Kabbalah. The Kabbalists taught of the ten *sefirot*, primal manifestations of the endless One that encompasses all of being. Each of these ten is represented in Kabbalistic language by one or more conventional terms and by a host of symbolic images. A certain face of the divine reality, to take one example, is conventionally called *hesed* or grace. But in Kabbalistic writings it is often referred to as "morning," "milk," "Abraham," "the right hand," "the priest," "love," "south," "lion (on the divine throne)," "myrtle twig," and a host of other names. Each of these terms, when used in the Kabbalists' symbolic reconstruction of the Hebrew language (for we are speaking of nothing less) has the same referent. What the Kabbalist has in effect created is a series of symbolic clusters, and when any member of a cluster is invoked, all the others are brought to mind as well. It is particularly important that each of these clusters contains elements of both classically Jewish and *natural* symbols. Though the Bible saw the variety and splendor of creation as the great testament to God's handiwork, nature was to a degree desacralized in later Judaism, which saw study, religious practice, and reflection on Jewish history as the chief areas where one should seek contact with the holy. The Kabbalist greatly reinvigorates Jewish language by this symbolic *resacralization* of the natural world. Rivers, seas, seasons, trees, and heavenly bodies are all participants in the richly textured description or "mapping" of divinity, which is the Kabbalist's chief task.

Jewish theology needs to find a way to repeat this process, to "redeem" the natural for our theology and to bring the religious appreciation of this world into central focus as an object of Jewish concern. We need to do this first and foremost for our own souls. We need to lead our religious parlance out of the ghetto that allows for the sacrality only of what is narrowly ours and allow ourselves to see again the profound sacred presence that fills all of being. We also need to do this as members of the human religious community, all of which is charged in our day with creating a religious language that will re–root us in our natural surroundings and hopefully lead to a deeper and richer appreciation—and therefore less abuse and waste—of our natural heritage. In this area Jewish theology is lagging far behind the

Jews, many of whom take leading roles in the movement for preservation of the planet, but with little sense that Judaism has anything to offer to these efforts.

The Judaism of Kook, Zeitlin, and Heschel is one that had begun to undertake this task. Shaken to our root by the experience of the Holocaust, our religious language took the predictable root of self–preservation by turning inward, setting aside this universalist agenda as non–essential to our own survival. We needed in those postwar years to concentrate fully on our own condition, first in outcry and later in the rebuilding of our strength, especially through the creation of Israel and its cultural and religious life. Now that time has begun to effect its inevitable healing on both mind and body, we find ourselves somewhat shocked and frightened by the rapid pace of this turn inward and the effect it has had on our people. In the face of these, we find ourselves turning back to the interrupted work of our nascent Jewish universalists and theologians of radical immanence, knowing that we need to resume their task.

The effect of these history–making decades is not lost, however. In adding "historical experiences" to the texts and symbols that comprise the sources of our Jewish learning, I mean to say that there has been a profound change wrought on the Jewish psyche by the events of this century. We are no longer able to ignore the lessons of our own historical situation, as Jews sought to do for so many years. Emancipation, Zionism, and persecution have all joined forces to drive us from that ahistorical plateau where the Jewish people once thought it dwelt in splendid isolation. We need a theology that knows how to learn from history, from our role among the nations, from our experiences both as victim and as conqueror. Without the ability to handle these real–life situations with moral integrity and strength, our Judaism of texts and symbols will become mere cant.

Finally, we need to insist in our definition that all these are "the shared inheritance of all Jews." Nothing in our tradition belongs to an exclusive group within the Jewish people. This includes groups defined by religious viewpoint, by national origin, by gender, and all the rest. The legacy of Hasidism is too important to be left to the *hasidim* alone; Sephardic ballads and Yemenite dance no longer belong to the descendants of those groups alone. Words like "*halakhah*" or "*yeshivah*" should not be left to the Orthodox; they are the inheritance of all Israel. So are observances like dwelling in the *sukkah*, bathing in the *mikveh*, and dancing with the Torah. None of the legacy belongs exclusively to men, and none of it exclusively to women.

All of this should be sufficiently obvious not to need stating here, but that is unfortunately not the case. The theologian should be committed to the entirety of the Jewish people, more than to any sub–group or denomination within it. This will mean an ongoing devotion to the endless task of educating Jews—all kinds of Jews—and bringing them home to their roots in the people Israel. It is both a *mitsvah* and a privilege to participate in this task. For having a key role in it, the theologian should be grateful.

Chapter 4

Faith and Method in Modern Jewish Theology

Eugene B. Borowitz

A principal category for Protestant Christian theology, the matter of faith arises in any account of the future of the theology of Judaism. Precisely what people mean by "faith" is what is defined: faith involves integrity in deed as much as in word; faith in God; faith in propositions. Since Borowitz forms a theology for Reform Judaism, he raises considerations of special interest to his Judaic system, the matter of "the regulating principle," or the reason why. And this matter of the authority of the Torah when worked out in the language and categories of the century now done— historic progress, idealism, naturalism—proves uncertain. Borowitz offers instead the paradox: "We know we do not arrive at the content of Judaism without faith. But we also believe that we cannot affirm everything to which believing Jews in the past centuries have been committed. Hence we seek to limit our faith in Judaism by some sort of regulating principle." From this point, Borowitz spells out his own, personal response: "What I must choose and of the method which derives from it." None can doubt that the important component of twenty–first theology of Judaism put forth by Reform Judaism will flow from the arguments of this paper.

***

I

My subject is the role of faith in modern Jewish theology. In this context, faith may have three separate though related meanings: faith as commitment to action, faith as commitment to content, and, mostly, faith as commitment to a beginning. Each level of definition has its particular implications for theological method and must therefore be treated on its own.

On the first level, to say that Jewish theology involves faith means, at least, that we expect the Jewish theologian to live what he teaches. Of the philosopher of religion we can demand only that he understand the reasoning of religious thinkers, not that he believe and live by all the diverse systems he expounds. A theologian should be no less academically competent and proficient, but in his case one critical requirement is added which radically changes the context of his scholarship. He shares the faith he expounds, and we expect his life to show his strength of belief in the truths he proclaims.

If faith for us must include both acts and thoughts, it is because of our frequent experience with those whose concepts are persuasive but whose behavior is repulsive. Not all men who think bright thoughts, not even those who are persuaded of their truth, actually live by them—even most of the time. This gap between cognition and decision, between idea and resolve, cannot be ignored. We may not ourselves believe much, but we will judge the man who says he believes more by his performance than by his preaching.

In Judaism, in which action has traditionally been valued above thought, the theologian's life must be the first evidence of his teaching. And for a Jew that must inevitably mean not just his private and familial existence, but his participation in the ongoing activity of the synagogue and of the Jewish people as a whole.

At this level there is virtual unanimity among us. The Jewish theologian should live his understanding of Judaism, and through his Jewish living he should test and refine his Judaism. But Jewish action stems from an understanding of the content of Judaism, and that content is itself established through faith. Surprising as it may seem, that is the almost unanimous conclusion of contemporary Jewish thinkers. Let us take, for example, the absolutely central question: How do we know there is a God? Even those Jewish theologians who are committed to the utmost use of reason acknowledge that at a given point reason will carry us no further. It may prepare the way. It may be necessary for clarification afterward, but reason itself does not lead us to the conclusion that there really is a God. The only way to get to Judaism's position is by faith.

Mordecai Kaplan has said that belief in God "is an assumption that is not susceptible of proof."[1] He has written, "Whence do we derive this faith in a Power that endorses what ought to be? Not from that aspect of the mind which has to do only with mathematically and logically demonstrated knowledge. Such faith stems from that aspect of the mind which finds expression in the enthusiasm for living, in the passion to surmount limitations."[2] Elsewhere he speaks of it as an intuition or an affirmation of one's whole being.[3]

Levi Olan similarly acknowledges that "the God faith is not subject to proof in the rational or scientific sense. . . . Ultimately, as Judaism learned at the beginning, God is an affirmation and postulate."[4] What affirmations and postulates involve is made clear by him in another connection: "Faith by its very nature involves affirmations *beyond the rational* [italics added] and the Hebraic spirit is not characterized by a rigid syllogistic encasement."[5] Similarly, Roland Gittelsohn, in the course of his argument for the existence of God, says: "The mind . . . by itself, unaided by the heart, . . . can never provide total answers. . . . We need faith. Man cannot live by reason alone. . . . Of course we need faith to carry us beyond the bounds of reason."[6]

We are so accustomed to hearing these men called "rationalists" that we tend to accept that appellation naively. We begin to believe that they are true philosophic rationalists, that if we follow their views we may hope to dispense with the kind of faith which they themselves categorize as "beyond the rational" or "beyond the bounds of reason." But we have only ourselves to blame for this illusion. The thinkers themselves have been far more rigorous and honest. They say plainly: "We need faith." Their claim to the title "rationalist" does not derive from their elimination of faith but from their effort to control faith by reason, as we shall see.

There have been Jewish thinkers in ages past—not only in medieval times, but as recently as Hermann Cohen—who were thoroughgoing philosophic rationalists. These men sought to demonstrate the truth about the existence of God by means of a rigorously logical argument. In this, the simple philosophic meaning of the term, it would be true to say that there are no rationalists among liberal Jewish theologians today.

This description is not limited to naturalists. Leo Baeck, often considered a rationalist by the uncritical, is rather to be found with those who clearly confess reason's inadequacy to establish a Jewish view of God. One might have expected Baeck, as a faithful if independent follower of Hermann Cohen, to restate Cohen's philosophical demonstration of the necessity of the idea of God. Baeck, however, completely avoids this and instead, following Schleiermacher, bases his discussion on inner experience, grounds which would have been repugnant to the neo–Kantian philosopher of Marburg. Thus it is not of God as idea, but of God as Exalted One, as Mystery, as Secret, that Baeck often speaks of Him. Moreover, Baeck does not wait for the end of a long, rationally ordered argument to introduce faith as the means of reaching a triumphant conclusion. God, in all His shroudedness as well as His righteousness, is present from the very beginning of Baeck's discussion. When, in his chapter on "Faith in God," he discusses faith directly, he says:

> In Judaism faith is nothing but the living consciousness of the Omni-present. . . . This Conviction is not sustained by speculation and gnosis, or by facts and proofs. Hence there is in it nothing subtly reasoned out, nothing demonstrated or expounded. On the contrary, it is the opposite of the faith which has to be set forth by arguments or established by victories.[7]

Only Martin Buber, among contemporary thinkers, finds God by knowledge, so to speak, rather than by faith. Buber manages this by positing an epistemology which has two categories of knowing, object–knowing and subject–knowing. The latter is as natural and everyday as the former. It involves no special state of consciousness and is clearly not to be compared with the mystic's special experience. Buber says we know God as we know other subjects, save that He is non–corporeal. Thus faith for buber is not a way of reaching convictions about God, but the life which comes from knowing Him.

Philosophically, we cannot insist a priori that it is impossible that knowledge is available in two modes, each with its appropriate structures and values. If Buber's categories are right, it would seem just as rational to know subjects by subject–knowing as it is to know objects "objectively." In those terms one might facetiously suggest that Buber is the only "rationalist" among Jewish philosophers today. But the title has now lost all meaning. Though faith has become knowing for Buber, what he has really shown us is that all subjects are known by faith, and that faith is more common to life than most modern men had thought.

Thus, there is almost universal agreement among contemporary writers that faith is basic to Jewish theology, not only on the level of action but on the more fundamental level of content as well.[8]

Once faith has been admitted to Jewish theology, we are led to a third and deeper plane of discussion. Faith brings us to such fundamental Jewish affirmations as the existence of God, His goodness and its eventual triumph. But what else will it bring us of Judaism? As modern Jews are we prepared to accept everything that has been characteristic of believing Jews over the centuries? Admitting faith to our religiosity raises the danger of Orthodoxy and sets the liberal Jew in search of a principle by which to regulate the content that faith may contribute to his liberal Judaism.

The need of a regulative principle is prompted, too, by our knowledge of human history. Summoning the deepest of men's passions, faith may lead to superstition, fanaticism, and oppression, and it has done so among Jews as among other peoples. Perhaps a liberal Jew could somehow reconcile Orthodox Jewish observance with his liberalism, if his personal decision so demanded. But that his faith might bring him into conflict with his sense of morality is as intolerable as it is a realistic possibility. For this reason, even more than because of Orthodoxy, a means of controlling faith must be found.

In traditional Judaism the search would quickly be over. The halachic tradition of authentic interpretation would do this in theory, even as the sanctions of the observant, organized Jewish community would do so in practice. But for us liberal Jews, who have neither a unifying law nor an observant community to channel our faith, but who rather require a firm faith so that we may rally our community and reestablish standards of Jewish living, the regulating principle must be found on the personal, not the communal, level.

How has this need been met over the past one hundred or so years of liberal Jewish theology? For Abraham Geiger, the progress which history displayed in its systematic evolution was the criterion of his Jewish faith. In its name he could abandon the personal Messiah. For Baeck, God's will is always understood as an ethical demand, and ethical monotheism is the test of Judaism. For this reason he makes the Jewish people a means to preserve and foster ethical monotheism, and

Jewish observance a secondary means to preserve that primary means. For Buber, though faith is a kind of knowing, one is commanded only as one encounters or is personally encountered. Thus Buber is halachically more radical than the most radical Reform Jew and rejects any practice which stems from community tradition rather than personal experience.

For Kaplan, the modern, naturalistic, particularly social scientific, understanding of man and society is indispensable. This, he believes, requires him to posit an impersonal God. Roland Gittelsohn's argument carries this view of reason as the arbiter of faith to its fullest and clearest exposition. Now, let us read the sentences which follow our previous citation and thus give his thought his own completion:

> Of course we need faith to carry us beyond the bounds of reason. But that faith must be built on a foundation of reason, must be consistent with the reasonable and the known, not contradictory to them. If the direction of the knowledge yielded by experience and reason be represented by a solid line, faith must be a dotted line which continues in the same general direction, not one which goes off at a capricious and contradictory angle.[9]

Here faith is strictly bound by reason, and Gittelsohn's reason can permit him to have faith in only a limited God.

We may, with some hesitation, summarize this cursory survey. Liberal Jewish thinkers have generally sought to regulate their faith by finding a universal standard of truth and reinterpreting Judaism in its terms. This standard has usually been borrowed from the philosophy current in the theologian's time and place, though Cohen and Buber created their own. If liberal Jewish thinkers, excepting Cohen, deserve to be called rationalists, though they rely on faith and cannot dispense with it, it is because they have regularly sought to control their faith by some rational principle.

II

Now let us turn to our own case. What principle is most appropriate to our day?

Before responding to this question, we must make very clear the responsibility involved in making our decision. The choice of a principle to guide the operation of faith is not a modest technical matter. It involves the very heart of our Judaism. As we select one concept pattern over another we are already committing ourselves to a certain character in our Judaism—not just its beliefs, but the balance and weight of its observances as well. This principle changes the nature of God, alters Israel's character, and reforms the hierarchy of Jewish values, as we have seen above. This is the most fundamental decision we can make with regard to our religion.

For some men the response is relatively easy. They recognize in one or another contemporary philosophic system man's best guide to truth, and they interpret

Judaism through it. But for most of us the choice is not that simple, particularly when we look at the views which previous thinkers have espoused.

If we turn to the vaguely Hegelian trust in historic progress of either an Abraham Geiger or a Kaufmann Kohler, we find ourselves in most uncongenial territory. History is not always progressive, and we find it difficult to say with conviction that we know the truth of man and God better and more clearly than did a previous age. We do know, however, that we cannot, as they did, unselfconsciously choose what we wish in history and, by calling it "the highest," "the noblest" or "the best," consider it validated by the historical march of truth.

The rational idealism of a Cohen, even as modified by Baeck, is similarly problematic. We are troubled by the former's relation to the real world. How shall we make the transfer from the philosophically necessary idea to the concretely existing reality? And in both cases, how can we today reestablish a philosophic certainty which derives from the clarity and independence of the ethical demand? We obviously do not wish to compromise the significance or the authority of the ethical. But it is another thing to make ethics the one sure and self–substantiating foundation of all our other affirmations of value. The varying apprehensions of ethical responsibility among different peoples, and even in different social classes within Western society itself, as well as the role education and personal exposure play in determining conscience, all make of the ethical a problem with which to deal, rather than an unshakable base on which to build.

Nor is the scientific naturalism of Kaplan, Olan, and Gittelsohn any less troublesome. Perhaps in the thirties it was possible to hold simply and self–evidently, as Kaplan did, that to be modern necessarily meant to think in terms of naturalism.[10] Today there are clearly other ways of being sophisticatedly modern, particularly since naturalism has floundered in dealing with the key philosophic problem of our time, the identification and authorization of values. One can take a thoroughgoing scientific view of reality and come up morally neutral, as the atomic bomb so dramatically illustrated. Such an uncommitted naturalism is far more "rationalistic," that is, internally consistent, than is Kaplan's theism. His response to this charge is that such a naturalism cannot motivate morality, and therefore must be rejected.[11] Philosophically, if the morality is prior, Kaplan should, like the neo–Kantians, first rationally establish the realm of the ethical, which he never does. Practically it is simply not true that naturalists, agnostic philosophically of god or ethics, cannot be morally active, as the cases of Bertrand Russell and others make clear.

Gittelsohn's more tightly drawn argument from science suffers from a similar difficulty. If scientific reason knows anything, it is that superfluous hypotheses are rigorously to be excluded. To add God to a strictly scientific view of the universe is therefore not to continue in a direction previously established but to add a new and rationally unnecessary direction. It is not just adding a bit of spice to the food, but radically changing the menu.

Of course, if what Gittelsohn means is that God seems a "reasonable" addition to the scientific view of the universe, that is another matter. It is a far cry from the philosophically ordered "rational" to what I personally can believe, the "reasonable." What makes the addition of God so "reasonable" to Gittelsohn is that he already believed in Him before the argument began. Indeed, it would be difficult to explain why Gittelsohn prefers the scientific data and opinions which will make the addition of God reasonable to all those which would not, if it were not that he begins with faith in God. Thus while Gittelsohn claims faith only completes a line which rationality itself drew, it seems clear to me that faith here preceded reason and guided it.

Levi Olan, who has given a similar argument about man's place in the universe, has been far more precise on the matter of presuppositions. While insisting that reason is a fundamental ingredient of truth, he has, in his discussion of faith and reason, frankly noted: "Reason, of itself, is never the source of truth."[12] Thus he correctly calls his evidence from modern science neither proofs nor even indications but resources. In other words, having established by faith that he believes in man, he can then find much substantiation in modern science for such a view.

These previous choices—historic progress, idealism, naturalism—do not easily commend themselves today as means of guiding our faith. Perhaps, then, we should turn to the current fashions in philosophy: linguistic analysis, Tillichian ontology, or one of the varieties of religious (not atheistic) existentialism? Or perhaps, dissatisfied with all the alternatives, we ought instead to begin by creating our own system of universal truth.

Which of these living, if troublesome, options shall we choose?

But considering what is at stake, should we not first ask: *How* shall we choose? On what basis shall we decide whether to adopt one principle or another to regulate our faith? This question may with equal significance be asked of the man who is not troubled by our uncertainty but knows which philosophy he must follow. How does he know it? How did he determine it?

Three possibilities suggest themselves. At one time it might have been possible to suggest that certain truths were self–evident, or so clear and distinct that one could not doubt them. Obviously a philosophy which based itself on them was sound. Such a view could be accepted by only a few in our day. We have learned to doubt everything, not least ourselves, our certainty, and our intuition. To be modern is, to begin with, to be critical.

Perhaps, then, we should prefer to see our choice more as a hypothesis, an educated guess, a temporary venture whose validity we will determine as we experience the results of its use and its application to life.

In many ways that is an attractive suggestion. Surely we do not consider ourselves in possession of absolute truth here and now. We, as liberals, do not want to take up a dogmatic stand, one which is not open to change and the possibility of whose further refinement is rejected in advance.

But while we are determined to remain open to new and keener truth, it is difficult indeed to call the principle we seek but a tentative surmise. Let us remember what is involved in this decision. On this "hypothesis" our whole religion hangs. What is at stake is simply—*everything*. A commitment of such intense involvement and immense consequence is not merely an enlightened hunch about what might possibly turn out to be right. In all its momentariness, in all its openness to re-adjustment, I do not see how we can call our choice less than an act of faith.

Indeed, the very structure of the decision itself makes that clear. When we are judging among alternative possibilities of reason (in fact, when we stand before any single system of reason asking ourselves whether we shall use it), we cannot use reason itself as the basis of decision. The criterion of the adequacy of reason cannot be reason itself, for it is precisely reason which is being judged. Or, to put the matter more directly, every philosophy begins with an act of faith. That is what we mean when we say that each one inevitably has its own assumptions. Assumptions are not validated by reason. They are an expression of faith.

On this point, too, Olan has been far more clear and consistent than other naturalists. Beginning in 1947 (as far back as I have been able to trace the matter), he has openly referred to liberalism as a "faith." An essay published in that year is appropriately entitled: "Rethinking the Liberal Faith."[13] And his address to the Central Conference of American Rabbis in 1962 was on the theme: "New Resources for a Liberal Faith."[14] Olan does not seek to prove the rational necessity of liberalism. He rather admits that liberalism is a faith, one which is consistent with reason but clearly not established by it. Faith first establishes a matrix, and then, within its frame, reason is free to operate fully.

In short, choosing a regulative principle involves a paradox. We know we do not arrive at the content of Judaism without faith. But we also believe that we cannot affirm everything to which believing Jews in the past few centuries have been committed. Hence we seek to limit our faith in Judaism by some sort of regulating principle. Only now is it clear that no self–justifying, autonomous principle exists, but that all the possibilities before us themselves involve a prior act of faith. Thus, we can delimit our Jewish faith only be acknowledging that we have a *prior faith*, in whose name we are willing to alter and revise traditional Judaism. This is the third and deepest level of faith on which the Jewish theologian must take a stand, commitment not only to action or to content but also to one particular beginning. Thus the structure of Jewish theology is tripartite, or even reduplicated. It begins in faith, and this makes possible the work of reason which, in turn, ends with faith—from this point on it is always faith followed by reason followed by faith in infinite, better messianic, progression.

So, to return to our theme, I ask again which approach shall we today choose?

III

From this point on I should not speak of what "we" should choose. Rather, in accord with what I said on the first level about the theologian's thought and life, I should rather speak of what I must choose and of the method which derives from it. If I say "we," it is in the hope that there are others who share my commitment and that I am articulating their views, consciously held or not, as well as my own.

My position is simple. I believe that the general method of Jewish theology over these past hundred years no longer makes sense. It reflects a point of view that may once have been necessary or even desirable but is so no longer. And it is time we consciously confronted this issue and radically altered our course.

Perhaps I can clarify my position by a question, hypothetical to be sure, but not unrealistic. Suppose that we follow the traditional method of liberal Jewish theology and choose an intellectual medium for our faith, say neo–Kantianism or existentialism. We carefully work out the meaning of our Judaism in its terms, adding some insights, on the one hand, but also refusing to believe this or observe that, on the other. Whereupon, over the years, we discover that the philosophy in which we had placed such faith is not nearly so adequate to life as we had thought. Indeed, we now wish to replace it with a better one. But wait. We had based our Judaism on that philosophy. In its name we had both justified and revised our Judaism. Once we have lost faith in our philosophy, do we lose our faith in Judaism as well? Would we, in the face of this intellectual setback, conclude that Judaism itself no longer had meaning for us?

Some men have indeed given up their Judaism under such circumstance, but I would like to believe that I would not and that the majority of Jews would not either. Despite such an intellectual catastrophe we would insist that we knew Judaism was still true. And we would do so despite the crash of reason and the tragedy of this experience, because our belief in Judaism was deeper than our trust in any philosophy.

Let me be blunt. Our theologians in the past century have acted as if they knew a truth superior to Judaism. But I do not know a body of knowledge or a system of understanding God and man and history superior to Judaism. I do not have a faith more basic to my existence than my Judaism. I believe in Judaism not because there are such good expositions of its content and its meaning, but despite all the inadequate and clumsy statements of its substance, including my own. I should be delighted one day to have a philosophically tenable exposition of the truth of Judaism, but I shall not wait for one to believe in it. I want faith in Judaism to come before any other faith, and I want to make this priority of faith in Judaism my methodological starting point.

Surely rabbis, students, teachers and servants of Judaism do not have to be reminded of their commitment to Judaism. But what is of critical concern to me is the level on which that commitment is made. This questions of primacy is not only crucial to our theological method, but explains the great difficulty rabbis often encounter in dealing with their congregants. Let me take two examples.

Every rabbi has had to deal with intellectuals whose approach to life was genuinely framed in terms of a given mental pattern. When such a man inquires seriously about Judaism, we are eager to tell him of its truth but usually have great difficulty in doing so. The reason is clear. This man has a prior faith. The only way we can make ourselves understood and, we hope, convincing to him, is to translate Judaism into the terms of his prior faith. And that is just the trouble. Often his private faith is so constructed that it does not make possible a belief in God or—to him, worse—an institutionalized religion. But whether he already has a hospitable or inhospitable point of view, we must recognize its priority in his life. We must talk to him in his terms, and that is why we have such difficulty doing so to our own satisfaction.

This task of explaining one's faith to a man with another faith has an old and honorable theological history. Its name is unfortunate. It is called apologetics. Much of our work not only with intellectuals but with our members as well is apologetic theology. And, in general, liberal Jewish theology this past century has been apologetic theology. Perhaps unconsciously, it seems to have assumed that it was addressing nonbelievers. It then took up its argument in terms the nonbeliever could perhaps accept and sought to explain Judaism convincingly in them.

Apologetics is an important practical task, not only for the Jew who does not believe but also for all those men of good will who seek its truth. We have a responsibility to share such truth as we have found. But apologetics cannot be our primary intellectual task today. Before we devise a theology for the outsider, we must clarify what those inside the circle of faith share.

If our faith in Judaism is prior to any other body of truth, then it is entitled to receive our attention in its own right, not just as explanation in terms of another point of view.

More critical to this issue of priority is the case of our more loyal members, those who have some faith in Judaism. Why does their Judaism generally have so little impact on their lives? Why do we so often find it difficult to communicate to them the over–whelming importance of Jewish belief and observance? Here, too, the answer may be found in analyzing the level of their Jewish faith. They do believe in Judaism, but they have other faiths of greater importance. As long as Judaism can be explained in terms of their private world of belief, they will accept it. We win their willingness to Jewish action when we explain it in their terms, say mental health or the image of themselves as good parents, dutiful children, or loyal Americans. But let the demands transgress their private norms—say we suggest mid–week Hebrew, daily prayer, or public agreement to racially integrated housing—and Judaism has become a bore, a chore, a nag.

That is the danger of marketing Judaism in the consumer's terms, of our informal apologetics. We are covertly endorsing the private faith by which our member lives. We never shake him loose from his more basic faith. We never make Judaism the foundation of his faith, and he lives out his days, using Judaism when it suits his purposes, rejecting it when it does not.

Many people are attracted to Reform Judaism for just this reason, not because it is "convenient," but because they know we stand committed to freedom of individual conscience. We will not deny each man's right to spiritual self–determination. The result in many cases has been that our members believe first in themselves, their needs, their goals, their image, and only on a secondary level in Judaism, its God, its commandments, is aspirations. And that is why every sensitive servant of the God of Israel suffers so as he works with his people. A religion that takes second place is no religion. Unless we make Judaism primary in our lives and in the lives of our people, we shall not have accomplished that first step on which all the rest of the journey depends.

Liberal Judaism is committed both to the self and to the tradition. Previous generations sought regularly to put the self first, to work from the self back to the tradition. In part they were right. The individual must always be the foundation of belief and thus retain the right to disbelieve. Our full respect for his freedom makes the right of dissent inalienable.

But many of our people have gone one step further. We taught them that Jewish tradition was not absolute, but that they had the duty to reach their own religious conclusions. They have transformed this, mostly unconsciously, into a whole view of life. They have made their selfhood the ultimate source of their religiosity, and their individuality the determinative principle of their faith. They confidently judge such truth as comes to them from without in terms of their goals and their predilections. They may occasionally find themselves confused and troubled, and they may then turn to Judaism for help. But mostly they seek a new fad, a new recreation, for they cannot abandon their operative faith that they personally know more about man and his destiny than does Judaism. "The anxious shall live by his faith in himself." This position is a logical outgrowth of liberalism, but it is at the same time the source of a superior, sometimes patronizing attitude toward Jewish belief and Jewish action. As long as Judaism is not primary to the existence of our people, we cannot hope to see their inertia and apathy disappear.

But can we give primary allegiance to a tradition we cannot accept as absolute? Can we retain the self's right to judge and to dissent, without turning it into a rival principle of faith? That is, indeed, what I am suggesting. By faith in Judaism I mean the conscious, personal assent to the unique meaningfulness and significance of the Jewish religious tradition for our lives. Such faith affirms a qualitative distinction between the body of truth given us about God, man, and history in Judaism and any other system or structure, without thereby insisting that Judaism is always right or cannot learn on this or that issue. Being founded on individual assent, it likewise guarantees the right to dissent without thereby raising the self to the status of a prior principle.

IV

The faith by which I seek to live as a liberal Jew is therefore a vigorous affirmation of the primacy of Judaism for my life if not of its absolute character. If I am consistently and rigorously to carry on the work of theology in its terms, a fourfold process suggests itself.

First, it should be obvious that such Jewish theology begins not with an idealist, naturalist, ontological, or linguistic philosophy, or an existential diagnosis of the self, but with the tradition and its affirmations. Nor will the disciplined detachment of a Büchler or a Marmorstein, or the quiet appreciation of a Schechter or a Moore, suffice us. They saw the Jewish past as an object of investigation. I see it rather as having a claim upon me and my life reasonably similar to that which it had upon other generations of Jews. Their careful objectivity can only be a beginning for a search which now must also ask: what did it mean once to believe such a faith? What did it mean to try to live such a faith? And, most important, what does it mean for me to join my forefathers in this belief? We begin with the tradition not as an interesting curio from the past or a source of quotations to illustrate some modern view, but as a living content of belief which confronts us in authority and challenge.

Nor can we, in the second place, say in advance that we should limit our attention and concern to just those aspects which are relevant to us. Because we assert no principle prior to Judaism we cannot know beforehand what no longer has the power to speak to us and to guide our lives. We must pay attention to the priesthood as to the other prophets, to the rabbinic apocalypses and mysticisms as to their ethics. And we must, if we would be true to our faith, remain as open as possible to what Jewish tradition can teach us, even if that means we might end up believing it all. The methodological principle here is that we seek to make our faith in Judaism self–regulating. Once prophecy was that judgement–from–within that helped the tradition transcend itself. Our hope is that a living Jewish faith can show the way to an ever truer Judaism.

Third, our openhearted search of the tradition may from time to time lead us to dissent. Because we do not wish to make a faith of dissent, we should not search to disagree nor study to disavow. In our affirmation of the primary value of Judaism we would not easily or peacefully dissociate ourselves from its teachings. When we are in all seriousness moved to disagree, the responsibility now rests upon us to justify that disagreement. Previous generations of liberal Jews often acted as if Judaism had to justify itself to the Jew. I am arguing that making Jewish faith primary calls on us to justify ourselves when we dissent from it.

Nor do I worry that this shift of responsibility will make it difficult for the liberal to remain free and selective. We can rely not only on his decades of autonomy and the influence of the American environment to strengthen his will to think for himself, but also on the instinctive human disinclination to accept duty and responsibility freely.

This affirmation of the right to dissent is the reason we cannot follow the theological methodology of Abraham Heschel. Omitting now all questions of the literary form in which he puts his arguments, the content does seek to be true to the Jewish tradition in its own terms. Heschel's favorite response to the questions of modern thought is to point out how the reverse may be asked if we only begin from within the circle of Jewish faith. But while he is no fundamentalist and makes allowances for the humanity of the channels of revelation, he does not understand genuine dissent. Again and again he asks whether it is believable that a biblical author should lie or misrepresent. Again and again he characterizes possible alternative thoughts as unthinkable, unbelievable, irrational, even insane.[15] We can recognize the consistency of his theology with one variety of Jewish believing, but it is one whose certainty liberals do not share. Perhaps this contrast with Heschel's full–fledged neo–Orthodoxy will make clear why I believe the position enunciated here with all its emphasis on the priority of faith in Judaism, is yet fully a liberal one.

Fourth, from this dynamic process of confronting the claims of the tradition in its fullness, and working out concurrence and dissent, the individual will come to know himself fully. It is not just that Judaism will teach him what a man is and ought to be. In thinking through his disagreements with the tradition, in seeking to justify and explain his necessary difference of opinion, he will find himself revealed. Both Judaism as accepted guide and as rejected standard will call forth the mixture of person and tradition that should mark the modern Jew.

This living interchange between the self and the tradition can thus provide the base from which the individual can reach out to all that diversity of modern life and culture which the tradition could not know. Again the order is reversed. We do not here begin with psychiatry or democracy and come to find what in Judaism agrees with them. Rather, in confrontation with the tradition we create a matrix of value with which to reach out to modern culture, willing to learn from it where we can, but sufficiently secure that we shall not also hesitate to criticize it. The firmer our roots are in our Judaism the freer we will feel to participate in modern society in its most varied activities. Knowing with reasonable clarity who we are and for what we stand, we can go our way as critics or enthusiasts with quiet confidence.

I have tried to make clear the way in which method in Jewish theology necessarily depends upon faith. The critical question then becomes: What is your primary faith? For some of us that faith is Judaism, and, as a result, we feel that a new methodology is needed in liberal Jewish theology. Men of other basic commitments will take other directions. That is their privilege and their right. If anything can characterize the proposal given here, it is this: for me and many others the crucial question of our existence has shifted from "How can a Jew truly be a modern man?" to "How can a modern man be truly a Jew?"

Notes

[1]Mordecai Kaplan, *The Meaning of God in Modern Jewish Religion* (New York: Jewish Reconstructionist Foundation, 1947) 28.

[2]*The Jewish Reconstructionist Papers* (New York: Behrman's Jewish Book House, 1936) 98.

[3]*The Meaning of God in Modern Jewish Religion*, 84.

[4]*Yearbook* of the Central Conference of American Rabbis for 1962 (New York, 1963) 238.

[5]*Judaism* 5/2 (Spring 1956) 114.

[6]Roland Gittelsohn, *Man's Best Hope* (New York: Random House, 1961) 61-62.

[7]Leo Baeck, *The Essence of Judaism* (New York: Macmillan, 1936) 118-19.

[8]Obviously this does not mean that all the content of Judaism is derived from or reached by faith, but that its major premises, such as the existence of God, His goodness, the ultimate triumph of righteousness, revelation, election, all involve faith.

[9]Gittelsohn, ibid., 62.

[1]Kaplan, *Judaism as a Civilization* (New York: Reconstructionist Press, 1957) 36-45.

[11]Ibid., 309-10.

[12]Olan, *Yearbook*, 114.

[13]Olan, "Rethinking the Liberal Faith," in *Reform Judaism, Essays by Alumni of the Hebrew Union College* (Cincinnati: HUC Press, 1949) 28ff.

[14]Reprinted below.

[15]Although I cannot associate myself with Ben–Horin's own exaggeration and the dogmatism which he brings to his pragmatic criteria, the reader will find a useful collection of some of Heschel's most disturbing habits in Meir Ben–Horin, "The Ultimate and the Mystery," in the *Jewish Quarterly Review* 51/1 (July, 1960).

Chapter 5

Has Judaism Still Power to Speak?
A Religion for an Age of Crisis

Will Herberg

"Crisis here means the perennial plight of man, who . . . sees the goal, is driven to motion, yet cannot find the way—who desperately needs the truth, strains to attain it, yet can never be sure that he has reached it." Written a half–century ago, Herberg's essay will still find its readers a half–century from now, because he provides perspective and defines where matters stand in relationship to the ages. His age of crisis is not the same as ours, and ours will not define that of our heirs. But the issue of crisis—turning, renewal, opportunity, danger, all at once—is sure to confront every generation, for that is what history deals as each age's lot. The main work, Herberg makes clear, pertains to "the fundamental problems of life." Theology comes from not recluses but persons of affairs, and theology is acutely contemporary or inert and merely academic. That does not mean theology is required to address for its agenda the current platform of a political party, but it does mean that theology is going to introduce God into the affairs of humanity, and human affairs into the realm of the transcendent. It is the mediating science. What makes Herberg's paper enduring in its interest lies in his mastery of the Protestant Christian and also Judaic theological traditions. He is able to see the Judaic in the context of the Christian framing of issues. But as a Judaic thinker, he insists, eternal Israel lies at the center of humanity: "The fate of the Jew has become essentially typical of the fate of contemporary man. The demonic evil and unreason which mankind loosed upon itself . . . found in the Jew its first and chosen victim. . . . In the Jew, the archetype of the outsider standing forever at the brink of nothingness, the alienation of contemporary man, his malaise and homelessness in the world, find their most intense expression."

$$***$$

The revival of creative theological thinking is generally recognized as one of the significant events in recent intellectual history. Theology, as we are beginning to learn, is not just a scholastic wordgame of abstract system–making, remote from life. It has something to say, something directly relevant to the fearful predicament in which modern man finds himself. "The Christian account of human motivation," Arthur M. Schlesinger Jr. points out in commenting on a work of Reinhold Niebuhr,

*Previously appeared in *From Marxism to Judaism: The Collected Writings of Will Herberg*, ed. David G. Dalin, published by Markus Weiner Publishing, New York, 1989. Copyright *Commentary Magazine*. Used by permission of B'nai B'rith.

"is massive, subtle and intricate, and it throws light on certain present dilemmas which baffle liberalism or Marxism. Whatever you may say about Augustine, he would not have been much surprised by the outcome of the Russian Revolution."

In the past generation, Christian theology has made an impressive effort to rise to its proper task—which is to interpret life and history, man and the universe, in ultimate terms. Without rejecting the insights gained on other levels of analysis, it has striven to include and transcend them, to fuse them into a single *Weltanschauung* that can serve at once as the ultimate logic and dynamic of life.

But what about Jewish theology? We have long prided ourselves on being universally recognized as the People of the Book. What have we done to make the Book relevant to the perplexities of our age? What has been our response in terms of creative religious think, theological interpretation, or prophetic witness? What word has Judaism had for mankind in agony?

The revival of Christian theology followed upon World War I, which put an end to the smug self–satisfaction of Western civilization and therewith to Western man's high illusions of approaching omnipotence and perfectibility. It may be said to date from that day in 1919 when Karl Barth stood in his little parish church in Safenwil, Switzerland, called upon to say something meaningful to a congregation still shattered by the impact of the war. He took up his Bible and preached. As he himself describes it, he was like a man who, uncertainly climbing the dark and winding staircase of a church tower, reaches for the bannister to steady himself, and gets hold of the bellrope instead.

The echoes of that bell, which reached the world in the *Römerbrief* that same year, have not yet died down. The steady stream of writings that have come from Barth's pen in Switzerland, in Germany, and then in Switzerland again, have had an immense effect in reshaping religious thinking on the Continent, in Britain, and in America. From Switzerland too has come the voice of Emil Brunner, the Zürich theologian, whose systematic works have had an even greater direct influence in the English–speaking world. Barth and Brunner are neo–Reformation theologians—that is, their work is primarily a reinterpretation of the Reformation tradition of Luther, Calvin, and Zwingli. Originally closely identified, they have now developed important and perhaps crucial differences. Both have found partisans and followers throughout Protestant Europe and America.

Concurrently, significant new trends have also appeared in the Roman Catholic and Eastern Orthodox communions. The Catholic revival in France predates somewhat the First World War but its major contributions fall in the postwar period, and the reworking of Thomism in contemporary terms, in particular the development of the idea of Christian Personalism, is linked with the name of Jacques Maritain. The intellectual renaissance in Eastern Orthodoxy is limited to a handful of Russian thinkers living in exile (the late Nicholas Berdyaev was perhaps best known), but is none the less brilliant for that.

In the United States, neo–Reformation theology has found its exponents among men like Reinhold Niebuhr, H. Richard Niebuhr, Paul Tillich (in this country since 1933), Robert L. Calhoun, and John C. Bennett. What they have had to say has perhaps had more meaning for Americans, so obviously is it cast in terms of our own experience.

Most characteristic of all these theologians, Catholic, Protestant, and Orthodox, is the immediate bearing of their teaching upon the fundamental problems of life. These men are very far from being the cloistered recluses theologians are popularly supposed to be; they are actively and deeply concerned with the world and the affairs of men. Their work is permeated with a profound sense of contemporaneity.

The one unifying motive in neo–Reformation theology has been the effort to find a "third way," a way free from the inadequacies of old–line fundamentalism and latter–day modernism. This third way, it has been felt, is to be gained not by eclectic compromise but by achieving a fresh synthesis of Reformation thought which would turn the insights of scriptural religion to bear upon life, human nature, and history.

Protestant neo–orthodoxy, as it has come to be known, thus begins with a double rejection from which it proceeds to a strong affirmation. Neither rationalism nor mysticism: dialectic theology—this is the first of its affirmations. The pretensions of reason to answer the ultimate questions of life are challenged. At the very most, Bruner says, reason is able to point to the transcendent reality, but it can never, unaided, apprehend or establish relations with it. (Barth is unwilling even to make that concession to human reason in the field of religion.) But if reason is challenged, so is mysticism, which claims immediate apprehension of the absolute and ultimate union with it. As against both rationalism and mysticism, these theologians take what has been called an "existentialist" position: *faith is decision*. Dialectic theology sees the thinker first of all as a man who has to make practical decisions in life, and among these decisions the most crucial is the one by which he stakes his life on his affirmation of God—it is a portentous "wager." "The truth concerns me infinitely now," said the early Barth, recalling Kierkegaard, and although Barth later abandoned the term itself, existentialist thinking remains basic to the best in neo–Reformation Protestantism. Out of the existential decision—out of the divine–human encounter in which man confronts God across the abyss which separates the human from the divine—is generated the tension of spiritual life. Neither reason nor mystic union can resolve it, in spite of their sweeping claims. Such tension is ultimately expressible only in paradox, which Reinhold Niebuhr defines as "a rational understanding of the limits of rationality, . . . an expression of faith that a rationally irresolvable contradiction may point to a truth which logic cannot contain."

The new Protestantism recognizes the service liberal theology has rendered in breaking the grip of a sterile fundamentalism, but it maintains that liberalism has been unable to meet the test. Theological liberalism—so runs the indictment—has systematically striven to break the tension that is the spring of spiritual energy by affirming the continuity of God with man instead of the "otherness" of God; by preaching an unwarranted confidence in the powers of human reason despite its clear limitations and corruptions; by insisting on the "innate" goodness of man and the essential unreality of sin and evil; by looking for the gradual realization of the Kingdom of Heaven in the course of social progress. Liberal theology is accused of having merely sanctified the relative standards of secular bourgeois society and having served as a sounding board for its prejudices, even to the point of virtually discarding the Bible except as "inspirational reading" or "great literature." In short, liberalism in theology has been a near–secular cult of "adjustment" and "peace of mind" at a time when these are counsels of spiritual death.

Against all this, the new theology takes Scripture seriously, though—and here it breaks with fundamentalism—not always literally. (How the Bible can be understood as revelation without danger of falling into bibliolatry is given profound theoretical treatment in Brunner's *Revelation and Reason* and H. Richard Niebuhr's *The Meaning of Revelation*.) It reaffirms Kierkegaard's insistence on the "eternal qualitative difference between God and man." The favorite preposition of liberal theology is *within*," H. Richard Niebuhr comments acutely, "that of post–liberal theology, *over against*."

This radical distinction makes possible a fresh appreciation of the meaning of sin and evil in human life, which has become, perhaps, the most familiar aspect of the new theology. The inordinate pretensions of the human spirit, man's efforts to deny and overpass his creatureliness—his pride, his egocentricity, deep–rooted tendency of each person to make himself instead of God the center of his universe—reflects the radical sinfulness of human nature ("original sin"). It is the other side to man's undoubted capacity for self–transcendence in reason, imagination, and moral freedom, and constitutes both a limitation and source of corruption of that capacity. In Reinhold Niebuhr's work we see excitingly described the insidious ways in which all motives, even the basest, are idealized, and all ideals, even the purest, are in fact compounded with the self–interest of those who promote them. It is a perspective capable of assimilating the best of Marx and Freud.

The new theology is preeminently a crisis theology. It was born in a time of crisis; it reflects the contemporary crisis of society; it expresses the permanent crisis in which man finds himself in this world.

Crisis here means the perennial plight of man, who, like Kafka's K., sees the goal, is driven to motion, yet cannot find the way—who desperately needs the truth, strains to attain it, yet can never be sure that he has reached it. But crisis also means judgment (Greek: *krisis*)—the divine judgment under which man and all his enterprises stand. "The worst sin is man," says Kierkegaard, "is self–assurance, the source of which lies in man's lack of realism in facing himself."

The Kingdom of God, as the neo–Reformation theologians conceive it, can never be simply identified with historical "progress." It always transcends and stands "over against" history, yet is always relevant to it as judgment and fulfillment. More, the power of the Kingdom breaks through into human existence. Every one of our achievements, it is true, is ambiguous; but each achievement nevertheless contains a genuine "hint" of the Kingdom. This is the source of the moral dynamic which makes possible working *within time* to speed the "grand consummation at the end of time." The final elimination of evil, it is recognized, is not possible in the life of man— "Prefection is an eschatological conception, and 'impossible possibility,' " says Paul Tillich—but, under judgment of God, man must never rest so long as there is evil in the world, while at the same time he must never permit himself to be deceived as to the quality of his achievement. Here we have a "utopianism" that can resist corruption, a theologically grounded social activism that can actually face and deal with reality.

Neo–Reformation theology is neither absolutist nor relativist in the usual sense; it holds to what may be called a God–centered relativism. Only God is absolute; everything else—literally everything, every idea, institution, or movement—is infected with relativity, for there can be no human situation that does not stand under the judgment of God. Once we confess and acknowledge God, Barth says, everything which is not God is "criticized, limited, made relative," and absolutizing the relative is idolatry. Such radical depreciation of everything short of God once drove Karl Barth to the utter devaluation of the world of nature and culture. It was this that led to his separation from Emil Brunner in the early 1930's. With the mounting European crisis and the war, Barth's attitude under–went a change, signified by his militant anti–Nazism. Apparently, however, the change was not a permanent one, for the same almost nihilistic tendency is to be detected again in his present–day attitude of unconcern for the fate of Western civilization as against Soviet Communism. Tillich was quite right, it would seem, when as far back as 1935, he criticized Barth's special type of dialectic theology in the following terms:

"When I am asked, what is wrong with the 'dialectic' theology, I reply that it is not 'dialectic.' A dialectic theology is one in which 'yes' and 'no' belong inseparably together. In the so–called 'dialectic' theology, they are irreconcilably separated."

Brunner, the Niebuhrs, and Tillich himself—each in his own way—has been able to maintain the dialectic tension so that the relativization of everything under God has not meant a turning aside from life and history, but rather the achievement of a standpoint from which both may be apprehended and dealt with. A relativism rooted in the absolute is the hallmark of neo–Reformation theology. It makes evident the tragic dimension of life for it does not hide the degree to which man's best aspirations are corrupted in his own soul and imperiled in the world. But it points beyond tragedy and despair—to the coming of the Kingdom, to the realization of the "impossible possibility."

The work of William Temple, the late Arch–bishop of Canterbury and easily the most distinguished Anglican theologian of recent times, may be conceived as an effective absorption of central neo–Reformation insights into the main body of Anglican tradition. His chief importance lies, perhaps, in his effort to work out a Christian social ethic that will be relevant to the times and yet refrain from identifying the church with any particular social program. His work in connection with the Malvern Conference (1941), in which he was the leading spirit, and his popular Penguin brochure, *Christianity and Social Order*, have made his point of view well known among large numbers in Britain and America.

The Catholic Humanism (or Personalism) of Jacques Maritain stresses the eminent dignity of the human person as a spiritual being and his transcendence over the total claims of society. It is rooted in the doctrine of "theocentric humanism," which Maritain finds in St. Thomas and which he opposes to the "anthropocentric humanism" that he asserts has brought contemporary civilization to the brink of disaster. He has had to contend with powerful resistance in Catholic ranks, for neither humanism nor personalism has ever been much stressed by the Church. Indeed, one gets the impression that what Maritain is attempting to do is to recapture a side of St. Thomas' teaching which has been rather consistently ignored since the 13th century. Closely linked with Maritain's thought is the Catholic existentialism of Gabriel Marcel and other French writers. Maritain himself has lately contended that St. Thomas' "philosophy of being" is existentialist in the true sense of the term.

The two leading Eastern Orthodox thinkers—Berdyaev and Father Bulgakov—were both Marxists to start with and have retained their social radicalism as part of their theology. Reflecting the diverse influences of Kant, Dostoevsky, Marx and the mystic Jacob Boehme, Berdyaev has developed, in a series of works—the best known of which is, perhaps, *Slavery and Freedom*—a personal theology widely different from Western patterns and rooted in the Russian Orthodox tradition. He is par excellence the philosopher of freedom, of free creativity. He condemns all types of *objectification*—that is, depersonalization—of man through institutions, organizations, laws, rites, or dogmas. In place of such "enslavement," Berdyaev calls for the free communion of love. His social philosophy is indeed one of Christian anarchism or personalist socialism, which recognizes the necessity of a certain degree of economic collectivism but categorically rejects the collectivization of any other aspect of life.

Bulgakov has sketched his own development "From Marxism to Sophiology" in an article under that title in the *Review of Religion* for May 1937. His criticism of Marxism is acute and realistic. His own "Christian humanism" or "social Christianity" is rooted in the Orthodox concept of *sobornost*, or free union, which brings him close to Berdyaev's sphere of thought. Both opposed the Bolshevik Revolution and were driven from Russia, but both regard the revolution as the perversion of a profoundly true idea and as punishment for the fearful sins of pre–revolutionary church and society. Berdyaev particularly is a firm believer in the Orthodox idea of the universalist–messianic mission of Russia: it is in Russia that "the way is being prepared . . . for the new Jerusalem of community and the brotherhood of man."

Virtually all the important figures in the renewal of Christian theology—Karl Barth, Emil Brunner, Reinhold and Richard Niebuhr, Paul Tillich, Jacques Maritain, William Temple, Nicolas Berdyaev, and Father Bulgakov—are to be classified as social radicals in the sense of being anti–capitalist and anti–totalitarian in their understanding of the Christian social imperative.

Indeed many of the leaders in the new theological movement took active part int he European resistance. As Horton (*Contemporary Continental Theology*) pointed out in 1938, "for a liberal Protestant, prepared to admit the reality of contemporary natural knowledge of God, it is a delicate question where to draw the line between the true and the false in this contemporary German [Nazi] sense of God. Not so for Karl Barth. He stands over against this in complete prophetic opposition, like Amos at Bethel or Elijah at Mount Carmel. . . . He calls upon all faithful Christians to take to the catacombs rather than bow the knee to the new Baal." To Barth and those who, after much hesitation, followed him in the German Confessional Church, to the church in Holland and Norway, the crisis of Hitlerism was no mere political, economic or cultural crisis. It was a religious crisis: it was man deifying himself, man establishing the God–state. That is why men who had never shown any interest in politics suddenly became rebels, why quiet, respectable citizens did not shrink from martyrdom. At that moment of crisis, the new theology became a force in history.

In a very profound sense, what goes by the name of the "crisis of our time" is a Jewish crisis. Not only has it brought frightful disaster to millions of Jews on the European continent; what is perhaps more significant, the fate of the Jew has become essentially typical of the fate of contemporary man. The demonic evil and unreason which mankind loosed upon itself in the course of the past generation found in the Jew its first and chosen victim: anti–Semitism has established itself as the projection of the deepest impulses of human sinfulness. In the Jew, the archetype of the outsider standing forever at the brink of nothingness, the alienation of contemporary man, his malaise and homelessness in the world, find their most intense expression.

Immediately after the First World War, a brilliant renaissance of Jewish thinking, ripened in the previous decade, came to fruition in Germany. Jewish religious existentialism, linked with the names of Martin Buber and Franz Rosenzweig, and in a sense too with that of Hermann Cohen, the great neo–Kantian philosopher, was born. In his *Religion of Reason from the Sources of Judaism*, published immediately after his death in 1918, Cohen had already, as Franz Rosenzweig was quick to see, transcended the abstract rationality of the academic tradition and achieved an essentially existentialist position.

It was Martin Buber, however, who developed the "new thinking" in a way that made it an immediate power in Western culture. Buber is probably the greatest religious existentialist thinker since Sören Kierkegaard; his philosophico–theological achievement is immense—his *I and Thou* is already an acknowledge classic—and his effect on contemporary thought deep and far–reaching. His affinities with neo–Reformation thought on the one hand and with Berdyaev's personalist approach on the other—so complex and many-sided is his thinking—have made him a powerful germinal force in contemporary theology, much more perhaps outside than within the limits of the Jewish community.

The central idea of Buber's thought is given in his celebrated distinction between the two primary attitudes, the two orders of living, the two fundamental types of relation, of which man is capable: I–Thou (person–to–person) and I–It (person–to–thing). Through the I–Thou encounter emerges the primary reality of the spiritual life: neither the I nor the Thou, says Buber, is ultimately real but the I–Thou meeting, the "between–man–and–man." The person—the "single–one"—is born of the I–Thou encounter: without a Thou there can be no I.

Yet man's attitude cannot possibly be cast permanently in the I–Thou relation. To survive, he must know and *use* things—and it is the intrinsic tragedy of life that he is only too often driven to treat persons as things. "Without It man cannot live. But he who lives with It alone is not a man."

To Buber, in his thoroughgoing existentialism, man's freedom is decision. "The man who thinks existentially," he says, "is the man who stakes his life on his thinking." It is through the decision of faith, upon which man does indeed stake his whole life, that in the last analysis he gains his freedom and becomes a person, a "single–one."

Though in his view, personality is generated out of the I–Thou relation and is therefore not ultimate in the sense of many radical individualists, Buber is insistent in her personalist emphasis. "Man can have dealings with God only as a single–one," he repeats. "The individual human person is unique and irreplaceable." Because of his personalist emphasis, Buber feels compelled to set limits to mysticism, which he has valued highly and to which he was personally attracted; it is communion, not union, with God that is the proper goal. He rejects too the rationalism that thinks it can "comprehend" God in an intellectual formula. "God may be addressed, not expressed," is Buber's profound insight. God as the transcendent Thou in the ultimate I–Thou encounter is, of course, "wholly other," as the Barthians have stressed; but he is also "wholly present." Buber, in the authentic Jewish tradition, refuses to suppress either the transcendence or the "hereness" of God.

Buber's ethic is rooted in his I–Thou philosophy. Evil in human relations is the conversion of the "other" from a Thou into an It—objectification or depersonalization, in Berdyaev's terminology—the utilization of a person as a means to an external end, in Kant's. Thus, Buber, like the neo–Reformation thinkers, finds the root source of human sin in the making absolute of the self. As against this, there is the self–giving love of a genuine I–Thou relation. Such love does not mean the suppression of self: "It is not the I that is given up, but the false self–asserting instinct. . . . There is no self–love that is not self–deceit . . . but without being and remaining one's self, there is no love."

In his social philosophy, Buber, like Berdyaev, sharply counterposes the free community "resting on self and self–responsibility" to the collectivity in which every person is institutionalized and turned into an It. In true community, he teaches, just as in true love for the "other," God enters as a "third": "The true community does not arise through people having feelings for one another (though indeed not without it), but through first, their taking their stand in living mutual relation with a living Center, and second, their being in living mutual relation with one another." He defines an important aspect of his social philosophy in a very telling polemic against Carl Schmitt and Friedrich Gogarten, who try to exploit a one–sided doctrine of the utter depravity of man to justify the authoritarian state. Buber eloquently vindicates individual man against the total claims of state and society. Man he sees as "essentially" neither good nor evil nor simply the indeterminate possibility of either, but in the most precise sense of the words, both–good–and–evil, "good and evil together." Only as against God can radical evil be ascribed to man, he insists, "because God is God and man is man and the distance between them is absolute."

This feeling for tension in the human situation appears strikingly in Buber's interpretation of the Messianic vision. "Redemption," he says, "occurs forever and none has ever occurred": the Kingdom of God is here among us as a power and a summons and yet always remains as the promise of fulfillment at the "end of days." Out of this polarity of the "already" and the "not–yet" is generated the dynamic of spiritual life. Buber, too, grounds his theology of social action—he is, of course, a convinced socialist—in his eschatology. "What he seeks," Ernst Simon points out, "is the 'demarcation–line' between the unconditional demand and the always only conditional realization."

Buber does see the possibility of a really "organic" community in which a We is formed through a complex of person–to–person associations. Such an organic community, he believes, was exemplified in the Hasidic movement, at least in its best days. Hasidism he regards as one of the great spiritual achievements of Israel, along with Prophetism and early Christianity—and Zionism too, the Zionism of the *halutzim*, who strove for the realization of the spiritual potentialities of Judaism. Buber's Zionism is linked with his conception of Israel. Israel is not just one of the "nations of the world": it is "something unique, unclassifiable, a community that cannot be grasped int he categories of ethnology and sociology." Israel is the people of spiritual creativity: "Salvation comes from the Jews; the fundamental tendencies of Judaism are the elements from which a new gospel for the world is always elaborated."

With Buber stands Franz Rosenzweig. Rosenzweig's tragic yet triumphant life—he died in 1929 at the age of 43 after eight years of an encroaching paralysis that finally deprived him even of the power of speech—constitutes a moving experience. His writings—*The Star of Redemption*, his one complete work; his shorter pieces and his letters—reflect a profound and penetrating intellect, in its very texture existentialist; it is humiliating to note that almost none of his writings has yet appeared in English.[1]

Having reached his existentialist position after a hard struggle with an idealist heritage, Rosenzweig traced, in life as well as in thought, the road that leads "from unimportant truths of the type 'twice two equals four,' to which men lightly assent, . . . through the truths for which a man is willing to pay something, on to those which he cannot prove true except with the sacrifice of his life and finally to those the truth of which can be proved only by the staking of the lives of all the generations." I say in life as well as in thought, for Rosenzweig's life—his existential decision for Judaism at the very moment when he was ready for conversion to Christianity—was precisely such a "wager" with destiny.

Rosenzweig too saw the ultimate reality in the I–Thou encounter, in "speaking and answering." The metaphysic of speech became a salient part of his philosophy: in a significant sense, his and Buber's translation of Scripture into German—or rather "re–translations of Holy Script into Holy Word"—was a work of theology, of an inwardly working theology of the world. His whole system, as elaborated in that strange work, *The Star of Redemption*, is based on a series of "correlations" between the primary elements of ultimate reality—God, man, and world—to which the divine–human encounter is crucial.

The "mystery of Israel" obsessed Rosenzweig, the passionate "life–thinker." For him, as for Buber, "salvation comes from the Jews." Judaism is the "eternal fire," Christianity, the "eternal rays"; Judaism, the "eternal life," Christianity, the "eternal way." While Israel stays with God, the Christian is sent out to conquer the unredeemed world. But he is always in danger of relapsing into paganism and when he does, when the pagan within him rises in revolt against the yoke of the Cross, he vents his fury on the Jew; that is the "secret" of anti–Semitism. "The fact of anti–Semitism, age–old and ever–present though totally groundless," Rosenzweig wrote to his mother, "can be understood only by the different functions which God has assigned to the two communities—Israel to represent in time the eternal Kingdom of God, Christianity to bring itself and the world toward that goal." Only when that goal is reached—at the "end of time"—will the final reconciliation and fusion take place; then all will indeed be one in the recognition of the unity of the Divine Name.

The time of Buber and Rosenzweig boasted of other names as well. There is Gershom Scholem, in whose scholarly studies of Jewish mysticism, suggestions of rich theological ideas may be perceived. In his writings on the "essence of Judaism," Leo Baeck has given the "liberal" viewpoint a new depth and power. And then there was Franz Kafka.

Perhaps in the current deluge of Kafka exegesis it is necessary to insist that Kafka was after all a creative artist, not a theologian. Yet it is not to be denied that, on the level of interpretation at least, *The Castle* is a powerful theological myth of man's search for salvation in a world marked, in Buber's words, by a "special human homelessness and solitude," while *The Trial* is an imaginatively projected study of human guilt and divine judgment. Nor will the perceptive reader fail to note the relevance of many of Kafka's episodes and symbols to the "mystery of Israel," to the position of the Jew in the world. However one may differ on interpretation—and no interpretation of a great creative artist can ever be final or exhaustive—I do not think it can any longer be denied that Franz Kafka was a religious thinker of a stature we are only now beginning to appreciate.

The ardent intellectual life of German Jewry did not cease with the triumph of Hitler. If anything, it grew more intense, for now it began to search for the meaning of the awful catastrophe that was overwhelming it. But the end came all too soon and the voice of German Jewry was silenced.

The center now shifted to Jewish Palestine. There an immense cultural work was going forward. Hebrew was being reborn as a living language; a rich literature was springing up, scholarly work of all sorts was being energetically prosecuted. But aside from the recent German immigration, only two figures seem to have made themselves felt as creative religious forces in the course of the past generation, Chief Rabbi Abraham Isaac Kuk and Dr. Judah L. Magnes.

Dr. Magnes was no theologian in the narrower sense of the term, but his pronouncements through the passing years had a genuine prophetic ring. In a cowardly age, he spoke out and no opposition or abuse was ever able to silence him. But what is perhaps most important, he spoke and thought in thoroughly religious terms. It is a great pity that so many have allowed factional heat or differences on what are, after all, secondary questions to obscure their appreciation of this great man. Rabbi Kuk infused the age–old Orthodox tradition with new energy. His writings are the reflection of a life of genuine sanctity and gain much of their power therefrom. His personal influence was perhaps even more potent than his writings; he has left a deep and lasting impression on important sections of the new Palestine.

Aside from these men, what Palestine has to show is hardly impressive. But how much less impressive is the picture presented by the United States, this land where lives the bulk of modern Jewry! It is true that the heritage of Solomon Schechter has been developed in new directions by such independent thinkers as Louis Finkelstein and Max Kadushin. It is true that Samuel S. Cohon has for more than a quarter of a century pursued serious theological work in the Reform–liberal tradition. It is true, too, that Reconstructionism, the creation of Mordecai M. Kaplan, has a notable achievement to its credit: it has evolved the only relevant "philosophy" of our Jewish existence in America. Its theology, however, still retains far too much of naturalism and pragmatic humanism so that it is always in peril of passing over into sociology on the one side or collapsing into mere ethical sentiment on the other.

Beyond this, what American Jews have to show in the way of theology and religious thinking is hardly more than routine reiteration of inherited formulas, Orthodox or modernist, the ostentatious parading of platitudes, the anxious effort to identify Judaism with the latest version of the "American way of life"—plus one or two less useful popularizations. The whole story is told when we not that the largest Jewish community in the world—numerous, active, and prosperous, involved in so many Jewish enterprises—does not possess one single significant journal of Jewish theology.

The fact is that neither the world catastrophe nor the Jewish disaster, with which it is so inseparably linked, has evoked any creative response on the part of present-day Judaism. The age of Buber and Rosenzweig, with all its achievement and promise, must be recognized as hardly more than an isolated episode in the almost unrelieved mediocrity of Jewish religious thinking in recent decades.

Is it primarily the desperate insecurity of Jewish existence during the past thirty years that is responsible, as so many have suggested? Has preoccupation with mere survival absorbed so much of Jewish energy as to leave little or none for reflective thought transcending the moment? Insecurity and disaster are nothing new in the history of Israel, but never in the past did they paralyze the sources of spiritual creativity. On the contrary, every great achievement in Jewish religious thought came into being in response to crisis.

Nor can the inadequacy of the Jewish theological response be attributed to the alleged anti–theological bias in Jewish religious tradition. This alleged aversion to theology is, to a large extent, nothing but a latter–day fiction. If theology is understood in terms more comprehensive than scholastic system–making, Jewish thought has almost always—at least until recently—been theological. From the scriptural writers and Prophets to Rosenzweig and Buber, Jewish thinking has been a continuing effort to interpret problems and events in terms of the divine–human encounter and the working–out of God's providence.

The renunciation of theology in modern times is not so much a continuation of Jewish tradition as a more or less definite break with it, although it must be said that there are aspects of the tradition itself that have made this break possible.

This abrupt break with tradition reflects the belated entrance of the Jews into the modern world. For the great mass of Jews in Eastern Europe, there was no Renaissance; within one or two generations, they passed directly from the Middle Ages into modern secularism. For all its great cultural achievements, Emancipation brought confusion and disorientation from which Jewry has not yet recovered. In the rout of traditional Judaism, the very notion of religious thinking was all but lost. More, in the self–hatred that this period of demoralization bred, theology was rejected not only because it was theology but also, and perhaps primarily, because it was *Jewish*, because it bore the ghetto–stigma of Jewishness.

The metaphysical climate of opinion has changed drastically since those days but the after–effects are still strong.

The religious tradition itself has not been entirely unambiguous. The polarity of Jewish religion has been noted more than once in the past. Over fifty years ago (1893), Ahad Ha-Am wrote his penetrating essay, "Priest and Prophet," in which he pointed out the reciprocal relation between the two contrasting types of Jewish spirituality. At one pole is the prophet, standing outside the sinning community—"over against" it, in fact—to denounce its evil ways. He is "a man of strife and of conten-tion to the whole earth." But he is also—and for that very reason—the inspired agent of crisis–creativity, the spiritual pioneer who conquers new frontiers of religious un-derstanding. Very different is the priest, who, in Ahad Ha-Am's words, "appears on the scene at a time when prophecy has already succeeded in hewing out a path for its idea." His task is not spiritual pioneering but everyday normalization, cultivating the ground gained by the prophet and reducing it to order. He is the respectable man standing at the head of—"within"—the respectable community to guide and rule it. "The idea of the prophet produces the teaching of the priest," but it is a teaching that no longer has the urgency and utter immediacy of the prophetic message.

Essential Jewish tradition takes as normative *both* prophet and priest, or rather the tension between them. It is a tension that manifests itself, not so much in the succession of historical epochs with varying emphasis, as in an ambivalence within each historical period and even within each genuine spiritual leader. But there is ever the besetting temptation to reduce the polarity to the one–sided routine of priestly "normalcy," thus draining Jewish spirituality of its originating force. Rabbinism was born out of the Pharisaic movement, which was clearly a prophetic protest against priestly superficiality and laxness, and many of the finest examples of post–scriptural prophetism are to be found in rabbinical ranks. Yet Rabbinism too, as Ahad Ha–Am indicates, only too often tended to lose its prophetic spirit and sink to the level of priestly routine.

For many generations now, priestly "normalcy" has been taken as the true spirit of Jewish religion and every suggestion of prophetic urgency impatiently brushed aside. A hidden "liberalism" permeates and enfeebles conventional Jewish religion, even the most orthodox. Judaism, we are assured, is not a crisis–religion but an affair of "everyday normal life." Yet if there is one religion in the world that owes every-thing to crisis, it is Judaism. Judaism was born out of crisis; Israel is the crisis–people par excellence. In tradition, it is the great crisis of the Exodus that is the central point of reference for everything Jewish. The crisis culminating in the fall of the two kingdoms and the captivity served as the background for the prophetic movement. The crisis under the Hasmoneans gave birth to Pharisaism. The crisis following the destruction of the Temple witnessed the far–reaching reconstruction of Judaism by Johanan ben Zakkai. Where is there another record of crisis so unrelieved and so continuous as that contained in the historical books of Scripture or indeed in the entire body of Jewish history.

Jewish existence itself is caught up in an inescapable ambiguity: is it ethnic or is it religious? Ideally, it is both, reflecting the universal and particularist components in the pattern of Jewish destiny. But this polarity too has been broken and reduced to a one–sided falsification, in the form either of old–line Reform Judaism or of secular nationalism.

The non–Jew striving to achieve a more profound, more significant spiritual orientation can do so only in religious, and usually one in specifically Christian, terms; the "scientific," aesthetic, and sociological cults of yesterday no longer have much appeal. The Jew too strives to affirm himself, but unlike the Gentile, he can affirm himself as Jew, at least up to a certain point, entirely in no–religious terms. To be a "good Jew"—how ambiguous is the phrase!—he need not affirm the religious tradition of Israel; he can be a fervent Zionist, an ardent Hebraist or Yiddishist, or a valiant fighter against anti–Semitism. Corresponding to the Christian affirmation of the non–Jew, there is, for the Jew, not merely Judaism or Jewish religion; there are also the *ersatz*–Jewish faiths—Jewish nationalism, culture, social service, "anti-defamatio"—all moving on the secular level, all unable or unwilling to break through to the religious.

Now all of these things—nationalism, culture, social service, "anti–defamation" —are fine things, worthy things, *in their place*. It is only when they make pretensions to absoluteness as *total* affirmations—it is only when, as I have said, they present themselves as *ersatz*–Jewish faiths in place of Jewish religion, rather than subordinate to it—that they become mischievous. To mistake the part for the whole, the relative for the absolute, is surely the most dangerous pitfall in spiritual life.

This atmosphere is so pervasive that it affects even those who sincerely believe themselves free from it. They too—rabbis, scholars, and theologians—make their interpretations and judgments, do their thinking, in wholly non–religious terms. It simply never occurs to them to make what they preach really and deeply relevant to the crucial problems of modern life; aside from a few platitudes, they have nothing to say that is not better said by the psychologist, sociologist, or political leader.

By the logic of compensation, it is precisely this failure that has given the *ersatz*-Jewish faiths, especially Zionist nationalism, the opportunity to claim with a great deal of cogency that it is they who are exercising the prophetic function, they who are saying the new and meaningful word. And in some sense they are—particularly in contrast to the sluggish mediocrity of conventional Jewish religion. But in the final analysis, it is merely a pseudo–prophetism.

It cannot remain so. It cannot be that Judaism has spent its force, that the ancient People of the Book possesses no religious, no theological, no prophetic word for our time. Perhaps events under way today may bring about a drastic change and release the creative forces of Jewish spirituality. But until then the matter must remain in the problematic form given to it by Dr. Magnes: "Has Judaism still the power to speak in these days of mankind's crisis?"

Notes

[1]A volume including a biography of Franz Rosenzweig and an anthology of his writings, prepared by N. N. Glatzer, is published by Schocken Books.

Chapter 6

What Can the Term
"Jewish Theology" Possibly Mean?

Manfred H. Vogel

We conclude with an essay worthy of the challenge of Dalferth's definition, given in the introduction to each of these volumes: "[Theology]" rationally reflects on questions arising in pre–theological religious experience and the discourse of faith; and it is the rationality of its reflective labor in the process of faith seeking understanding which inseparably links it with philosophy." Precisely what that work requires, and how theology differs from philosophy of religion, are the questions answered in the programmatic essay with which we conclude our direct and immediate encounter with theologians at work. Here is the last, best model of how the work is to be done. Joined to the first five chapters' systematic efforts at doing theology, this chapter now defines the task. Since, in the first five volumes, Vogel's systematic theology has found for itself a central place, his account of what he conceives the theological enterprise to be provides a fitting conclusion to this glimpse at theologians at work. What makes his definition important is that he defines the work awaiting the next generation of theologians of Judaism, spelling out for them their task in their hour. He asks the fundamental question, is there a difference between theology and philosophy of religion? His answer lies in precisely the core of particular faith on which we concentrate here: philosophy speaks in general terms, theology in particular ones: "in the case of natural theology the nature and character of the divine which it attemps to establish is already known a priori from the outside—natural theology merely attempts to show that one can arrive at it also by the path which comes from human experience." This is not an easy essay, but it raises the fundamental issues of definition that each generation must resolve for itself. In insisting upon the priority of revelation ("the Torah," "tradition") in establishing the truths of religion, Vogel sets forth the task for the rational inquiry into faith that theology in age succeeding age accomplishes.

***

Clearly, the answer to this question must consist in clarifying what we take the noun 'theology' to signify and the adjective 'Jewish' to designate. Namely, answering the question is tantamount to clarifying the significations of these two terms. For if we

*Previously published in *Problems in Contemporary Jewish Theology*, ed. Dan Cohn-Sherbok. Copyright 1991 the Edwin Mellen Press, which has granted permission for its reprinting here.

are clear about the significations of these two terms we certainly should also be clear about what the notion of Jewish theology should mean. Indeed, we can go even further and say that the crux to the answer to the question before us really lies specifically in determining the signification of the term 'theology' rather than determining the designation of the adjective 'Jewish'. For, as we shall see, the signification of the noun 'theology' will determine to a great extent what the adjective Jewish can meaningfully designate. The signification we give to the term 'theology' will have already prescribed in considerable measure what the designation of the adjective 'Jewish' can be.

I

So what do we mean by 'theology?' What does it signify? What is its definition? Well, what readily comes to mind and what, indeed, seems eminently reasonable, is to derive the definition from the literal meaning of the word 'theology'. Now, the Greek word 'theology' when taken literally signifies a *logos* with respect to a *theos*, namely, it signifies a body of discourse, of knowledge, a 'science' (*i.e.*, a *logos*) about God (*i.e.*, the *theos*). Thus, its signification parallels the signification of any number of Greek terms such as psychology (a *logos* about the psyche, *i.e.*, a body of knowledge about the mind) or geology (a *logos* about geo, *i.e.*, a body of knowledge about the earth). Theology is thus a body of knowledge like all the other bodies of knowledge, *i.e.*, the other logi; it is differentiated, as indeed all the other logi differentiate themselves from each other, by the object to which it refers itself—it impinges upon the object God while other bodies of knowledge impinge upon such objects as the earth, the mind, society (*i.e.*, sociology) or man (*i.e.*, anthropology). This, of course, implies that the body of knowledge that one establishes in theology is of the same kind as the body of knowledge that one establishes in any of the other logi and that the object with respect to which this knowledge is established, *i.e.*, God, is the same kind of object as the objects of the other logi. Thus, the sum–total body of knowledge is subdivided according to the objects it investigates and God is taken here as one of the multiplicity of objects constituting our world; likewise, the knowledge that can be obtained of Him is the same kind of knowledge that can be obtained of the other objects within our universe.

Now, in terms of this signification the enterprise of theology is, in the last analysis, really tantamount to what is commonly referred to as natural theology or rational theology. For what constitutes our various bodies of knowledge, *i.e.*, our various logi or 'sciences', are collections of propositions with respect to various objects, propositions that are established by inference from our experience of our world, *i.e.*, our experience of nature and of ourselves, such inference being carried out in conformity with the requirements of our rationality, *i.e.*, the canons of our logic (indeed, to the extent that the propositions are established in this way they are taken to be true and thus constituting knowledge rather than illusion). But this is precisely what natural or rational theology is commonly taken to signify. The qualifications natural or rational are there precisely in order to signify that the body of knowledge with respect to God, *i.e.*, theology, is established on the basis of our experience of the world and in conformity with the requirements of our reason, *i.e.*, in conformity with the dictates of the canons of our logic. They signify that we constitute our knowledge of God, *i.e.*, theology, by proceeding from the experience of our world, *i.e.*, of nature and of ourselves, and inferring from this, in conformity with the canons of our rationality, certain truths about the object God. Thus, it would follow that if theology is to signify a body of knowledge about God (where God is an object like all the other objects in our world and the knowledge is secured in the same way as the knowledge of the other objects is secured), then for all intents and purposes it is really equivalent to being a natural or rational theology; theology as such is merely an abbreviated expression for natural theology or rational theology. And, indeed, there is no denying that in the history of religion the enterprise of theology has very often been nothing else but the enterprise of a natural theology.

In this context, however, it is only natural that the question would arise as to whether or not there is a difference between the enterprise of natural theology and the enterprise of the philosophy of religion and, if there is a difference, as to what that difference might be. It is important that we take a moment and address ourselves to this question because in the process we may very well come up with an additional qualification that may prove very significant in delineating the enterprise of natural theology. Thus, it would seem to us that the very fact that we have this difference in terminology should drive us to look for a difference in substance, *i.e.*, for there being two distinct enterprises. And if there are two distinct enterprises, what can the difference between them be?

To begin with, one can, of course, say that the difference here is the same as the difference that obtains between the philosophy of science, on the one hand, and the various particular sciences such as chemistry or physics, on the other hand. Chemistry or physics establish propositions, *i.e.*, describe or delineate certain characteristics or qualities, with respect to certain objects, e.g., molecules or atoms, while the philosophy of science examines and establishes the structure of the underlying methodology by which the various particular sciences establish their objects. In a likewise manner the philosophy of religion would examine and establish the structure of the underlying methodology by which the particular science of theology would establish the propositions which describe and delineate its object, *i.e.*, God. Such a difference, *i.e.*, such a division of labor, is certainly feasible in principle. But since such a division of labor was rarely, if at all, practiced in the past, it can be valid only in a programmatic sense, namely, it can be valid only as a commendation for future activity but not as a description of past activity. In practice, the philosophy of religion throughout its long history proposed to do, in overwhelming measure, precisely what we attribute here to theology, that is to say, establish propositions with respect to the object of religion, *i.e.*, with respect to God.[1]

But if this be the case, then one must press the question as to what possibly could be the difference between the philosophy of religion as it has been overwhelmingly practiced thus far and theology, *i.e.*, natural theology? Well, it may be suggested that the difference lies in the observation that while natural theology takes a positive and constructive approach to its object, *i.e.*, to God, the philosophy of religion takes a negative and critical approach to the same object, *i.e.*, to God. Thus, while in both cases the object remains the same (*i.e.*, God) and the basic delineation and direction of the approach remain the same (*i.e.*, proceeding from the human experience of the world or of ourselves to the divine), natural theology and the philosophy of religion differ in that the intention of the former is positive and constructive while the intention of the latter is negative and critical. Now, in a way this distinction certainly seems valid. Most of us would no doubt find it very odd and unacceptable to attribute a critical, negative approach to the enterprise of natural theology and, indeed, there are no such instances in what is commonly taken to constitute the field of natural theology. Clearly, there is a linkage between the enterprise of natural theology and a positive, constructive approach to the divine object. On the other hand, it is not at all strange to encounter the negative, critical approach in the philosophy of religion and, indeed, one can encounter many such instances in the history of this enterprise. Certainly, most of us are not put off by a linkage between a negative, critical approach and the enterprise of the philosophy of religion. Thus, in this sense, and to this extent, there is some validity in this distinction. In the last analysis, however, this differentiation too breaks down and it breaks down because while the philosophy of religion *may* be negative and critical in its approach it *need not* be so. Namely, the negative and critical approach is not an essential and thus all–encompassing characterization of the enterprise and, therefore, it cannot be used as a criterion for differentiation. Certainly, one can think of any number of formulations that most of us would want to relegate to the philosophy of religion and yet which are in no way negative or critical in their approach. Indeed, the negative and critical approach has by and large found its expression in Anglo–Saxon philosophy rather than in Continental philosophy and even then most prominently only in recent times. And while it certainly constitutes a very important expression within the philosophy of religion, it cannot be equated with it. It certainly would leave out some very significant formulations. Thus, shall we leave out of the philosophy of religion such formulations as those of Plato, Aristotle, Descartes, Hegel, or Schelling? And if not, then in what sense are these formulations an expression of the enterprise of the philosophy of religion and not of the enterprise of natural theology? Clearly, to take care of these formulations and many others that most of us would want to relegate to the domain of the philosophy of religion we must come up with a better criterion for differentiation.

We would suggest that the criterion for differentiation should be constituted by the source which is to determine and delineate the kind of being at which the processes of natural theology and the philosophy of religion would come to rest, *i.e.*, the source which would define what kind of a being constitutes the object that natural theology and the philosophy of religion respectively attempt to establish. Namely, while both the philosophy of religion and natural theology proceed from human experience and attempt to establish the divine in terms of this experience, *i.e.*, using this experience (albeit with the additional help of inference) to provide a way of arriving at the divine, the matter remains still open as to what kind of a being this divine, *i.e.*, the divine implicated in this process, is going to be. And here a viable distinction may well suggest itself. For in the context of a philosophy of religion the character and nature of the divine will be determined by the overall character and implications of the philosophic system in whose terms the divine is delineated; the character and requirements of the philosophic system as a whole (of which the enterprise of the philosophy of religion is but one part among others—the other parts may well be such enterprises as metaphysics, ethics, aesthetics or epistemology) will determine the kind of being (*i.e.*, will describe and delineate the characteristics and attributes) which the philosophy of religion attempts to establish. As against this, in the context of the enterprise of natural theology the character and nature of the object to be established (*i.e.*, the characteristics and attributes of the divine) will be determined by the orientation and requirements of a particular historical religious tradition such as Christianity, Judaism or Islam. Namely, in the case of natural theology the nature and character of the divine which it attempts to establish is already known *a priori* from the outside—natural theology merely attempts to show that one can arrive at it also by the path which comes from human experience. Given the kind of being the divine is (this being determined by the particular historical religious tradition involved), natural theology merely attempts to show that it can also be established by inference from human experience. In contrast, in the case of the philosophy of religion of the nature of the object (*i.e.*, the characteristics and attributes of the divine) evolves from the overall philosophic orientation of the philosopher; the philosophy of religion attempts to establish not an object that is given to it from the outside but rather an object that it evolves from within its own workings. It clearly follows from this that while in the case of the philosophy of religion there is, strictly speaking, no connection to a particular historical religious tradition, in the case of natural theology there is a very intimate relation. Indeed, there *must* be such an intimate relation to a particular historical religion if the enterprise of natural theology is to be feasible—it cannot be carried out without such a connection. Unlike the philosophy of religion, natural theology cannot stand by itself—it must always be qualified by an adjective designating a particular historical religion.[2]

This being the case, the adjective 'Jewish' is here by no means superfluous. It is required as the enterprise of natural theology cannot stand by itself. But the adjective here clearly designates and refers to 'Judaism', *i.e.*, the religious tradition that is Judaism, and not to 'Jews', *i.e.*, the members of the community of faith that is Jewish. For clearly, while there is an indisputable linkage between the enterprise of natural theology and the formulation regarding the divine being in a religious tradition (in this case, the religious tradition of Judaism), there is no linkage whatsoever between the enterprise of natural theology and members of a community of faith. And this is so, seeing that the formulation of a religious tradition clearly delineates what kind of a divine being the enterprise of natural theology is attempting to establish, while membership in a community of faith provides no such substantive and meaningful information. Thus, a divine being delineated by the religious tradition of Judaism is in all likelihood different in some important respects from the divine being delineated by the religious tradition of Christianity and consequently a Jewish natural theology would be attempting to establish a different being than a Christian natural theology; in contrast to this, anyone can do natural theology and membership in a community of faith should as such have no bearing on the matter. Indeed natural theology is like mathematics—the affiliation of the practitioners does not impinge upon the execution of the enterprise. And just as it should make no difference to the enterprise of mathematics whether the mathematician is an Englishman, Frenchman or Russian, so also it should make no difference to the enterprise of natural theology whether the natural theologian is a Jew, Christian or Moslem. Of course, natural theologians, like mathematicians, physicists, chemists and so on, can be classified according to some other criteria, such criteria as nationhood, religion, physical properties, etc. In this sense qualifying mathematicians, physicists or natural theologians by nationality or religion does give us some information (it certainly gives us data that would be of interest to the sociologist). But the point is that the information it gives us is completely beside the point as far as the nature of the enterprise is concerned. For doing natural theology (as indeed for doing mathematics, physics, chemistry, etc.) this information is completely beside the point. Any rational human being should in principle be able to do it (and this in no way undermines the great difference that talent can make here, for we are not talking here about how well it is done but only whether or not it can be done in principle). Thus, any rational human being should be able to do any natural theology regardless to what historical religious tradition it may belong, *i.e.*, regardless of which religious tradition delineates its God–object. In principle, not only a Jew but anyone, *e.g.*, a Christian, a Moslem, indeed an atheist, should be able to do Jewish natural theology and the same should apply to Christian, Moslem, or any other natural theology[3]

Thus, to take the term 'Jewish theology' as signifying the doing of a natural theology that is Jewish is to give the term a signification that is meaningful in that it ascribes to it an activity that is feasible and arrogates to it a domain that is legitimate. Indeed, there is no denying that throughout much of the history of religion the pursuit of theology was taken all too commonly and naturally to be nothing else but the pursuit of a natural theology. As such, the pursuit of natural theology is a very widespread and a very venerable enterprise in the domain of religion. True, it is much more widespread and central in other religious traditions (the glaring example would, of course, be Christianity) than it is in Judaism. Still, one can also encounter it in Judaism, particularly in the Middle Ages. Indeed, from Isaac Israeli at the end of the ninth century to Joseph Albo in the middle of the fifteenth century we have a whole array of very notable figures such as Saadia Gaon, Maimonides, Crescas, Gersonides and many others who pursued natural theology. It is the period when the doing of natural theology really flourishes within Judaism.[4]

In theory, therefore, we have a clear distinction between the signification of 'natural theology' and that of 'philosophy of religion'. True, the line of distinction is fairly thin and its applicability in actual practice may be very difficult and problematic. After all, the distinction is constituted in terms of intentions and not in terms of hard, observable facts. It is very hard to ascertain from the outside what the intention is and consequently we should not be surprised that with respect to any concrete particular instance there would, in all likelihood, be controversy and even more that the controversy, in the last analysis, cannot really be resolved. Thus, for example, is Aquinas or Hegel with respect to what they have to say about Christianity natural theologians or philosophers of religion? Likewise, is Maimonides with respect to what he has to say about the religion of Judaism or Averroes with respect to what he has to say about Islam a natural theologian or a philosopher of religion? Granted, the line of distinction is thin and it is very difficult to decide. Still, we must insist, that difficulty in applying the criterion does not mean that the criterion is invalid—difficulty in application is one thing, meaningfulness and validity another. And we would submit that the criterion we proposed, in spite of the grave difficulties in applying it, is a meaningful and valid criterion. It meaningfully delineates for us a specific kind of enterprise which we name natural theology and which we can now use to stand for the notion of theology—theology means doing natural theology in the way we have delineated it.

But granted that the term "natural theology" has a distinct signification and that, therefore, it delineates a distinct activity and appropriates a distinct domain for itself (so that it is quite meaningful to suggest that the notion of theology should be equated with that of natural theology), there are still two questions that are very pertinent and which must be addressed before we can close the books and accept the equation between theology and natural theology. First, it must be asked whether it is wise and, indeed, advantageous for a religious tradition, specifically a religious tradition that belongs to the theistic mould, to resort to and utilize the enterprise of natural theology. And secondly, it must be asked whether, irrespective of the previous question and the answer we may give it, a specific particular religious tradition (in our case, the religious tradition of Judaism) can in terms of its very structure of faith resort to and utilize the enterprise of natural theology. Clearly, only after being able to give an affirmative answer to these two questions can one proceed with equanimity and confidence to accept the identity of theology with the enterprise of natural theology. Otherwise, even though the notion of natural theology is meaningful and valid in its signification, it would still not be operative with regard to the religious tradition in question.

So, let us turn to the first question. Here, a case can be made that although the enterprise of natural theology is in principle feasible, it would be unwise, indeed, detrimental in the long run, for a religious tradition in the theistic mould to resort to it. For natural theology undertakes to establish its knowledge of the divine in the same manner and fashion as other sciences establish their knowledge of their respective objects. But this opens up the religious tradition which resorts to natural theology to two very serious and devastating criticisms. For natural theology builds itself on a fundamental inner contradiction when it applies itself to a theistic God, namely, to a God which transcends the system (*i.e.*, the world) and thus locates Himself beyond the system, over–against it. The inner contradiction lies in the fact that it utilizes a method of establishing knowledge that applies to objects *within* the system but applies it to an object that transcends the system. This obviously is not valid and the enterprise may give the appearance of validity only because it smuggles in, hopefully unnoticed, a leap in its rationale which is not legitimate. As a result, the theistic religious tradition in turning to natural theology opens itself up to one of two alternative devastating criticisms (and both forms of this criticism have been actually mounted against theistic religion in modern times).

On the one hand, it opens itself up to the criticism that its God is a chimera, that such an entity which it calls God simply does not exist (this form of the criticism is raised, in the main, in the Anglo–Saxon tradition of philosophy from Hume on). For if the existence of God depends on its being established by the method of natural theology and this method is shown to be untenable it follows that such a God simply does not exist. The other form of the criticism (and this found its main expression in Continental philosophy from Ludwig Feuerbach on) is to adopt and pronounce explicitly what natural theology may be taken to imply implicitly and that is that the divine being does not really transcend the system. It is only the faulty and misleading language of religion that leads to this confusion. The theistic religions are guilty of using misleading and invalid language, to wit, that there is a being transcending the system; in reality, in truth, what they really mean to say (and in this respect they are quite valid) is that the being which the traditional language refers to as God is really within the system and as such it is no other than the being of man projected to its idealized status. In Feuerbach's famous cry, 'theology is nothing else but anthropology', God is nothing else but 'man writ large'. We judge the religious tradition by what it does and not by what it says, namely, we judge it by the fact that it resorts to natural theology which clearly implies the reduction of theology to anthropology rather than by the theistic language which it continues to use. Thus, the method of natural theology makes an illegitimate leap in transferring its application from an object within the system to an object outside the system. In consequence, one can either take the method at face value and conclude that it is false and invalid and, therefore, that there is no such object as it claims to establish (this is the first form of the criticism); or one can interpret the method to be saying that what has been taken to be an entity beyond the system (*i.e.*, the theistic god) is in reality and truth an entity within the system (*i.e.*, man) and, therefore, that what has been said about the theistic God is really quite valid when applied to man (this being the second form of the criticism). In either form of the criticism, however, the theistic religious tradition is clearly undermined in the most fundamental way–its lynchpin, *i.e.*, the theistic God, is abrogated.

Turning to the second question, a similarly strong case can be made that even if it were not inadvisable for the religious tradition to resort to the enterprise of natural theology, in the case of biblical religions and, specifically, in the case of Judaism the very structure of faith operating here would make the resort to natural theology simply self–defeating. For the very crux of distinctive Judaism, *i.e.*, prophetic and subsequently halachic Judaism (and for that matter, of other biblical religions such as Christianity and Islam to the extent that they remain faithful and authentic to their distinctiveness in biblical faith) is the notion that the divine being is a personal being, *i.e.*, a Thou–God, and not an impersonal, blind power, an It–God. But if this is the case, if the very essence of biblical faith is that its God is of necessity a Thou–God, then this clearly forecloses as far as biblical faith is concerned any meaningful resort to the enterprise of natural theology. For a Thou–being, thus a Thou–God, can only be an ontological subject and never an ontological object. At the same time, however, the object of natural theology, *i.e.*, the divine being which natural theology attempts to establish, cannot be anything else but an ontological object, namely, it cannot be anything else but an In–God. The very method, the very approach, of natural theology dictates that the divine being which it attempts to establish can only be an ontological object.

Thus, even if natural theology is completely successful in its enterprise it can only be successful with respect to a God that is an It–God; it has nothing to say and in no way impinges upon a God that is a Thou–God. We clearly have here an irreconcilable difference, a totally incommensurate partnership. For, on the one hand, the very essence of biblical faith is to insist that God be a Thou–God and not an It–God while, on the other hand, the inescapable end–result of natural theology can only be an It–God. Thus, even if natural theology is completely successful, it would come up with the very God that biblical faith negates and rejects—it can only come up with what for biblical faith is merely an idol which is to be destroyed. For biblical faith therefore, to resort to natural theology in order to establish its God can only be an act of insanity, an act of committing suicide. So, even if it were advisable for theistic religion to resort to natural theology (which is not the case), other religions may do it but biblical faith, and thus specifically Judaism, cannot do it.[5] For natural theology in its very approach and method collides head–on with two of the most fundamental and essential aspects of biblical faith, namely, the personhood of God and His theistic relation to the world. In view of this, it is obvious that there is an inherent and inescapable incompatibility between the method of natural theology and the content of biblical faith—natural theology in principle cannot really serve biblical faith.[6]

II

But if in the context of biblical faith one cannot utilize theology when it is taken in the sense of natural theology, is there another sense in which theology can be taken and still be utilizable by biblical faith? Well, an alternative sense that readily suggests itself is the sense connected with the term 'revelatory theology'. For the notion of revelatory theology seems to preserve the basic signification of the notion of theology while at the same time it appears to avoid the serious difficulties which natural theology presented with respect to biblical faith, *i.e.*, the difficulties which arose with respect to a God who is a Thou–God and thus a God theistically related to the world. Thus, revelatory theology maintains the signification of theology as a *logos* of the *theos*, *i.e.*, a body of knowledge, a discourse, with respect to the divine being. Where it differs from natural theology is in the method, the way, by which this body of knowledge, this discourse, is established or attained. In natural theology, it was attained by proceeding from human experience, from the world, to the divine; in contrast, in revelatory theology it is attained by proceeding from the divine to man. The divine communicates a body of knowledge about Himself to man—we have a body of knowledge about the divine because the divine has communicated to us this body of knowledge. Thus, while in natural theology the knowledge about the divine is discovered or inferred, here it is disclosed or imparted. The only difference between natural and revelatory theology is with respect to the method by which knowledge about the divine is attained—revelatory theology reverses the direction pursued by natural theology. But this reversal of direction makes all the difference in the world as regards the difficulties which natural theology presented with respect to biblical faith.

Thus, with respect to a Thou–God, it would appear that there should be no problem with establishing knowledge about Him on the basis of His revealing Himself. A Thou–being, a person, can certainly disclose, impart of himself/herself. Indeed, the only way in which we can come to know another person would appear to be through such a disclosure or impartation. Unlike the way we gain knowledge of an impersonal being, we cannot gain knowledge of a personal being through investigation and discovery. So while the way of discovery through sense–perception and inference, the way which characterizes the method of natural theology, is very problematic when directed to a Thou–being, a Thou–God, the way of disclosure and impartation, *i.e.*, of revelation, would seem to be not only not problematic but actually the only valid, viable way by which knowledge with respect to such a being can be established. Thus, with respect to biblical faith, resorting to revelatory theology would appear to be the only way by which any knowledge of the divine can be established.

Similarly, resorting to revelatory theology should also remove the other problem that arose in connection with natural theology, *i.e.*, the problem connected with the theistic dimension of biblical faith, to wit, the problem precipitated by the fact that God cannot be reduced to just another object among the many other objects of this world. God cannot be another object in this world (no matter how quantitatively great or powerful he may be); He must be qualitatively distinct and different. And this, of course, means that God cannot be known in the same way as the other objects of this world are known. Now, it would seem that this, indeed, is safeguarded by resorting to revelatory theology. For by resorting to revelatory theology, knowledge of the object, *i.e.*, of the divine, is established on the basis of the object, *i.e.*, the divine, disclosing and imparting of itself. But this is certainly not the way in which knowledge of all the other objects of the world is established. Knowledge of all these objects is established on the basis of discovery, *i.e.*, on the basis of sense–perception and inference. Objects of the world do not disclose or impart of themselves; they are there to be handled, examined and investigated and as such to become known. Thus, the method which revelatory theology introduces, *i.e.*, the method by which knowledge of the divine is established on the basis of the divine disclosing and imparting of Himself, adequately safeguards the qualitative distinction and difference of the divine–object from all other worldly objects.[7]

Clearly, the approach of revelatory theology possesses significant strengths with respect to biblical faith. However, for this revelatory theology to be effective, *i.e.*, for its strengths to come into play, the divine being must be taken, must be perceived, by the religious tradition involved here as having revealed Himself, *i.e.*, as having disclosed and imparted Himself to man. Otherwise, we would have the instrument of revelatory theology but with no material for it to work on—we would have revelatory theology as an instrument, but an instrument that stands idle, that is out of work. For clearly, if we do not have a God who has revealed Himself, revelatory theology, notwithstanding all its strengths, would not be able to tell us anything about that God and consequently such a God would remain a totally unknown God, a *deus obsconditus*. Since in revelatory theology God is the only source for all possible knowledge that we may possess about Him, if this God does not disclose to us who and what He is, we cannot possibly possess such knowledge about Him. Namely, if God does not disclose Himself, there is no revelatory theology or, more accurately, the revelatory theology which in principle is feasible must remain totally devoid of any content, totally empty—a revelatory theology which has nothing to say.

Thus, if one is to work with revelatory theology, then the central question that must arise with respect to the religious tradition involved is whether or not it perceives its God as disclosing Himself (and if yes, then in what way and to what extent). For clearly, without disclosure the very possibility of establishing a revelatory theology is not available; furthermore, the very nature and extent of the revelatory theology that can be established will depend upon and be commensurate with the nature and extent of the divine disclosure, the divine revelation, that the religious tradition in question provides.

Thus, for example, Christianity is a religious tradition that lends itself very readily and, indeed, extensively to revelatory theology. Here, God by incarnating himself into a specific human being who lived, walked, and talked in our midst, discloses a great deal about who and what He is. Thus, the religious tradition here provides plenty of material, of content, for the enterprise of revelatory theology.

In Judaism, on the other hand, the situation is much more complicated and indeed ambiguous. Thus, as to providing material, content, that would be relevant to the question of who and what God is, the tradition is not at all forthcoming, indeed it is reticent. It clearly rejects the possibility of incarnation. For Judaism God is in no way concrete and consequently He can be in no way visible or palpable in any fashion. Indeed in this sense God is not accessible. Thus, when Moses asks to see God the classic reply is 'No man shall see my face and live' (see Exodus 33:18–23) or when Moses asks for God's name (the name constituting the disclosure of who and what God is) the reply is evasive in the extreme—'Eheye asher Eheye' (I shall be that which I shall be), 'Eheye (I shall be) sent me' (see Exodus 3:13–14). Clearly, the Bible sets here the fundamental pattern that is to characterize Judaism, to wit, the conscious and knowing rejection of any possibility of the divine disclosing or imparting any information regarding who or what He is. Thus, to the extent that one would expect to have precisely such matters dealt with within the enterprise of theology (theology being constituted by knowledge regarding the being of the divine), Judaism does not have and, indeed, cannot have any revelatory theology or, to put the matter more precisely, any revelatory theology that is in principle feasible will have to remain completely empty of content as regards this kind of knowledge.

But if we wish, in a sense, to expand the signification of the notion of revelatory theology by moving away from the stricture that the content must be specifically limited to who and what the divine is and instead make *any* disclosure or impartation from the divine a legitimate content for revelatory theology, then there is indeed a real possibility for a revelatory theology within Judaism—indeed, Rabbinic Judaism, by its very essence, grounds itself in such a revelatory theology. For although in Judaism God does not disclose any information about Himself, He does disclose a great deal about His expectations and wishes regarding the conduct of man, specifically, how man should lead his life—how man should act and behave with regard to God, to other people, to himself, to inanimate and animate nature. Thus, while God does not disclose His being He very definitely discloses His will. With respect to the latter Judaism has plenty of content for a revelatory theology. But clearly, the revelatory theology here cannot be of a metaphysical nature and orientation; it can only be of an ethical–legal nature and orientation (legal being here just the other side of the coin to the ethical—it is the objective, public side of the intentional, subjective side of the ethical). This is, indeed, the case with Rabbinic Judaism. It clearly does not have a revelatory theology that is metaphysical in nature and orientation. But just as clearly, it does have *Halacha*, *i.e.*, an ethical–legal system that covers every aspect of human life and conduct and is ultimately derived from the divine disclosure of His will. But in view of our comments above, it should be possible to view *Halacha* as constituting revelatory theology; for, after all, it represents the human exposition and interpretation of a divine disclosure, except that the disclosure is not of His being but rather of His will for man.

Now, we would submit that in this context, *i.e.*, in the context where 'theology' is used in the sense of revelatory theology, the only significant and meaningful signification that the adjective 'Jewish' (the adjective that qualifies the notion of theology, *i.e.*, revelatory theology, here) can have is the signification which designates the religious tradition that is Judaism. Namely, the adjective 'Jewish' in the term 'Jewish theology', when theology is used in the sense of revelatory theology, can have meaningful and relevant signification only when it refers to Judaism. Thus, it signifies a revelatory theology that operates in the context of the religious tradition that is Judaism. As such, it provides meaningful, relevant and, indeed, necessary and essential information with respect to the revelatory theology. For, as we have seen, the content of revelatory theology (*i.e.*, the material, the information, which revelatory theology is to describe and interpret thus transforming it to a 'body of knowledge') is provided by the particular religious tradition in which it operates. As such, it does not make any sense to speak of revelatory theology as such, of revelatory theology in general, devoid of any qualification designating a religious tradition (*i.e.*, to speak of a universal or global revelatory theology). There is no such thing. Revelatory theology, if it is not to be empty, must be attached to a particular religious tradition. Indeed, different religious traditions provide different contents and consequently give rise to different revelatory theologies—a revelatory theology that arises in the context of the religious tradition of Judaism is bound to be different from a revelatory theology that arises in the context of the religious tradition of Christianity. The adjectival qualification that signifies a particular religious tradition is thus a necessary and essential qualification as regards the enterprise of revelatory theology.

As against this, the adjectival qualification, when it signifies not a religious tradition but membership in a community of faith, gives us at best information that is peripheral and unessential to the enterprise of revelatory theology, for membership in a community of faith does not impinge on the doing of revelatory theology. Thus, for example, being Jewish does not, in principle, qualify one in any special, essential way to do the revelatory theology that is constituted in terms of the religious tradition that is Judaism. In principle, any human being should be able to do it; any human being should be able to describe and interpret what Judaism presents as a divine disclosure to man. One does not have to be a Jew to describe and interpret what Judaism claims is the divine revelation nor a Christian to describe and interpret what Christianity claims is the divine revelation. In principle, a Christian should be able to describe and interpret what Judaism presents as the divine revelation and a Jew should be able to describe and interpret what Christianity presents as the divine revelation. True, it is much more likely that a Jew will do the revelatory theology that arises in Judaism and a Christian will do the revelatory theology that arises in Christianity. But this is brought about by sociological and psychological factors, factors that are peripheral and contingent. They thus may determine what in fact may be the case but not what must be the case in order for revelatory theology to be done. Thus, to merely signify that the practitioners of a revelatory theology happen to be Jews or Christians or Moslems is not to signify anything that is essential or necessary to the doing of that revelatory theology. Clearly, we have here the same situation that obtains as regards the doing of natural theology. In both cases, it makes ample sense to take the adjectival qualification as referring to a religious tradition and not to membership in a community of faith. So, the adjective 'Jewish' in the notion of Jewish revelatory theology is to be taken as referring to the religious tradition that is Judaism (the factor that provides the content of this revelatory theology) and not to the fact that the practitioners of this revelatory theology may be Jews.

But to return to the further examination of the notion of theology when it is taken in the sense of revelatory theology, the all–important question must finally be addressed, namely, whether theology taken in this sense, *i.e.*, revelatory theology, is really, in the last analysis, workable in the context of Judaism? Our answer must be no and this for two reasons. First, as we have seen, revelatory theology appears in Judaism only in the form of *Halacha*. Namely, the only divine disclosure that Judaism presents is a disclosure of the divine will as it is directed towards man. Judaism does not know of a divine disclosure regarding who or what the divine is. To the extent, however, that our pursuit of theology is the pursuit of knowledge regarding who and what God is, Judaism in its presentation of divine disclosure simply does not give us the necessary information. Thus, to the extent that we want revelatory theology to tell us who and what God is, it is not available in Judaism—the format, the structure, is available but it is empty as the content is missing.

The second reason is even more powerful and fundamental. Indeed, it inheres in the very nature of the enterprise of revelatory theology as such and is not merely dependent on the external contingency of whether or not the revelatory theology is provided by a religious tradition with material to constitute its content. It lies in the fact that a being that is exclusively a person, *i.e.*, a being that is purely a Thou (what one might call an Absolute Thou), cannot really communicate or transmit to another being any contentful knowledge of any kind. This is so because a Thou–being, by its very essence *qua* Thou, can communicate only with another Thou–being (more precisely put, a Thou–being can come into being only from within such a communication with another Thou–being), and this communication, *i.e.*, this relation, must by its very essence be a relation of mutuality—a relation which does not move one–way from one pre–existent being to another preexistent being but rather, ontologically speaking precedes both beings (these beings arising as the poles of the relation) and oscillates with true mutuality in the in–between. But any communication of content must immediately and inescapably reduce the relation to a one–directional relation, *i.e.*, to a relation that transmits, that moves, from one being to another thus abrogating the required mutuality. Any transmission of content whatsoever, be it cognitive information or the expression of feelings, desires, wishes, necessarily excludes the possibility of the relation being an I–Thou relation of mutuality and reduces it to being a one–directional I–It relation. Thus, a being that is a pure Thou cannot communicate content of any kind; it can only confirm.[8] In as much, therefore, as the structure of faith of mainstream Judaism requires, by its very essence, that its God be a personal being, a Thou–God, this means that we cannot have revelatory theology here because such a God, *i.e.*, an Absolute Thou–God, cannot impart any content to man—He can only impart pure confirmation.

Thus, we must conclude that revelatory theology is not a satisfactory explanation for the notion of theology when it formulates itself as Jewish theology, *i.e.*, as the theology that expresses itself in the context of the religious tradition of Judaism, not only because in the religious tradition of Judaism God does not really disclose any information regarding Himself (He discloses only information regarding His will concerning man) but, much more fundamentally, because God is constituted here as an Absolute Thou, as a pure Thou, and as such He cannot, in principle, be implicated in a revelatory theology. And this, in turn, means that the move from natural theology to revelatory theology does not really resolve the problem before us.

Indeed, a moment's reflection may indicate to us why this is so. For after all, the move from natural theology to revelatory theology only succeeded in changing the role of the divine from being a *grammatical* object (in the case of natural theology) to being a *grammatical* subject (in the case of revelatory theology). And while this is, in its own way, an important change, it does not impinge on the fundamental problem that faces us here and that is the divine must be an *ontological* subject (*i.e.*, a Thou) and can never be and *ontological* object (*i.e.*, an It). For after all, a grammatical subject can still be an ontological object (as was illustrated in the foregoing analysis of revelatory theology). Indeed, to be an ontological subject, the divine (or, for that matter, any other being) must be implicated exclusively in a relation that is truly mutual, a two–way relation. But this is precisely what the move from natural theology to revelatory theology fails to accomplish—revelatory theology implicates a one–way relation as much as natural theology does. What the move changes is only the direction of the relation—while in natural theology the direction is from man to God, now in revelatory theology it is from God to man. But change in direction is not enough here. Indeed, in as much as revelatory theology continues to be a one–way relation, the fundamental difficulty is not overcome by the move. Revelatory theology continues to confront us with the same fundamental difficulty which we encountered in the case of natural theology, namely, that the divine being which it implicates cannot be constituted as an Absolute Thou. To the extent, therefore, that we want to insist that the very essence of the distinctive expression of Judaism (as, indeed, of authentic biblical faith in general) lies in its claim that the divine be constituted as an Absolute Thou, neither natural theology nor revelatory theology will do, in the last analysis, as the format in which the theological enterprise can express itself.

III

The only way, we would suggest, by which we can extricate ourselves from this impasse and arrive at a delineation of the theological enterprise that can function in a meaningful and acceptable way when used in the context of the notion of a Jewish theology is by removing the divine from being the direct, the primary or the immediate object of concern for this enterprise. What we are suggesting is that the divine be made a secondary object of concern, *i.e.*, an object once removed, at which the theological enterprise can arrive only by moving first through another object of concern. The divine should be moved, so to speak, from the first line of exposure to the theological search–light to the rear, to a secondary line, so that the theological search–light must first pass through another object, (*i.e.*, the object placed in the first line of exposure) before it reaches the divine object. Namely, we are suggesting that we shift God from being the immediate, direct object of the *logos* of theology, making Him a secondary, once removed, object of this *logos*. But what, then, would be the primary object of this *logos*, the object placed on the first line of exposure, the object through which theology must move in order to get to the divine object? Our suggestion is that it be the content of faith of the religious community.

Of course, this means that we are suggesting moving away from delineating the theological enterprise in terms of the literal meaning of the word 'theology'. The enterprise now would no longer consist in establishing a logos regarding the divine being but rather in establishing a logos regarding the content of faith of a religious community. But such a shift in the usage of terminology occurs all the time and is not too objectionable. Indeed, in this case it can be readily justified. For after all, God is certainly a part of the content of faith—indeed, it is in all probability the most central and most prominent part of the content of faith. Thus, by using the term 'theology' as we propose to use it here, we would be identifying the enterprise as it impinges on its whole object by a term that signifies its impingement on only a part of that whole object. This is done not infrequently and should be quite acceptable. Particularly in the case here, seeing that the part, *i.e.*, God, is the most central and prominent part of the whole, such a transfer in usage should be quite justifiable. It is certainly not a radical or abusive shift in the usage of language.[9]

But be this as it may, a good case can certainly be made that using 'theology' in the sense that we are proposing here, *i.e.*, as the enterprise of describing and interpreting the content of faith of a religious community, has a clear and substantive advantage over using 'theology' in the alternative senses available, *i.e.*, either as natural theology or as revelatory theology. The advantage lies in the fact that using 'theology' in the sense proposed here cancels out and neutralizes the problematics encountered when natural or revelatory theology are used. For any problematic that the method of theology may precipitate when it impinges directly on the divine (and this, indeed, is the nature of the problematic presented by natural and revelatory theology) is cancelled out and neutralized here because its direct impingement is diverted from the divine to the content of faith (the divine is affected only because and to the extent that it constitutes part of the content of faith but in this capacity the impingement of the method of theology does not precipitate a problematic). Essentially, what we are saying is this: the problematic is precipitated because the very essence of distinctive mainstream Judaism lies in the fact that its God is a Thou–God and a Thou–God is fundamentally incompatible with either of the two alternative methods that theology uses, *i.e.*, either with the method of demonstration and inference (the method used by natural theology) or with the method of description and interpretation (the method used by revelatory theology and by the theology proposed here). For, as we have seen, either method abrogates the thouness of God, when applied to Him directly—a Thou–God cannot be demonstrated, inferred, described or interpreted without being reduced in the process to an It–God. The great advantage of the usage of theology proposed here is that it applies itself and thus its methodology not the Thou–God directly but to the content of faith of a religious community, an entity that is not a Thou to begin with but an It and consequently no problematic is precipitated by such an application.[10] The problematic arises only when the method of theology is made to impinge directly on the divine. This, indeed, is the basic short–coming of both natural theology and revelatory theology. In contrast, it is the great strength of the usage of theology proposed here that its method does not impinge directly on the divine but rather on a content of faith and only through it on a notion of the divine as perceived in that content of faith.

Still, before we can settle on this as our final word on what the definition of the term 'theology' signifies, we must take care of yet another question that is bound to arise. Namely, we must encounter the question of how our delineation of the enterprise of theology differs from the enterprise of the phenomenology of religion.

For, at first glance, it would certainly seem that the task we have assigned to theology here is precisely the task that the phenomenology of religion is purported to carry out. Have we, then, to all intents and purposes, reduced theology to the phenomenology of religion or can we establish a legitimate distinction between the two terms so that, in the last analysis, we are still left with two different and distinct enterprises rather than with one enterprise possessing two names? What distinction, if any, can we establish by which to differentiate the two enterprises?[11]

Well, it may perhaps be suggested that the distinction lies in that the phenomenology of religion undertakes merely to *describe* the content of faith of a religious tradition while theology in the sense proposed here undertakes not only to describe but also to *interpret* the content of faith of a religious tradition. So, the differentiation would revolve here around the distinction between mere description, on the one hand, and a description accompanied by interpretation, on the other hand. But, in the last analysis, is this distinction really valid or viable? It would not seem so. For, in the first instance, the very supposition that there can be a separation between description and interpretation (what the distinction here clearly implies) would be challenged. It would be argued that we cannot really have a description without interpretation—the very act of description already implicates an interpretation. Thus, the very possibility of there being a distinction in principle between these two activities is challenged. But even if we reject this challenge and maintain that there is a valid distinction in principle between mere description, on the one hand, and interpretation, on the other hand, it is certainly a very difficult undertaking to maintain and carry out such a distinction in practice. Indeed, there can be no denying that much of the work of the phenomenology of religion is not purely descriptive but is also (and, indeed, more than one would like to admit) interpretative. Thus, if we are to compare the phenomenology of religion with theology in terms of their very practice, then this line of distinction would not hold. But even if we insist on being theoretical purists and thus continue to hang on to some kind of validity for the distinction between pure description and interpretation, what shall we do when the enterprise of phenomenology consciously transforms itself to the enterprise of a hermeneutical phenomenology, namely, when it consciously proposes not only to describe but also to interpret? The distinction between pure description and interpretation would clearly not hold here. Do we want then to grant that the enterprise of theology, as we have delineated it here, is nothing else but the enterprise of a hermeneutical phenomenology of religion? Do we really want to maintain that, in the last analysis, the enterprise of theology is reducible to the enterprise of a hermeneutical phenomenology of religion? It would not seem so. But, then, what can the distinction between them possibly be?

Well, it may perhaps be further suggested that the distinction lies in that the phenomenology of religion deals with such aspects of the content of faith of a religious tradition as cult, ritual and institutions, namely, that it deals with the concrete, practical expressions of the religious tradition, while theology deals with such aspects as tenets of faith and doctrines, namely, with the speculative, intellectual expressions of the religious tradition. What is one to say to this? Well, it may well be true that as a matter of practice, of fact, there is considerable validity to this observation. The phenomenology of religion does seem to concentrate very often on ritual, cult and institutions while theology does seem to concentrate equally often on doctrines and tenets of faith. Thus, by and large, there is something to the claim that there is, so to speak, a 'division of labor' between the phenomenology of religion and theology and the suggestion here clearly builds on this in proposing that this 'division of labor' be taken as the criterion by which to distinguish these two enterprises.

But this suggested distinction is really, in the last analysis, not acceptable. For first, it must be noted that the criterion for distinction here is constituted not in terms of the structure or methodology of the enterprises involved but rather in terms of what aspects of the content of faith are being examined by these enterprises. Thus, the criterion for distinction resides outside the enterprises which are being distinguished, which means that in their own terms, *i.e.*, in terms of their structure, methodology or activity, they are not distinguishable. This clearly is not satisfactory. And indeed, this, in turn, leads to a second and by far the more decisive consideration for finding this proposal unacceptable. Namely, this distinction need not actually take place. For it is quite possible that a phenomenology of religion would deal with tenets of faith and doctrines and that a theology would deal with institutions, cult and ritual. Indeed, some phenomenologies of religion and some theologies do precisely this. The fact that the criterion for distinction resides in some factors outside the enterprises themselves removes the element of necessity and compulsion, making it merely contingent and accidental. It just so happens that the phenomenology of religion focuses on these aspects while theology focuses on those aspects of the content of faith (but there is nothing in the structure or methodology of these enterprises to force them to focus the way they do). Clearly, as such, the criterion we have here is not applicable in a sufficiently rigorous manner.

In terms of what criterion, then, can we establish the distinction between these two enterprises? We would suggest that the criterion which would clearly establish a viable and valid distinction is the criterion of adoption. Namely, according to this criterion, in theology the theologian would be expected to adopt as his own the claims of the content of faith which he is describing and interpreting while in the phenomenology of religion no such expectation would exist with respect to the phenomenologist. Put slightly differently, we can say that the essential distinction between the phenomenology of religion and theology arises with regard to the question of the truth–value of the object, *i.e.*, the truth–value of the content of faith which they describe and interpret. Thus, we would want to say, that the theologian, by the very essence of his vocation, is expected to adopt, profess and defend the content of faith with which he is dealing as true and valid while the phenomenologist, by the very essence of his vocation, must reject any such expectation. The very commitment of the phenomenologist *qua* phenomenologist is solely to the original intent and expression of his object. His concern is focused solely on recapturing and representing as accurately and authentically as possible the practices and thoughts of the religious tradition he chooses to describe. His sole commitment is to accuracy of representation. It is the accuracy of describing, for example, how a religious tradition celebrates its ritual, the accuracy of capturing its meaning for its celebrants, that is the sole concern of the phenomenologist. The question of the truth–value, of the universal validity of the data he describes, does not concern him. Certainly, and this is the crux of the matter, he himself *qua* phenomenologist does not have to appropriate the truth and validity of the data he describes; he does not have to commit himself to the truth–value of his data. Of course, he must be able to empathize with those who do appropriate the truth and validity of the data. But precisely, this requirement clearly indicates that he, the phenomenologist, is standing outside the circle of faith of the phenomenon (those who are inside the circle need not empathize; they possess and share in the faith directly).

As against this, the theologian, by the very essence of his vocation, is vitally concerned with the truth–value and validity of the data he undertakes to interpret. Indeed, he appropriates and identifies himself with the data. True, he is interpreting someone else's *Weltanschauung* but at the same time, through his act of appropriation and identification, he is also interpreting his own *Weltanschauung*. His interpretation becomes self–interpretation, and as such it comes to contain a claim to it validity and truth. The theologian must put himself on the line. He must not only, like the phenomenologist, subject himself to the body of data given him by a religious tradition, undertaking to interpret it in a way faithful and authentic to its own intent, he must also (unlike the phenomenologist but like the philosopher) be an advocate claiming its truth and validity. Thus, his task, in a sense, combines the role of both the phenomenologist and the philosopher.

It follows from this that the theologian must be within the circle of faith of a religious tradition. And this, in turn, means that the theologian must be a member of the community of faith in as much as the carrier of the religious tradition is the community of faith.[12] Thus, membership for the theologian in the community of faith is necessitated not because as such the data of the religious tradition is made accessible to him but because the very nature of the theological enterprise requires it. The theological task cannot be carried out outside the community of faith, specifically, outside the particular community of faith of the religious tradition whose *Weltanschauung* the theologian has appropriated.[13]

We must conclude, therefore, that a theologian must be qualified by the specific religious tradition that he undertakes to interpret. There is no such thing as a theologian in general but only a Christian theologian, a Jewish theologian, etc. In a sense, of course, the qualification here (as we have argued above) signifies the subject–matter of his theologizing. But now, we can see that this qualification assumes yet another signification equal in importance to the foregoing signification, namely, it signifies the community of faith to which the theologian belongs. To say that a theologian is Jewish or Christian is thus to say not only that his theologizing consists in interpreting the Jewish or Christian religious tradition but that he belongs to the Jewish or Christian community of faith. And the two significations are inextricably bound to each other in a one to one relationship. A member of the Jewish community of faith cannot be a theologian of the Christian religious tradition and vice versa a theologian of the Christian community of faith cannot be a member of the Jewish community of faith.

Now, such a requirement of affiliation is totally absent in the case of the phenomenologist. In the case of the phenomenologist the belonging to a community of faith is of no consequence whatsoever and totally beside the point. Thus, a Christian can be a phenomenologist of the Jewish religious tradition and, vice versa, a Jew can be a phenomenologist of the Christian religious tradition. Indeed, a phenomenology of non–living religious traditions is quite feasible. Also, a phenomenologist can change the religious tradition which he undertakes to describe—describing one religious tradition at one time and another religious tradition at another time. Or indeed, he may, when engaging himself in a comparative study, describe concurrently a number of different religious traditions. And all these changes in no way implicate a change of status in the personal standing of the phenomenologist.[14]

A helpful analogy to this difference between the enterprise of phenomenology and that of theology may be taken, perhaps, from the field of music. According to this, the enterprise of the phenomenologist may be compared to that of the musicologist. The musicologist does not have to identify himself with the music he undertakes to analyse; the music does not have to affect him; he does not even have to enjoy and appreciate it; he can analyse any and all music. On the other hand, the enterprise of the theologian can be compared to that of the performer. The performer must identify himself with the music, make it his own expression; he must enjoy and appreciate the music.[15] The analogy is suggestive because, in the last analysis, the enterprise of the musicologist is to describe while that of the performer is to interpret (by the way, the analogy may be even more suggestive if we keep in mind that a religious tradition is ensemble and not solo music and the performer, therefore, can perform only when participating in the ensemble).[16]

Thus, we do have a viable and valid distinction between the enterprise of the phenomenology of religion and that of theology in the sense proposed here and this means, we would submit, that we can claim that our proposed delineation of the signification of the term 'theology' is a viable and valid delineation. Furthermore, this, in turn, clearly implies, as we have seen, that the adjectival qualification 'Jewish' designates here both a religious tradition, *i.e.*, Judaism, and membership in a community of faith, *i.e.*, Jew. For to do theology in the sense proposed here one must have not only a content of faith that is provided by a particular religious tradition but also the practitioners of this theology must be members of the community of faith which carries that religious tradition. For after all, the doing of theology in the sense proposed here implies the adoption of the truth–value and validity of the content of faith that is to be interpreted and this, in turn, clearly implies that the interpreters must be members of the community of faith that carries the religious tradition which provides the content of faith. This is so inasmuch as the adoption of truth–value and validity on behalf of a content of faith is tantamount to assuming membership in the community of faith that is associated with this content of faith, seeing that membership in a community of faith is determined by the appropriation of the truth–value and validity of the content of faith associated with that community of faith. Thus, for example, 'Christian' signifies a member of the Christian community of faith by virtue of the person's adoption of the content of faith of Christianity as true and valid and 'Moslem' signifies membership in the Islamic community of faith by virtue of the person's adoption of the content of faith of Islam as true and valid. As such, this would mean that a Christian who would want to do Moslem theology or a Moslem who would want to do Christian theology would be a person who would have to adopt simultaneously as true and valid two contents of faith which may not be compatible at all with each other. This is clearly an untenable situation. Indeed, to the extent that the contents of faith of biblical, monotheistic religions are, so to speak, monogamistic, *i.e.*, demanding exclusive loyalty, it is clearly not possible for a member of any of these communities of faith to undertake to do theology in the sense proposed here with respect to the content of faith associated with any other religious tradition, for this would make the person a member at one and the same time of two different communities of faith and this is not possible. Thus, doing theology in the sense proposed here must be restricted to members of the community of faith which carries the religious tradition that provides the content of faith for the doing of the theology—only a Christian can do Christian theology, only a Moslem can do Islamic theology and only a Jew can do Jewish theology.[17]

Now, this conclusion is in clear contrast to what we had to conclude regarding the signification of the adjective 'Jewish' when dealing with natural theology and revelatory theology. As will be recalled, in these two latter instances, the adjective 'Jewish' could be used only in terms of its designation of the religious tradition which provides the content of faith and not in terms of its designation of membership in a community of faith. Clearly, the use of the adjective "Jewish" in conjunction with the notion of theology in the sense proposed here has a clear advantage over its use in conjunction with either natural or revelatory theology. For in the former case, and in contrast to the latter two cases, its possible range of designation is utilized to the fullest extent without any kind of compromise.

One last observation before bringing this essay to a close. The notion of Jewish theology in the sense proposed here is not merely prescriptive, it is also descriptive. Namely, it is not just that we are recommending that this be the way in which Jewish theology is pursued; a good case can be made that Jewish theology in the sense proposed here has actually been pursued in the course of Jewish history. In the main, we would suggest, this has been done in what is commonly referred to as modern Jewish thought of philosophy, *i.e.*, in Jewish thought pursued (mainly in Germany) since the times of Moses Mendelssohn. Indeed, if one examines this body of thought in the light of our analysis, one would have to conclude, in all likelihood, that a considerable–part of this body of thought conforms to theology in the sense proposed here, to wit, it is essentially a description and an interpretation of what can be taken as the content of faith of Judaism or, more broadly but also more vaguely, as the content of the phenonomenon of Judaism. Thus, while Jewish theology in the sense of natural theology exemplified itself, by and large, in what is commonly referred to as medieval Jewish philosophy and Jewish theology in the sense of revelatory theology exemplifies itself in the *Halacha*, Jewish theology in the sense proposed here exemplifies itself, we would submit, in what is commonly referred to as modern Jewish thought. No wonder that the use of the term 'theology' has come to the fore only in our time and that it is with reference to modern thought that we feel most comfortable using the term.

IV

Thus, in conclusion, we can give our answer to the question posed at the beginning of this paper in one sentence. Yes, there is a possible meaning to the notion of Jewish theology—it means that enterprise which undertakes to describe and interpret the content of faith of the religious tradition of Judaism from a vantage–point that adopts and defends the truth–value of this content and which consequently can be carried out only by members of the community of faith that carries the religious tradition of Judaism.

Notes

[1]There may be a few exceptions to this, *i.e.*, some philosophies of religion which actually manifest interest in the underlying methodology of approach rather than directly in its object, *i.e.*, in constituting the divine being, but they are to be encountered mostly in our time.

[2]We have qualified our claim that the philosophy of religion establishes its divine object without connection to a particular historical religious tradition by the phrase 'strictly speaking' for it might be argued that the philosophy of religion too must in a way have a connection with a particular historical religion which as such would determine the nature of its divine object. After all, the philosopher pursuing a philosophy of religion is a human being who as such must live and act in the context of a certain particular culture and consequently this culture in which he lives and works will inescapably condition and influence his philosophical creativity in all its forms, including

specifically his philosophy of religion. Now, to the extent that this culture is suffused with a certain religious tradition (and almost all cultures are suffused with one or another religion tradition), this philosophy of religion and specifically the kind of divine being it establishes will in all likelihood be influenced by the religious tradition connected with the culture underlying it. Indeed, one can make a fairly good case that there is a correlation between the conception of God developed by various philosophies of religion and the conception of God operating in the cultures in which they are embedded. But although this is in all likelihood true, it should not undermine the distinction we are attempting to establish here. For the distinction we are attempting to establish is on the level of consciousness and in terms of intention and not on the level of the subconscious and in terms of the workings of certain forces and influences that are unbeknown to their agent. And consciously, the philosopher of religion does not see himself subject to any religious tradition or, for that matter, to any culture. Consciously, he does not accept that the end–result of his philosophy is already established by another agency. Consciously, he is beholden only to his experience and to his reason. That his experience and reason are, in all probability, conditioned by the culture to which he belongs and by the religious tradition characterizing this culture, does not alter this commitment. Consciously and intentionally he is still committed only to his reason and experience. As against this, we would want to argue that the natural theologian does see himself consciously and intentionally, beholden to a particular religious tradition. He consciously accepts from another agency the end–results of his enterprise. It is not only that he is subconsciously conditioned by a certain religious tradition; he consciously interacts with it.

[3]Of course, since the God–object is delineated by the religious tradition it is natural that the practitioners of that religious tradition would be more likely to pursue the natural theology which is linked to their religious tradition rather than the natural theology which is linked to a foreign religious tradition. Thus, it is only natural that, by and large, Jewish natural theology would be done by Jews, Christian natural theology by Christians and so on. But this linkage is completely contingent, determined by sociological, psychological or historical factors; it is not essential and in principle it need not be so. If we take, then, the adjective 'Jewish' to designate Jews we would get at best a very minimal and really insignificant qualification of the enterprise of natural theology; as against this, we do get a much more meaningful and indeed significant qualification of the enterprise if we take the adjective to designate the religious tradition of Judaism. We must conclude, therefore, that the expression 'Jewish theology' in the sense of being a Jewish natural theology refers to a natural theology that is carried out in connection with the religious tradition of Judaism in that the religious tradition of Judaism delineates the nature of its object, *i.e.*, it delineates the characteristics and attributes of the divine. Indeed, while the expression 'a Jewish natural theology' or 'a Christian natural theology' is awkward, a much more comfortable way to express this is to say 'a natural theology that is Jewish' or 'a natural theology that is Christian' thus indicating quite clearly that the adjective Jewish or Christian refers here to the religious tradition itself and not to the members, *i.e.*, practitioners, of that religious tradition.

[4]And even so we should really qualify this by adding 'relatively speaking', for we can say that it flourishes only in a relative sense to what is going on in other periods when there is very little, if any, doing of natural theology. Also, it is true that we usually refer to this literature as embodying not the doing of natural theology but rather as embodying the doing of Jewish philosophy. That is to say, one normally uses the term 'Jewish philosophy' rather than the term 'Jewish theology' or 'Jewish natural theology'. Now, when one examines this literature one would have to say that while, indeed, there is a certain part of it which deals with issues in general philosophy (particularly in such areas as epistemology and cosmology), the overwhelming bulk of the material deals with issues that properly belong to the area of religion (the bulk deals with

various aspects of Judaism as a religion, *i.e.*, with various aspects of the tenets of faith of Judaism) and here, most significantly, the approach is, given the distinction we have proposed, that of natural theology and not that of the philosophy of religion. So, when judged by what is actually done and using the terminology in terms of the significations that we have proposed above, a good case can be made that what we are encountering here is in the main not a Jewish philosophy of religion but rather a natural theology that is Jewish. The reason why, not withstanding this, this enterprise is nonetheless usually referred to as Jewish philosophy and not as Jewish theology (*i.e.*, as a philosophy of religion that is Jewish rather than as a natural theology that is Jewish) is the reluctance among many Jews, particularly in the past, to grant that the enterprise of theology is feasible within Judaism, namely, that such a thing as a Jewish theology is at all possible. There is a fairly widespread though vague feeling of being uncomfortable with the notion of theology and consequently the tendency to resort to the notion of philosophy. We shall try to clarify below the rationale that underlies this feeling. Still, whether or not we succeed in accounting for this misuse of terminology, on the basis of the delineations we proposed above we would have to argue that what we have here is clearly a natural theology and not a philosophy of religion. And in essence this is so because while proceeding from human experience to the divine, these various so–called medieval Jewish philosophers knew very well in advance where they wanted to come out, this being determined for them by their religious tradition *i.e.*, by the religious tradition of Judaism. Given our definition, this constitutes the enterprise of a natural theology and not of a philosophy of religion.

[5]It is most probably this consideration which half–consciously underlies the thinking of those who claim that Judaism has no theology. They equate theology with natural theology and on this basis claim that Judaism has no theology. Now, they are wrong in making this equation as there may be, as we shall presently see, other forms of theology (though, given the actual history of doing theology, such identity is not all that outlandish). At the same time, however, they would be, in our judgement, completely justified if all they mean to say is that Judaism does not have *natural theology*.

Indeed, distinctive, mainstream Judaism does not show much appreciation for natural theology. True, as remarked above, we do witness, particularly in the Middle Ages, a very impressive manifestation within Judaism of doing natural theology. But it should be noted, first, that this pursuit of natural theology comes about in Judaism in consequence to and in emulation of the pursuit of natural theology within Islam. It does not originate from within Judaism but comes to it from the outside. Indeed, it is in the outside, *i.e.*, in Islam, that the innovative, creative work of formulating the various strategies to be employed by natural theology is done; in Judaism, on the other hand, the work with respect to this enterprise is essentially one of emulation and copying, with the additional work of adaptation necessitated by the specific needs and requirements that the religious tradition of Judaism introduces into the picture. Secondly, and much more significantly, it should be noted that, essentially, the medieval Jewish natural theologians were preserved and honored by the tradition not because of their work in the domain of natural theology but rather because of their work in the domain of *Halacha*, *i.e.*, Jewish law. Namely, such persons as Maimonides or Nachmanides are honored in the tradition not because of their work in and contributions to the domain of *Halacha*. Indeed, their work in the domain of natural theology is tolerated and preserved by the tradition because of the stature and reputation that these men have achieved within the tradition by virtue of their work in and contributions to the domain of *Halacha*. It is only in the last century or so, in the context of the Emancipation (no doubt in conjunction with the assimilatory forces that are inevitably linked to the emancipatory process), that these people are greatly honored not so much because of their contributions to *Halacha* but rather by virtue of their work in and contributions to natural theology (the nomenclature commonly used, however, is Jewish philosophy rather than natural theology). Thus, for example, it is only in modern times that the greatness of Maimonides is linked to his being the author of the *Guide to the Perplexed* i.e., to his main work in natural theology); traditionally, in the past, his greatness was linked to his being the author of the *Mishne Torah* (*i.e.*, to his main work in *Halacha.* Indeed, it is only the high status which Maimonides attained as a halachic scholar that safeguarded his position in the tradition against the serious attack directed against him because of his authoring of the *Guide.* Thus, our reservation above regarding the status and importance of the theological or philosophical activity of medieval Judaism is not without some justification.

Also we should note that quite clearly, though implicitly, the natural theology which arises in the context of medieval Judaism often appears to wish to distance itself from the cover–up the necessary implication that the God of natural theology, *i.e.*, the God with which it is dealing, is of necessity an It–God. The consistency of the logic derived from the orientation of natural theology which requires that the God involved be an It–God is broken and a kind of a thou–God is smuggled in. Thus, all of a sudden, at the end of the road (*i.e.*, after attempting to demonstrate the existence of a God who is an uncaused First cause or an unmoved mover) one encounters a God who hears prayers, who is providential and who pursues justice. Clearly, it shows that the concerns of the religious tradition of Judaism come to prevail over the considerations of natural theology. It is the interests of natural theology that give way to the requirements of biblical faith—the needs of biblical faith prevail even though it is at the cost of consistency. Indeed there is no escaping the conclusion that in this context the pursuit of natural theology is feasible only at the cost of such a price and this is really tantamount to saying that, in the last analysis, the pursuit of natural theology in its own terms is really not feasible with respect to biblical faith.

[6]It must be admitted, however, that apparently this was not clearly seen in the past. Hence, the repeated attempts in the past to somehow ignore or fudge the incompatibility and thus allow one to resort to natural theology. It is really in our time that the incompatibility is fully and clearly realized and brought into the full light of consciousness, thus allowing one to mount a devastating attack against any attempt to use natural theology in conjunction with biblical faith. The two who lead the charge most prominently are Buber and Barth. The former comes from the religious tradition of Christianity; the former focuses his attack in terms of the theistic aspect of the divine, *i.e.*, God being a Thou–God, while the latter focuses his attack in terms of the theistic aspect of the divine, *i.e.*, God being wholly other; the former is somewhat implicit and *ad hoc* in his attack while the latter is quite explicit and programmatic. Thus, while the two differ in their method of attack (by the way, they also differ in the solutions they offer, the former offering what might be termed a 'dialogical theology' while the latter is offering a form of a 'revelatory theology', *i.e.*, dogmatics), between the two of them is clearly covered the waterfront. The two put together mount a most telling critique of any possibility of linking natural theology with biblical faith.

[7]The one entity that may appear as a possible exception to this claim, thus threatening to compromise God's unique distinctiveness from all the beings of this world, is the human being. For the human being is clearly an entity of this world, and entity existing inside this world; and yet, on the other hand, by virtue of it being a person (though not by virtue of it being a body) the human being can be known only to the extent that he/she chooses to reveal himself/herself. Thus, it would seem that the divine being has a partner, a companion, who, like the divine being, can be known only on the basis and to the extend of its choosing to reveal itself, this partner being the human being *qua* person. This is true, and yet we can argue that it does not really undermine the unique distinctiveness of the divine being from all other worldly beings. This is so by virtue of the following two observations: the first attempts to overcome the possible problematic that the existence of man may present regarding this claim of the'unique distinctiveness' of the divine being

from all other worldly beings by attaching itself to the aspect of 'unique distinctiveness' in the claim while the second attempts to do the same by attaching itself to the aspect of worldly beings' in the claim. Namely, the first observation attempts to remove the problematic by preserving the distinctiveness of the divine with regard to man while the second observation attempts to remove the problematic by removing man (the being with whom a similarity with the divine can be established) from being a worldly being pure and simple.

Thus, first, one can point to the fact that the human being is not only a person but also a body, while the divine being is exclusively a person. Thus, the human being parallels the divine being only in part but not in the totality of its being. The similarity is with respect only to one dimension, one aspect and not the totality of that other being. As such, we cannot really say that the unique distinctiveness of the divine being has been dissolved and done away with, for in terms of its being in its totality, the divine being remains uniquely distinctive—there is no other being whose *totality* of being can be known only on the basis of its self–disclosure and impartation. What might not escape the sting of the criticism raised here is the further claim that the divine is not only a uniquely distinctive being but that it is a wholly other being. For, after all, there can be no denying that a bridge, a linkage, is clearly established between the divine and the human at a certain point in the ontological makeup of the human. And in this sense, and to that extent, this undermines the wholly otherness of the divine. Thus, while the constitution of the human being *qua* person does not undermine the unique distinctiveness of the divine being it does undermine its wholly otherness.

Secondly, one can point to the fact that while it is certainly true that the human being is part and parcel of the world, a being that exists in the world, this is so exclusively by virtue of its body. But in terms of its body the human being does not share any similarity with the divine. The similarity is shared only in terms of the human being being also a person; it is only in terms of the dimension of personhood that a similarity, indeed, an identity between the human and the divine can be established. But it is precisely by virtue of his/her personhood that the human transcends the world and is not a worldly being. Thus, the similarity or identity established here between the divine and the human (due to the fact that both can be known only on the basis of and to the extent that they choose to disclose themselves) is a similarity or identity that is established in a realm transcending the world rather than in the world. It does not, therefore, pull the divine into the world; rather, it pushes man to transcend the world. If already, it implies the apotheosis of man rather than the incarnation of the divine. But from the theistic perspective the problematic lies with divine incarnation and not with human apotheosis.

[8]Such confirmation, let us stress, does not involve the transmission of content. Rather, it is established by mere presence, a presence, however, which constitutes itself as an address, a challenge—the challenge to an other to confirm it. In communicating this challenge, this address, one confirms the other while at the same time and in the very same act the other, in taking up this challenge, confirms the challenger in return. Now, this constitutes a true relation of mutuality from which a Thou–being can arise. By the way, it is Buber who makes the point that in an authentic I–Thou relation there can be no transmission of content, utilizing this point in mounting his criticism and rejection of *Halacha*, *i.e.*, of the claim of Rabbinic Judaism that in the revelation at Sinai God transmitted to Moses the body of laws constituting the *Halacha* (no content can pass in revelation, seeing that revelation is but an I–Thou encounter between the divine and man). But clearly, this point can be raised (as indeed we are doing here) against any kind of revelatory theology inasmuch as it necessarily involves a Thou–God and thus an I–Thou encounter.

One further point needs clarification in this connection. When we established above the analogy between knowing the Divine as a Thou–being and knowing the human being as a Thou–being (in both cases the knowledge being feasible only through the disclosure coming from the Thou–being), we clearly implicated that a human being as a Thou–being, as person, discloses himself/herself to us through the passing of contentful information—I know another human being as a person only to the extent that he/she chooses to impart to me through speech or other forms of communication what he/she thinks, wills, and feels. This is true and, indeed, it is feasible because a human being is constituted not only as a Thou–being but also as an It–being. Thus, human beings communicate not only in the context of the Thou but also in the context of the It where the passing of contentful information is not only feasible but required. Indeed, in this context the Thou can be communicated, transmitted, only by its refraction through the domain of the It (how this comes about is a myster, indeed, one may claim that it is the ultimate mystery). Thus, in the case of a being who is not constituted exclusively as a Thou but rather is constituted as both a Thou and an It, disclosure of the Thou dimension can be, nay must be, through the mediation of the It domain. Of course, what is disclosed here is not a pure Thou–being but rather only a refracted Thou–being, *i.e.*, a Thou–being whose Thouness is constituted by his/her thinking, willing and feeling. A pure Thou–being has none of these dimensions but only pure awareness which can be disclosed only through an act of pure confirmation (it is only when pure awareness is refracted through the It–dimension that it expresses itself as thinking, willing or feeling). Thus, a disclosure through the passing of content (and thus the establishment of a revelatory theology) is feasible only with respect to a divine being who is constituted as a Thou–It being, *i.e.*, as a being which is both a Thou and an It (both Consciousness and Power); in short, it is feasible only with respect to a divine who is constituted, in the last analysis, as nothing but man writ large. It is not feasible with respect to a divine being who is constituted as an absolute Thou and is thus qualitatively distinct from man. It may be, therefore, that those expressions in biblical faith which resort to revelatory theology may unwittingly implicate a divine being who is constituted not as an absolute Thou but rather as an It–Thou being, a divine who, therefore, in the last analysis, is not really wholly other but merely man writ large.

[9]Indeed, a case can be made that much (though, true, not all) of what is in actuality being pursued under the name of theology is precisely of this nature, namely, the establishment of a *logos* regarding the content of faith of the religious community. Thus, indeed, theology very often deals with subjects, *i.e.*, categories, other than that of the divine. It very often deals with such categories as salvation, sin, history, politics, etc.

Indeed, it is in this sense that we should understand the usage of expressions such as 'theology of history' or 'political theology' (though, regarding the latter, it would, most probably, be more accurate to use the expression 'theology of politics'). Thus, such expressions would signify a logos regarding a content of faith of a particular religious community as it focuses on a specific theme, category, *e.g.*, history, politics, society, salvation, liberation, etc., within that content of faith; they would refer to parts, sub–divisions, of the content of faith as a whole. Indeed, it is in this sense that we can also understand the term 'theology' when taken in its liberal signification (*i.e.*, *logos* about the *theos*)—it would parallel such expressions as 'theology of history', 'theology of politics' etc. Namely, 'theology' in its literal sense would signify a logos of the content of faith of a particular religious community as it focuses on its specific category of the divine. Thus, the expression 'theology' in its literal sense would stand in the same relation to the notion of theology in the sense proposed here as such expressions as 'theology of history' or 'theology of politics'. Indeed, if one would want to articulate the signification of 'theology' in terms of its literal meaning one would say that it is a logos of a theos that is refracted through the content of faith of a religious community.

[10]Even in the case of revelatory theology as it operates in Rabbinic Judaism, where its description and interpretation do not impinge upon the very being of the Thou–God but only upon

His communication to man (so that one may rightly argue that the method of description and interpretation does not really undermine here the thou–ness of the Thou–God), a serious problematic is precipitated by the fact that, as we have seen, a Thou–God cannot communicate content and consequently in as much as this theology implies that the Thou–God did communicate content it undermines the thouness of the Thou–God. But again, when moving away from impinging directly on God to impinging instead on the content of faith the problematic is removed.

[11]Of course, there is no denying that there are also a number of very important similarities between the two enterprises (similarities which are all the more striking when contrasted with the differences that obtain in these respects when one compares, as we did above, the enterprise of theology with that of the philosophy of religion). Thus, for both theology and the phenomenology of religion, the body of data constituting their subject–matter is predetermined by an outside agency, *i.e.*, the various religious traditions; their data, their subject–matter, is not generated by them but is prescribed for them by an outside agency. Thus, both must subject themselves to a body of data that is presented to them from the outside and consequently for both the fundamental criterion which regulates their respective enterprises is the criterion of authenticity, *i.e.*, authenticity to the given body of data. As such, both theology and the phenomenology of religion must depend on particular, concrete religious traditions to provide them with their materials.

[12]The structure of the religious phenomenon is such that it can express itself not in the isolated individual but only in the collectivity of a community and, therefore, the appropriation of a religious tradition necessitates membership within its community of faith.

[13]In view of this we would have to say that with regard to non–living religious traditions, *i.e.*, to religious traditions that are no longer carried by existing communities of faith, the theological enterprise cannot be, strictly speaking, fully pursued. Thus, such appellations as biblical theology or the theology of Greek religion may not be happy choices. These enterprises may be ascribed more appropriately to the domain of phenomenology or to the domain of intellectual history as, indeed, the whole field of historical theology should be.

[14]Of course, it is also conceivable that, for example, a Jewish theologian would become a Christian theologian, but then such a change would necessitate a conversion of faith, *i.e.*, a change of membership in the community of faith, which change would at the same time exclude him from continuing as a Jewish theologian. It is not possible to be a theologian of more than one religious tradition at one and the same time. Thus, a comparative theology, *i.e.*, a theology of a comparative nature, is not feasible.

[15]Of course, musical performing differs from theologizing in that the various musical styles are not as stringently exclusive of one another as are the various religious traditions and the musical performer can perform, *i.e.*, identify with and appropriate, more than one musical style. Still, even in performing, a kind of conversion–like change is required in the performer when he moves from one style to another.

[16]One further but rather important comment regarding the theological enterprise. It is possible, if one were to dwell exclusively on the subjection of theology to the *Weltanschauung* of the religious tradition, to arrive at a very wrong conclusion, namely, that theology is a finite enterprise that can come to a close. After all, if the sole purpose of the interpretation which constitutes the theological enterprise is to authentically and fully explicate the content of a religious *Weltanschauung*, then, seeing that this content is finite, once this has been achieved the work of theology would end and one would just have to repeat the perfected theology from generation to generation. But such a conclusion would be very wrong for it leaves out the other fundamental consideration dwelt upon in our deliberations above, namely, that the interpretation that is theology appropriates the *Weltanschauung* of the religious tradition and in doing so claims truth–value and

validity for the *Weltanschauung*. Including this consideration, however, as indeed we must, changes the picture radically. For now, the claiming of truth–value and validity for the religious *Weltanschauung* must necessarily imply establishing the religious *Weltanschauung* as meaningful and understandable, seeing that in the absence of such an establishment the truth–value and validity of the religious *Weltanschauung* cannot be established. But the establishment of meaningfulness and understanding refers to the present; it is with reference to the *Zeitgeist* of the present that these are established. Thus, the interpretation that is theology is committed not only to the past but also to the present. The interpretation is committed not only to doing justice to the finished content and intent of the religious tradition (*i.e.*, to the past) but equally to making this content and intent understandable and meaningful (*i.e.*, to the present). Theology has the task of making the *Weltanschauung* and the way of life of the religious tradition, originating in the remote past, meaningful and valid to the *Zeitgeist* of the present. The *Zeitgeist* of the present, however, is ever–changing and so the work of theology, the work of bridging the finished past and the ever–changing present, is never ending. As every generation must re–write its history anew, so every generation must rework its theology anew.

[17]It may be argued that the considerations raised above may indeed be valid with respect to Christianity or Islam but that they are not valid with respect to Judaism. And this is so because unlike in the case of Christianity or Islam, in the case of Judaism the adjective 'Jewish' designates not only membership in a community of faith but also membership in an ethnic–national entity. Now, this is true and it certainly complicates the picture and the analysis that would be required to sort things out. Evidently, this cannot be done here. Let us, then, merely state our conclusion that, notwithstanding the complications, the considerations raised with respect to Christianity and Islam would also apply just as validly to Judaism. This is so because, in the last analysis, in Judaism, membership in the ethnic–national community is subsumed under the membership in the community of faith, namely membership in a community of faith implies a necessary and simultaneous membership in the ethnic–national entity and as such in the context of the content of faith of Judaism membership in the ethnic–national entity is made synonymous with membership in the community of faith and vice versa. This being the case, one should already be able to glimpse the thrust of our argument that the introduction of the additional membership in the ethnic–national entity should not really interfere with the considerations raised above which impinge upon the community of faith.

Part Two
Three Long Perspectives on the Theology of Judaism Beyond the Holocaust

Chapter 7

Contemporary Jewish Theology

David Novak

The next three descriptive papers on how theology has been done in diverse ways show us the road that has been traveled. Looking backward with the reliable guidance of the present and the next two writers, we can project into the future a cogent tradition of thought. The first of the three gives us a fine introduction to the place, in the history of the theology of Judaism of the past half century, of many of the writers we now have studied. Heschel, Borowitz, Cohen, Herberg, Steinberg, and Fackenheim now are placed into the context of their age. The important themes of their writing—covenant, Torah—are highlighted. Novak introduces other names, not represented here, and has the further merit of spelling out what he conceives to be the next stage in an on–going and unending labor. He stands on the border between the participant and the onlooker; he does more than pass his opinion, but less than compose an ambitious construction.

***

Jewish Theology after the Enlightenment

When speaking Jewish theology, one should be aware at the onset that many Jews are uncomfortable with the word "theology" altogether as a designation of Jewish religious thought. Therefore, before dealing with contemporary Jewish theology, one should try to indicate the reasons for this discomfort and why they are invalid, though understandable.[1] Only in this way can one present Jewish theology as a perfectly

*Previously published in *Problems in Contemporary Jewish Theology*, ed. Dan Cohn-Sherbok. Copyright 1991 the Edwin Mellen Press, which has granted permission for its reprinting here.

legitimate Jewish intellectual pursuit. Thereafter, one can then indicate some of its major contemporary manifestations, as well as its most promising direction in the near future.

In its literal sense, "theo–logy" means what is now called by philosophers "God–talk." It should not be forgotten that for many centuries before the rise of the Enlightenment in the eighteenth century and the Emancipation of West European Jewry, the predominant modes of Jewish religious thought were medieval rationalist theology and kabbalistic theology. Medieval rationalist theology, especially the greatest part of it which was heavily Aristotelian, was largely God–talk inasmuch as its major concerns were proving the existence of God from the nature of the universe and describing the intelligible attributes of this God. Kabbalistic theology was even to a greater extent God–talk inasmuch as it viewed all reality to be contained within the divine reality and all relationships to be in essence interdivine relations. Even is the actual term "theology" was not used either by medieval rationalist thinkers or kabbalists during the premodern period, probably because of its predominant use of Christian thinkers in designating their own religious thought, there can be little doubt that what they were actually doing was indeed theology in a quite literal sense.

It was the enlightenment, which brought West European Judaism into the universe of modern intellectual discourse, that for the most part made both medieval rationalist theology and kabbalistic theology implausible.

In the case of medieval rationalist theology, the implausibility came from the radically new view of nature that has arisen from (or was presupposed by) the great shift of scientific paradigms during the preceding seventeenth century. Proofs of the existence of God made on the basis of the general Aristotelian– Ptolemaic view of nature were considerably less plausible when one now viewed nature from a Copernican–Galilean–Newtonian perspective. After Kant had given philosophical expression to these assumptions, rationalist theology was never again able to make the intellectual case it had been able to make for itself during the long Middle Ages (which for Jews, even in the West, did not actually end until the middle of the eighteenth century).

In the case of kabbalistic theology, its implausibility came from the new emphasis on human history, which began in the eighteenth century and which came to full expression in the nineteenth century. In Kabbalah, the historical element of Judaism so evident in the Bible and even in the rabbinic writings became almost totally sublimated into an elaborate topography of the inner life of God. All seemingly external events involved in the relationship between God and Israel became symbols of interdivine processes. Any independently human realm was basically precluded by Kabbalah. The emphasis of external relationships which is so predominant in historical thinking, however, made Kabbalah appear to most modern Jewish thinkers as an area of extreme irrelevance to their contemporary situation, if not an acute embarrassment in it. And, despite the fact that Gershom Scholem succeeded in rescuing Kabbalah from its intellectual oblivion in the West, it is important to remember that he did so as an historian not as a theologian. Even though some have argued that Scholem's historical project was one that had normative intent, Scholem himself never developed it theologically or otherwise.[2] Scholem's researches thus created a whole field of inquiry into the history of Kabbalah, but they did not create or recreate kabbalistic theology as the thriving normative enterprise it has been before the Enlightenment.

After the radical intellectual changes brought about by the Enlightenment, Jewish theology assumed new forms, however, In the nineteenth century, there was the attempt by certain post–Kantian Jewish thinkers, most notably Hermann Cohen, to recreate Jewish theology by justifying it within the context of the new post–Enlightenment rationalism. This was done largely on the assumption that the ancient Hellenic priority of metaphysics (*theoria*) over ethics (*praxis*) had now been inverted, in the West, in favor of ethics. The inversion seemed to come quite close to what Judaism had always been preaching.[3] Thus this type of Jewish theology saw the very essence of Judaism to be its idealistic ethical teaching and attempted to show that Judaism has something unique to offer to philosophical ethics in general.

With the breakdown of the cultural confidence in historical progress which idealistic ethics seems to presuppose, early twentieth century Jewish thinkers such as Martin Buber and Franz Rosenzweig attempted to present Jewish religious teaching in the light of a new philosophical anthropology that emphasized the existential contingency of the human condition. Indeed, they and certain Christian religious thinkers were actually in the forefront of developing this new philosophical approach with its emphasis of human subjectivity.[4] It was Rosenzweig, especially, who reemphasized the Jewish need for theological reflection. Thus it is no accident that he is the single most powerful influence on those contemporary Jewish thinkers who have considered themselves to be theologians. Furthermore, what emerges from the post– Enlightenment theological project of a thinker like Rosenzweig is that Jewish theology cannot return to either of its premodern manifestations, that is, it cannot reason in the way of medieval rationalism or in the way of Kabbalah. It cannot return to the view of the premodern rationalists that the human relationship with God is within the context of the natural order because God's existence is no longer a factor in the modern view of nature. As such, the primary locus of this relationship has to be constituted elsewhere by post–Enlightenment theologians, either Jewish or Christian. And it cannot return to the view of the kabbalists that the human relationship with God is in truth an inter–divine relation because the modern emphasis of the independence of human historical reality is one which has become too much a part of our discursive milieu to be precluded.

Postwar Jewish Theology

After the Second World War, when European Existentialism was at the height of its influence in Western Europe and was being discovered by American intellectuals, one can see the beginnings of a distinct Jewish theology among some American Jewish thinkers especially. For Jews, this discovery of Existentialism was aided by the recent arrival in American of Jewish refugees from Western Europe, including some of the most distinguished disciples of Martin Buber and Franz Rosenzweig. Newly transplanted Western European scholars such as Nahum N. Glatzer and Alexander Altmann—as well as Abraham Joshua Heschel, who was an original Jewish theologian in his own right—both by their writings and their personal teaching enabled a generation of young American Jewish thinkers such as Eugene Borowitz, Arthur A. Cohen, Seymour Siegel and Michael Wyschogrod to connect themselves to the theological project of Buber and Rosenzweig. In this context, the names of American Jews of an older generation such as Milton Steinberg and Will Herberg, who had also connected themselves to this project, should be mentioned. Finally, one should mention the name of the young Emil Fackenheim, who might be considered to be the last Jewish thinker who was educated in Germany. In his writings until the early 1970's, he was certainly part of this general theological movement.

The task of Jewish theology in this postwar period, as well as that of Christian theology, was to convince thoughtful people that the human relationship with God is not only possible, but that it is necessary to take it seriously in any fully adequate view of the human condition. In other words, Jewish theologians were attempting to do much the same thing for Jewish faith as Paul Tillich and Reinhold Niebuhr were attempting to do for Christian faith.

It was during this postwar period that Jewish theology came into its own in America. This does not mean, however, that there have not always been those who questioned the whole Jewish validity of the theological enterprise in Judaism. Secularist critics of Jewish theology have long been convinced that any God–talk is impossible after the Enlightenment. Therefore, Jewish thought, for them, can only be adequately conducted along sociological lines, concerning itself with such issues as Jewish survival and Zionism. Certain Orthodox critics of Jewish theology, at least in its modern version, have seen it as implying a denigration of Halakhah as the primary locus for Jewish intellectual endeavor. Furthermore, the fact that Rosenzweig and especially Buber could not be considered halakhic Jews made the whole project suspect in their eyes. However, this Orthodox suspicion usually became more a critique *ad hominem* than a critique *ad rem* since Halakhah itself clearly requires a theological foundation for its very authority to be cogent. Also, the leading Orthodox religious thinker in American, Joseph B. Soloveitchik, even if he did not call himself a theologian, certainly spoke and wrote using decidedly theological categories, heavily influenced by Existentialist philosophy. and the fact that his main source of inspiration has always been Maimonides, probably the greatest theologian in Judaism, belied the notion that concern for Halakhah was only concern for its practical applications. Moreover, as we shall soon see, some of the most explicitly theological work today is being done by Soloveitchik's disciple, the American–Israeli thinker David Hartman.

Covenant Theology

Certainly in an open society such as that in North America, theology is going to be influenced by changes in the cultural and intellectual environment in which it operates. Jewish theology is no exception.

During the postwar period, much theology saw it cultural role to be that of emphasizing the transcendent horizon of human subjectivity in an age when the individual person seemed to become lost in "the lonely crowd," to use the title of a widely influential book in the 1950s by David Riesman, Nathan Glazer and Reuel Denney.[5] However, beginning in the late 1960s, with the societal and cultural upheaval of that period, intellectual attention began to be more and more concerned with the nature and content of human community. It is no accident that this same period saw a growing interest in religious traditions, not just the religious experiences of individuals. For religious traditions have developed highly intricate ways of structuring and directing relationships both interhuman and divine–human. The communal character of so much of Jewish religion, of course, easily lent itself to this new interest. Along these lines, during the 1980s especially, a number of Jewish theologians began dealing with the concept of covenant as that which designates the communal character of Judaism most profoundly. It seems to me that the most interesting work in recent Jewish theology could be accurately designated "covenant theology." A brief look at the thought of two of the most prominent of these theologians, Eugene Borowitz and David Hartman will give some conception of the various ways the theme of covenant has found expression in contemporary Jewish theology.

Eugene Borowitz

Eugene Borowitz, for many years a professor at the New York school of the Reform rabbinical seminary, the Hebrew Union College—Jewish Institute of Religion, was mentioned earlier as one of the young American Jewish thinkers who during the postwar period was decidedly influenced by the existentialist Jewish theology of Buber and Rosenzweig. His early work surely bore the stamp of their strong influence, especially that of Buber.[6] Borowitz's theology has remained quite consistent with that original impetus and he has developed it by an increasing concern with the question of covenant.

Borowitz's covenant theology is quite lucidly presented (a characteristic of all his writing and teaching) in his 1984 article, "The Autonomous Jewish Self." In this article, Borowitz sees his task as a contemporary Liberal Jewish theologian to "recapture a compelling particularism without sacrificing the gains of the universalization of Judaism."[7] Borowitz is well aware of how earlier Liberal Judaism, which had almost totally accepted the Enlightenment view of the universality of individual autonomous reason, played down Jewish particularism, whether it be that of Jewish nationalism or that of much of traditional Jewish religious practice. Borowitz is concerned that too much of what is unique to Judaism and worth preserving in it was lost in this fascination with universalization. However, he is not willing to turn away from this trend totally, for to do that would be an admission that Liberal Judaism has fundamentally been a mistake. That is an admission Borowitz is most definitely unwilling to make. What he wants to do is to balance this trend with a renewed emphasis of the value of Jewish tradition, most of which is decidedly particularistic.

At this point in his argument, Borowitz's project sounds quite similar to the slogan favored by many of those associated with the Conservative Movement, "tradition and change." The problem with this bipolar approach is that without a mediating term it quickly becomes an oxymoron. Tradition and change are mutually exclusive terms if tradition means that which does not change. If tradition is that which does change, then the slogan is a tautology. Thus there must be a third term which determines just how much is to remain the same (tradition) and how much is to become different (change). So similarly, universality and particularity are mutually exclusive terms unless there is some third term which determines just how much is to be universal in contemporary Liberal Judaism and how much is to remain particularlistic.[8]

To his credit, Borowitz seems to be aware of this problem and offers the following solution to it, stating that "where the biblical–rabbinic Jew had essentially a theocentric existence, the modern Jewish self may better be described as theorelated in ultimate depth."[9] What I think he means by this is that in the premodern period the Jewish relationship with God was almost exclusively determined by what was discerned to be God's revealed will in the Torah. Since there is no universal revelation in any direct sense, God's revealed will can only be known through the experience of a particular people, in our case the Jews. Nevertheless, as Borowitz has insisted, the postmodern Jew cannot return to this earlier position, even though its certitude often looks quite attractive in retrospect. He or she cannot return to this position because the Enlightenment with its concurrent Emancipation of the Jews gave us an experience of universality. That experience of universality came with the emphasis of individual moral autonomy, namely, that every human being is only morally bound by those norms he or she has rationally willed for himself or herself. This general view of moral autonomy is the theoretical basis for democracy. It was in democratic societies where Jews actually experienced this universalistic autonomy and it was in democratic societies where they became fully equal participants in a larger world (at least in theory, if not always in actual practice), something they had never experienced before. For the overwhelming majority of modern Jews, the experience of autonomy afforded by democracy is considered to be a great boom. Virtually all of those Jews who have experienced life in a democracy are among its most ardent defenders, whether in the diaspora or in the State of Israel.

Theologically, this raises the challenge of how this universal autonomy can be related to the very particular historical relationship between God and the Jewish people. For Borowitz, theo–relatedness rather than theocentricity is what mediates between universality and particularity here. It is the individual Jew's experience of being related to God not as an anonymous autonomous self but, rather, as an autonomous *Jewish self* which mediates between the particularity of the Jewish experience and the universality of the modern democratic experience. Basically, as I understand him, Borowitz argues that Jews can and should appropriate as much of the Jewish tradition as possible in their covenantal relationship with God. Indeed, without such an appropriation, contemporary Jewish existence loses the true depth of which it is capable. But it is still autonomous because the individual Jew must being from his or her own experience and his or her own free choice in response to it. This means, of course, that the source of the authority in this covenantal relationship is no longer the will of God per se. Unlike the earlier universalism, though (especially in its more Kantian expression), the source of authority is not the will of man either. Rather, the source of authority in the relationship lies in the relationship itself. In essence, it generates its own norms. The norms emerge in the autonomous decision of the individual Jew not so much to obey God as to respond to God. Furthermore, the autonomous aspect of this covenantal reality requires the elimination of those factors in the tradition which entail an authoritarian relationship between individual covenant members.

Here is where Borowitz is still quite close to the influence of Buber, for whom an I–Thou relationship, of which the God–human relationship is the very epitome, is never one where one party simply wills what the other party should be or do.[10] Thus Borowitz as a Liberal Jew, albeit more existentialist than rationalist, cannot accept the authority of Halakhah in the same way traditionalist Jews still do precisely because it does not admit enough autonomy for the human participant. Nevertheless, he is hopeful that this new autonomous Jewish religious existence will be able to create an ordered Jewish life. He is undoubtedly sensitive to the charge long made by the detractors of Liberal Judaism that it is antinomian or anarchic in practice. As he puts it, "A richly personal yet Jewist– grounded and communally–created Jewish style or way would be the autonomous Jewish self's equivalent of '*halakhah*'."[11]

The questions I would address to Borowitz are as follows: If revelation is not an act of divine lawgiving, but only the experience of God's presence, then on any specifically practical issue, is the authority of the covenant not going to be just as anthropocentric as it was for the older, modern rationalist, form of Liberal Judaism? In the end, is it not man and not God who speaks norms?[12] How can any norm emerging from the covenantal ethos be considered anything more than human–made law? If so, how can such a law be practically binding on autonomous individuals together in one community short of some formal contract accepted by each one of them?

As it has turned out, those aspects of the ethos of the Liberal religious Jewish community which have assumed a normative character—I think especially of egalitarianism—are not presented as norms resulting from an experience of revelation, but rather as norms required by the divinely created status of all humans. In other words, it does not seem that the drive for normativity within the Liberal religious community, a drive very much encouraged by Borowitz, is one based on revelation of any kind. Hence, can it be considered covenantal in the classical sense of that term?

Davie Hartman

As was mentioned in the treatment of Borowitz's movement theology, this type of theology can be best understood looking at how it emerged from the religious Existentialism that had been imported from Western Europe after World War II and that had influenced a number of younger American Jewish thinkers. Nevertheless, this religious Existentialism is not all of one type, anymore than all nonreligious Existentialism is all of one type. In terms of Jewish religious Existentialism, one can see a divide between those Jewish existentialists who take Halakhah to be antithetical or secondary to authentic Jewish religious life and those Jewish existentialists who take it to be the very foundation of Jewish religious life. Of the former type, Martin Buber is the leading figure; of the latter type, the leading figure if Joseph B. Soloveitchik.[13] It is important to see how different covenant theologies begin from these two respective poles and how they must move beyond them to properly constitute the idea of covenant.

In Borowitz's case, the task is to show how one can move from a position of relational autonomy, strongly influenced by Buber, to a position of communal normative structure, without surrendering the sense of the universal entailed by the experience of moral autonomy. As we have seen, he is willing to grant more to the communal tradition that Buber does, but he is still unwilling to acknowledge the authority of the Halakhah as a full system of governance. To do so, Borowitz would cease to be a Liberal Jew in any real sense.

In the case of the American–Israeli thinker David Hartman, the move from existentialist to covenant theology is to begin from the theology of his teacher Solveitchik and then move beyond it without, however, severing his connection with the Halakhah as a full system of governance. And, whereas Borowitz sees his problem to be how beginning from autonomy one can consistently embrace traditional norms, Hartman sees his problem to be how beginning from a normative structure

one can consistently embrace autonomy. In popular terms, one might say that Boro-
witz is a liberal thinker attempting to move in a more traditional direction, and that
Hartman is a traditionalist thinker attempting to move in a more liberal direction.
Each of them uses the idea of covenant to effect this transition.

The location of Hartman as a theologian in the State of Israel is as important a
contextual consideration as is the location of Borowitz as a theologian in the United
States. Hartman's theological problem is essentially that of an American Jewish
religious Zionist (from the community for whom Soloveitchik has been *the* spiritual
mentor) who has made *aliyah*. As a Zionist, he is living and teaching in a society
which has already achieved the general Zionist goal of Jewish sovereignty in the land
of Israel, but as a religious Zionist, he has not yet seen the specifically religious goal
of a sovereign Jewish state in the Land of Israel fully governed by the halakhic
system (*at pi torat yisrael*). Finally, as an American who has experienced the benefits
of democratic pluralism, he is no doubt troubled by the fact that in those areas of
Israeli life where Halakhah does govern, those governing in its name—the religious
and the rabbinical establishment—are decidedly undemocratic, antipluralist, and often
authoritarian in their whole approach.[14] Thus, there is a real poignancy when he sees
the problematic of his book, *A Living Covenant*, to be how to creatively develop
Jewish life in a Jewish society in a situation where there is "tension between the
dignity of the autonomous self and unswerving commitment to the community."[15]

In response to this situation, Hartman presents an extensive theology of covenant,
attempting to demonstrate that there are resources from within classical Jewish
tradition which can be developed into a theory that emphasizes what he calls "human
adequacy."[16] This emphasis, however, is to be one which does not eventually cul-
minate in a type of secular humanism where the divine factor gets lost altogether.

Hartman sees the extremes he wants to avoid as being epitomized by the
respective positions of Erich Fromm and Yeshayahu Leibowitz. Fromm represents the
emphasis of human adequacy which can find no place for the acceptance of divine
authority. Leibowitz, on the other hand, represents the emphasis of divine authority
which can find no place for human adequacy, that is, for human autonomy. Hartman
sees the theology of his teacher Soloveitchik as the starting point for a position that
successfully avoids the two extremes he has delineated.

Despite the initial influence of Soloveitchik's religious anthropology on Hartman's theology, he is uncomfortable with Soloveitchik's emphasis on the submission
of human will to the will of God as the leitmotif of his view of Jewish religious life.
Clearly, this type of emphasis is not going to provide much of a base for the
autonomy Hartman wants to constitute out of the classical Jewish sources. Thus, he
moves away from Soloveitchik's religious anthropology to that of Maimonides. That
in and of itself is a tour de force inasmuch as Soloveitchik has always presented
much of his own theological reflection as being rooted in the thought of Maimonides.
Hartman has quite boldly turned to the very same source as did his teacher and has

indicated that he has developed a theological position out of it that is more in keeping with its own project and more relevant to the contemporary need to incorporate a more humanistic element into traditionalist Jewish thinking, especially thinking above the covenant.

At the center of Hartman's development of his covenant theology is an extensive and highly original phenomenology of the whole experience of Jewish prayer. Unlike many other Jewish thinkers, who have seen the essence of Jewish prayer to be submission to the will of God and self–abnegation, Hartman emphasizes what he calls "the mood of covenantal intimacy before God."[17] Here, in a way quite similar to Borowitz's emphasis of theorelatedness rather than theocentricity, he calls attention to the experience of *being before God*. As I understand him, this means that the human participant in the covenant brings *before* God all of his or her experience and achievements at least as much as he or she relies on help *from* God. In this whole discussion, Hartman continually makes analogies with the reality of interpersonal relationships between humans, especially those involving love between two human partners.

Because of this continual use of these analogies with interhuman relationships, which have, of course, been the subject of so much discussion in an age seen by one astute observer to be that of "the triumph of the therapeutic"[18] Hartman is well aware that he might be accused of psychologizing religion, of simply reducing religious reality to the level of a metaphor for what is essentially an interhuman reality. Thus he is emphatic that "religious statements also suggest existence claims."[19]

Hartman has succeeded in working out of the classical Jewish sources a view of an intimate divine–human relationship. This view can be defended against the charge that the use of psychological metaphor automatically leads to the reduction of the covenant to something purely human. However, it seems to me that Hartman's psychological emphasis is at the expense of a needed metaphysical emphasis that an adequately Jewish view of the covenantal reality also requires. The psychological emphasis is clearly quite helpful when theologically constituting the intimate, immanent aspects of covenant. Here, as noted earlier, Hartman's treatment of prayer in the context of covenant produces many important insights. Nevertheless, there is also a transcendent aspect of the covenant.

Whereas Israel has no real existence outside of the covenant because it is only by the covenant that she is created as a unique people, God does have a real existence outside it, for God is also the creator who continually transcends everything he has created. Without the emphasis of this transcendent dimension, the covenant comes to be constituted as a symbolic relationship between two essentially equal partners. Clearly, the whole thrust of classical Jewish theology— biblical, rabbinic, medieval rationalist and kabbalistic—has been to deny that type of intimate enclosure of God in the covenant, God and Israel are never equals in any real sense.

Hartman is surely aware of this problem, but he deals with it in a bizarre, theologically unsatisfying way. Also, he deals with it in a way that strongly suggests a break with one of the most important aspects of classical Jewish theology.

In classical Jewish theology, especially in is rabbinic development, God's transcendence of the covenant as a reality here and now was emphasized by the doctrine of reward and punishment beyond the limits of this world. This doctrine teaches that Israel's participation in the covenant is only fully justified eschatologically. The essential truth of the covenant is not what is experienced in this world, but it rather lies in the final effect of the keeping or neglect of the commandments of the Torah in the world–yet–to–come (*olam ha–ba*). This ultimate effect will be experienced by the participants in the covenant *then* because God has the power even *now* to bring it about. As a reality here and now the covenant often appears to be untrue inasmuch as the experience it presently entails is to usually outweighed by the collective and individual meaninglessness of the acts it continually requires. Many times these acts appear to be counterproductive to the welfare of the very people performing them. The doctrine of reward and punishment does not teach that the whole created universe is to be seen as being for the sake of the covenant as the human reality it is here and now. That would be an anthropocentrism quite uncharacteristic of Judaism. Rather, it means that faithfulness to the covenant here and now will ultimately be justified as being in total harmony with God's full governance of the universe. That final harmony is redemption (*ge'ulah*).

Hartman, on the other hand, is only interested in God's transcendence to point out the essential limits of the covenant. Thus he writes, "It would be arrogant to presuppose that the whole scheme of creation exists merely for the sake of the relationship between God and Israel."[20] However, it is not at all arrogant if creation is not for the sake of the covenant as experienced here and now, but rather for the sake of the covenant as fulfilled by God in the end–time (*ahareet ha–yamim*). Hartman, it seems to me, cannot deal with the whole eschatological dimension of Judaism because it has no analogue in the essentially psychological model that is ubiquitous in his theology. Only a metaphysics can provide one with the theoretical structure necessary for an adequate constitution of this indispensable aspect of Jewish theology. The doctrine of revelation, as Franzx Rosenzweig more than any other modern Jewish theologian showed, must be constituted in correlation with the doctrines of both creation before it and redemption after it. By not making the necessary correlation, Hartman cannot consistently treat the asymmetry of God and man even in the intimacy of the covenant experienced by the Jewish people living by its norms in the present. For this reason, he has no cogent theory of revelation. Why is God needed to reveal covenantal norms? That is certainly a question every traditionalist Jewish theologian must seriously address.

Jewish Theology in the Near Future

The covenantal turn of Jewish theology during the past decade or so shows no signs of abating in the near future. Moreover, I believe that the vitality of Jewish theology in the near future depends on working out the deeper implications of this concern with the whole reality of the covenant between God and Israel. However, this process requires a much more extensive use of political philosophy than we have seen heretofore. More than anything else, the covenant is a political idea and a political reality. By "political" I mean the whole range of human communal existence and its place in the very nature of things, the overall kind of political philosophy suggested by such earlier modern thinkers as Leo Strauss and Eric Voegelin and now being carried on by such contemporary thinkers as Alasdair MacIntyre and Charles Taylor. It is only within Jewish political theology that the questions of ethics entailed by emphasis of the covenant can be properly treated.

In the brief look at the covenant theologies of Borowitz and Hartman the question of human autonomy within covenantal reality is raised continually. The task, however, for both Borowitz and Hartman, as well as for other covenant theologians, is to more extensively constitute the idea of autonomy and offer a Jewish alternative to the way it has been constituted by philosophers and non– Jewish theologians. Both autonomy and covenant are political ideas before they are issues pertaining to ethical norms. It behooves Jewish theologians to now begin devising theories which show how these ideas can be cogently developed in tandem. Not only is this a theoretical desideratum, it also has immediate practical import. The most emotionally wrenching issue of the decade was the ongoing debate over "who is a Jew?" Ambiguities about this issue have had the most profound ethical ramifications as pertains to specific relationships between Jews and between Jews and non–Jews. But the ethical question of "who is a Jew?" cannot be answered adequately unless the prior political question "what is the Jewish people?" is answered. The political question especially calls for Jewish theology. It alone can deal with the most fundamental question: How are Jews to be related to God? Jewish theologians, who carefully incorporate a perspective of political philosophy in their enterprise, will be in a unique position to be in the leadership of those devising cogent answers to this great question.

Notes

[1]See D. Novak, "Toward A Conservative Theology" in *The Seminary at 100*. ed. N. B. Cardin and D. W. Silverman (New York: Jewish Theological Seminary of America, 1987) 315–18.

[2]See David Biale, *Gershom Scholem: Kabbalah and Counterhistory* (Cambridge, MA: Harvard University Press, 1979) 100–103, 109–12, 148–70.

[3]See Kenneth Seeskin, *Jewish Philosophy In A Secular Age* (Albany: State University of New York Press, 1990) 4–7.

[4]See Rosenzweig, "Das Neue Denken," *Kleinere Schriften*, ed. Edith Rosenzweig (Berlin: Schocken, 1937) 373–98.

[5]*The Lonely Crowd: A Study of the Changing American Character* (New Haven: Yale University Press, 1950).

[6]See esp., *A New Jewish Theology in the Making* (Philadelphia: Westminster, 1968) 123–46.

[7]"The Autonomous Jewish Self," *Modern Judaism* 4/1 (1984): 43.

[8]See Novak, "Toward a Conservative Theology," 317.

[9]"The Autonomous Jewish Self," 45.

[10]See *I and Thou*, trans. W. Kauffmann (New York: Chas. Scribner & Sons, 1970) 160–68.

[11]"The Autonomous Jewish Self," 47.

[12]See D. Novak, *Jewish–Christian Dialogue: A Jewish Justification* (New York: Oxford University Press, 1989) 89–92, 142–48.

[13]See his *Halakhic Man*, trans. L. Kaplan (Philadelphia: Jewish Publication Society of America, 1984), beginning where Soloveitchik cites such existentialist thinkers as Kierkegaard and Barth.

[14]Along similar critical lines, see Eliezer Berkovits, *Not in Heaven* (New York: Sanhedrin Press, 1983), especially chapter 4.

[15]*A Living Covenant: The Innovative Spirit in Traditional Judaism* (New York: Free Press 1985) 4.

[16]Ibid., 3, 126.

[17]Ibid., 133.

[18]See Philip Pieff, *The Triumph of the Therapeutic* (New York: Harper and Row, 1966) 232–44.

[19]*A Living Covenant*, 302.

[20]Ibid., 266.

Chapter 8

The Vocation of the Jewish Mind

Arthur A. Cohen

Cohen's introduction to theology of Judaism ends with a long account of where, in his view, matters have been and where they are heading. As does Novak, he stands on the border between description and participation. He begins with the category of "Israel," then defines as his problem "a metaphysics of history." Starting with the category of eternal Israel, he quite reasonably asks the history of that eternal Israel to define the terms of thought for his own reflection. And that conforms to the pattern of the classical thinkers we have examined here as well of those we have neglected. For the theological question of the Holocaust is made plausible not by secular facts, subject to description, but by fundamentally religious convictions, demanding advocacy. If the history of eternal Israel, which is the Israel after the flesh of the Holocaust, forms a chapter in the covenant with God, then the primacy of theological thinking about the history is established. Cohen has therefore selected for himself the central issue of the age in which he lived, which was the meaning of catastrophic events. And the consequent focus of his thought then shifted to the matter of the Messiah—history without an end in the coming of the Messiah forming mere chaos. The logic of his thought produced a theological novel of enormous proportions, In the Days of Simon Stern, as well as the important essay before us, "theology as the science of sacred history." Here, Messianism finds its place at the apex of thought, and Holocaust-theology reaches its most explicit, most sophisticated formulation.

***

Catholic Israel

Undoubtedly Solomon Schechter—that luminous and profound Anglo–American Jewish theologian[1]—intended to adumbrate with his famous phrase "Catholic Israel" something of the essence of Judaism. The only passage in Schechter's writings which treats at any length of "Catholic Israel" makes clear that its catholicity consists in its consensus. What counters or distorts consensus—the rigorism of a tenacious fundamentalism, the authoritarianism of schools and movements, the rising sacerdotalism of the rabbinate—conceals the catholicity of Israel. Schechter underscores this observation with characteristic vigor and precision:

*Originally published in *The Natural and the Supernatural Jew: An Historical and Theological Introduction*, copyright 1962 by Pantheon Books, New York. Used by permission.

This living body . . . is not represented by any section of the nation, or any corporate priesthood or rabbihood, but by the collective conscience of Catholic Israel as embodied in the Universal Synagogue. The Synagogue, with its continuous cry after God for more than twenty–three centuries, with its unremittent activity in teaching and developing the word of God, the only true witness to the past, and forming in all ages the sublimest expression of Israel's religious life, must also retain its authority as the sole true guide for the present and the future. . . . Another consequence of this conception of Tradition is that it is neither Scripture nor primitive Judaism, but general custom, which forms the real rule of practice. . . . The norm as well as the sanction of Judaism is the practice actually in vogue. Its consecration is the consecration of general use—or, in other words, of Catholic Israel.[2]

Schechter's understanding of Catholic Israel suggests something of the nature of authentic Jewish theology. The conscience of Israel is informed by canons of tradition and practice, which are indifferent to the reticulated and complex constructions of rational religion. This is not to say that Catholic Israel is of necessity unreasoning Israel. It is merely to suggest that catholicity consists in that more delicate fabric which historical consciousness and the instructed conscience devise.

Historical consciousness receives the continuous narrative of tradition which comprehends an "uninterrupted succession of prophets, Psalmists, Scribes, Assideans, Rabbis, Patriarchs, Interpreters, Elucidators, Eminences, and Teachers, with its glorious record of Saints, martyrs, sages, philosophers, scholars, and mystics";[3] it is of the essence of Catholic Israel, for it marks the Jew as a creature of history and the bearer of the instruction of an historical God. Consciousness, however, defines only the superficies of catholicity; it suggests only the outer limits which are compassed by tradition. What transforms consciousness from recipient into bearer, from passive receptacle into creator, is that what passes through the filter of consciousness informs conscience. As conscience is the especial faculty of the religious man, so historical consciousness is the instructor of conscience. There is no catholicity unless consciousness is open to the whole of tradition and conscience is susceptible to the demands and obligations of tradition. The catholicity of Judaism is a union in which history and anticipation are joined in conscience. Each Jew decides for himself; out of his assent to tradition the constantly renewed catholicity of Judaism is affirmed.

Catholic Israel manifests the living substance of the Jewish people. But Catholic Israel, as both concept and reality, does not go far enough. Rich and suggestive as it is, Schechter's understanding of catholicity is limited. To the obvious retort that his conception of catholicity and universality, Catholic Israel and Universal Synagogue, is but an adaptation of glorious, but palpably inappropriate, formulations of Roman Catholic theology, Schechter was monumentally indifferent. Schechter could hardly by accused of "Christianizing" Judaism. Schechter's understanding of Catholic Israel is defective because his conception of historical Judaism as its source results in a restriction of its catholicity to the private task of self–definition. Catholic Israel emerges as a retrospective judgment upon the history of the Jews. It serves as a device of argument against dissidents and assimilationists, extreme reformers and narrow–minded fanatics; but it does not aid us—in Schechter's definition—to locate ourselves in that vaster universe of human culture to which Catholic Israel must lay claim. Catholic Israel is much more a weapon in a war against destruction by attrition and desuetude than it is a conception—metaphysical, mystical, eschatological— which might suggest something of the eternal nature of Judaism and the vocation of the Jew.

We wish to transform the catholicity of Israel from a *deduction from a specific history* into a *category of all history*, from a rallying standard of factional and sectarian movements within Judaism to a reality with which Judaism may confront the world.

To accomplish such a transformation, to redefine Catholic Israel in such a way as to maintain what Schechter achieved but to extend its claim to the whole of human culture, requires that our catholicity be founded upon more than the narrative of history and the voluntary affections of conscience. Schechter was painfully aware of the one problem which his view could not compel: as he defined Catholic Israel, history could *educate* consciousness and *form* conscience, but it could *command* neither. Catholic Israel has no apodictic force. It is that fitful, unpredictable, indeed, on occasion, capricious response of the Jewish people to its collective history and obligation. Jewish catholicity too often degenerates into the vulgar response of mere collectivity—kinship feeling and camaraderie.

Catholic Israel issues from and returns to the attitude of the tradition and the individual Jew toward the God who called them forth. Israel is catholic in the sense that the truth of Judaism has relevance and bearing upon the destiny of mankind and in that it is the obligation of the Jew—not for himself alone, but for mankind—to preserve, transmit, and communicate that truth. Catholic Israel is therefore both comprehensive and universal. It cannot be either without being both. Its catholicity is founded upon truth believed, possessed, and transmitted. Those truths are not saving truths; they have neither sacramental power nor sufficiency, for their efficacy lies only in their ability to transform conscience and inspirit acts. The sinner is not saved by faith, but neither is he saved by ignorance. He may believe correctly but be damned for the indifference and insufficiency of his acts, or he may behave rightly by accident or through self–interest and be damned as well. There can be little right action without purity of heart and spirit; there can be little purity of heart and spirit unless both be formed by the beliefs and hopes of tradition.

The beliefs and hopes of tradition are exhibited by the action of Judaism, by observance and practice, by prayer and works. It matters little how much the consensus of tradition (that is, its definition of appropriate acts and habits of action) may suffice the inner life of the Jew, for if it contributes little to that communication between Jew and pagan, Jew and Christian, Jew and Moslem, Jew and Oriental, which defines the relations of the Jew to world culture, its catholicity is reduced from an historical reality to a self–delusive phantasm. It is one thing to conceive of catholicity as an expression of the spirit, as a manifestation of the organic unity of Jewish life; it is quite another when this same spirit and this same unity confront an alien time and an inhospitable history, when the Jew must live in the presence of the Gentile. The Jew can no longer afford the luxury of isolated sanctity, cut off and disinclined to share the history and time of his environment.

Indeed, part of the crisis of the modern Jew is that the catholicity of Judaism was restricted for so long to the consensus of acts and observances, to the language of inner life and destiny, that it lived without connection with the world that surrounded it.

The essential problem which underlies all our concerns is the evident withering of the Jewish vocation and the vanishing supernatural consciousness of the Jew. As we stated in the Introduction, we are disinclined to ask whether it is better that the Jewish vocation pass and the supernatural Jew disappear. We regard both as beyond our discretion to confirm or disprove. The destiny of the Jew and the historical function of Judaism cannot be regarded as issues of religious controversy. They are objects of faith and silence. They are not urged upon the disbeliever; but they are affirmed for the believer. They are doctrines which give substance to the concept of Catholic Israel, for they define the sense in which our catholicity is related to the culture of the West. Were our catholicity restricted, as it has been, to an encapsulated unity of the spirit, we could not hope to speak before the West. Ours would continue to be a silent witness, a mute presence in the world, exhibiting the sanctity of "an uninterrupted succession" of prophets and priests, scholars and saints, but incapable of shaping the stream of history in whose currents we move and by whose tides and undertows we are not threatened.

We do not imagine that we have presented in the fore–going pages a conventional history of modern Jewish thought. Few is any of the normal canons of intellectual history have been observed. Ours has been less the task of definition than that of presentation. It would be fool–hardy to attempt a formulation of the nature and characteristics of the Jewish mind. What such a procedure might have accomplished would have been offset by the unavoidable tendentiousness, abstraction, and historical condensation involved. Rather it has been our concern to indicate that the Jewish mind has been in constant interaction with other cultures than its own. To speak of the Jewish mind without reference to its surrounding environment would be to create a hypostatic fiction, an essence of little use to those who are genuinely preoccupied with Jewish life and destiny. The pursuit of definition as such is only useful to those who are indifferent to the reality defined—it enables them to file a history of experience, to classify and categorize, as in some intellectual lepidoptery, the various, multicolored, but now dead events of the past.

History is only dead when the living discard it. Moreover, history can only be written when the living succeed in distinguishing—at least to some extent—their own present from the past under view. We have been unable to do this, as the Jewish past is very much our present and future. We can only speak of the history of the Jewish mind as a living inheritance, for the situation of the modern Jewish mind differs only in degree from that of Jehuda Halevi or Maimonides. The general character and environment of our problem is the same. We can, perhaps, no longer profit from their specific solutions—we cannot really reconcile Scripture with Aristotle and the *Kalam* or interpret Judaism to the neo–Platonist, Sunnite orthodox, or triune Christian—but we can examine with great profit why in some ages the Jewish philosopher instructed the masses and why in others he was totally repudiated; why in some ages rabbis were the mystics, poets, preachers, and philosophers and why in ours few rabbis are numbered among our major thinkers; why in some ages Judaism was a universal religion, sensitive to the claim which it made upon all history, and why in ours that claim is all but buried beneath the pride of patriotism and the secure comfort of assimilation; why, in effect, in some ages Judaism lived—even though the people suffered—and in others Judaism waned.

In short there is nothing in the historical display of the modern Jewish mind that is worth recalling other than as a reminder and instructor to this moment. Although we could well recall thinkers and their systems, innovators and their innovations, we should be recalling not the history of the Jewish mind but the concrete achievement of individual Jewish minds. We are not interested, however, in Jewish minds apart from their participation in the whole of Jewish history; moreover, we are not interested in the whole of Jewish history—as but a department of the history of religions or the history of Christian and Islamic civilization or the history of sovereign national cultures—except insofar as that history informs us the better of providential history, of that which makes the Jewish people a chosen people.

It is necessary, therefore, if we are to profit from what has come before, to summarize its consequences. We propose to draw together the lines of argument which have defined our narrative and to inquire whether they are in fact relevant to the present. The considerations which have recurred throughout shall be treated here explicitly, no longer as points of suggestion and argumentative relief, but as explicit ideas which are thought to characterize the Jewish past and have significance for the Jewish present and future. Those specifically Jewish realities—Exile, Dispersion, prophetic judgment, messianic trust, and such like—are articulated in the context of history, theology, culture, and messianism. These four subject matters of Jewish thought are intimately related; moreover, we can speak very little of any one without animadverting to the others. They form a unity which suggests something of the vocation and destiny of Judaism and the Jewish people.

History is the substance of Jewish theology, and culture is the substance of Jewish messianism. Culture is a partial consummation of history; messianism is the trust and consummation of theology. But as the lines and markers of our intellectual disciplines converge, texturing and interpreting each other, they point to that reality which is bound and limit to our own, out of which ours takes its origin and through which ours is fulfilled.

There is little use in theory except as it orders life. If theory does not result in life—richer and more prescient life—it is but a tiresome exercise. We are less concerned, therefore, with *proving* that our theory is right than with stating it in such a way as to adumbrate something present in our lives. This is not to say that chimerical theory is to be excused merely because it has proved to be an instructive chimera. Not at all! It cannot assist life if it is a fiction; however, any "fiction" which informs life with greater richness and seriousness is, to that extent, no fiction but reality! The truth may be inadequately stated; it may be insufficiently rigorous to the demanding; it may only indicate by indirection that about which it speaks; it may be only symbolic truth; but it is still truth and for that we can be thankful.

Reflections upon a Metaphysics of History

The image of Exile has, like the cord of Theseus, passed through each chamber of the historic Jewish mind, imparting unity and continuity to disparate and seemingly unrelated moments of creation and despair.

The Exile has been not only a rationalization of historical events, an effort to elevate disaster into national triumph, a neurasthenic sublimation of pain and defeat; it has been a source of permanent meaning. To be sure, the naturalization of the Exile, accompanying as it did the naturalization of the Jew—his rejection of supernatural vocation and destiny and his conventional, frequently unresisting, acceptance of the hostility of the non–Jewish world—has made of Exile and physical diaspora an opprobrious reality for both Zionists, who revile the Exile, and Diaspora Jews, who would willingly exchange it for adjustment.

It is not our purpose, however, to prolong the war with Jewish nationalism or with Jewish assimilationism. That war is really over. It raged passionately in the last century and was continued in the present, but it is now over. The rhetoric of Zionist repudiation of the Exile lingers on, a reminder of this dead but eloquent war. It is a dead war because Zionism is now triumphant and yet millions of Jews are unwilling either to go up to the Land or to be assimilated. The situation of the modern Jew is substantially as it was before. There is limbo, an indeterminate stasis, where nothing appears changed, other than the fact that the present situation is clearer, more sharply etched, false and inadequate alternatives having been removed by the outcome of historic events.

It would appear that however much the controversies of the nineteenth century have been silenced by decisive historical fortune, the perpetual crisis of Jewish survival continues. It is a problem formed out of the pull and drag of events. It is a natural problem in the most immediate and meaningful of senses, for the issue of Jewish survival, so seen, is an issue of population and numbers. To be sure, Jewish survival is qualitative as well, since one would not be willing to settle for Jews in name only. But let us be equally clear that we will not be asked to settle for Jews in name only, if Jews indeed survive. It is hardly thinkable that the Jewish communities of the Dispersion could survive if every Jew intermarried, if there was no interest in raising one's children as Jews, if those powerful "symbols" of identification— Sabbath, the High Holy Days, the Kaddish of praise and mourning—were all discarded. Since we are not a race, marked off by ineffaceable physical characteristics, we cannot rest confident that race will enable us to survive; nor are we simply an ethnic community whose cultural artifacts are so agreeable, harmless, and undivisive that they can be perpetuated as links of sentimental continuity. No racial or ethnic unity—unless so minimally defined as to be all but worthless—helps us to survive. We are destined to disappear if our existence depends solely upon the slow action of history. The ethnic ties tray and rot, the cultural artifacts are abandoned, and our religion, cut off and separated from the whole of our life, becomes a formal piety— itself a fashion of history to be abandoned when the climate of opinion heralds the time of abandonment.

It is exceptionally difficult to articulate the lines of Jewish intellectual history from the beginnings of the Hellenistic world to the present day. The stages of Jewish history do not conform to the stages of Western history. Its middle ages were not followed by a renaissance, a reformation, an enlightenment, and an age of scientific rationalism and political ideology. Such historical periods have at best contingent validity. They reflect, not merely man's assessment of himself in the moment of his renaissance or enlightenment, but more intensely, the retrospective appraisal of later ages, seeking either to praise or blame, to epitomize and condense, to adjudge, define, and transmit their characteristics and accomplishments to later ages. Historical generalization apostrophizes an age, setting forth its emphases and directions; but it cannot report with accuracy the daily life which textured and gave relief to what men actually thought and felt. Systems of historical tagging, at best mnemonic devices, are useless to the historian, particularly to the historian of Christianity or Judaism! To lay the history of Judaism over the history of the West in the hope that it will fit is vain exertion and profitless history. It assumes that the intellectual history of Judaism and the development of European thought pass through identical stages. It assumes moreover that the history of Israel is similar to the history of the nations of the world. The first assumption is rendered implausible by the fact that the conditions of European history were relevant to the life of the Jew only recently and then only when his Judaism had radically changed or disappeared. Marx and Freud, whatever their Jewish syndromes, reacted to conditions which the West defined, not to presuppositions which the religion and culture of Israel imposed. Jewish culture cannot be said to exist *wherever* one finds Jews (though to be sure we may learn much about how the Jew considers himself in separation from Judaism by reflecting upon the Jewish genius sundered from his Judaism). Jewish culture can be said to exist only where one finds the Jew whose Judaism is the energizing center of his life and activity. It is equally implausible for the Jew to consider his own history to be like that of the nations. The scientific historian (who has problems enough of his own) may be unable to tolerate such a metaphysical bias; but the historian of Judaism cannot interpret many of the most shocking and scandalous assumptions of the Jewish religious mind unless he acknowledges that the Jew considered his own history to be the central event of a divine drama—a drama of covenant, sin, and purgation; a drama of divine dispersion and promised ingathering; a drama in which natural history was raised up to God and relocated within the order of providential causation.

If natural history does not supply the medium of Jewish survival, it is to sacred history that we must turn. If ours is not a history according to nature, then it must be considered as history according to God. Having affirmed this, we should nevertheless beware the sundering of all connection, indeed all intimacy and interaction, between natural and supernatural history. To determine our history according to God is not to repudiate our history according to nature. It is merely to suggest that history according to nature—separated from God—and time—independent of eternity—are insufficient. History cut off from its transcendent source and arbitration becomes either historicist phenomenalism, where all of life becomes history without the Archimedean point of judgment, or else a passionless and formal recurrence of events with which past history has already prepared and bored us.

History and the metaphysics of history are indispensable to the Jew. We need not expand upon the Greek indifference to history and the Hebraic preoccupation with history. History was meaningless to the Greek for the reason that concrete and immediate events were essentially meaningless; it was possible, as Ernst Troeltsch suggested, for the Greek to adumbrate a science of history precisely because the laws of fate (*vide* causality) were rigid, but it could not ask the question of meaning because such would be a metaphysical question inappropriate to nature and its animated presentation in history.[4] The Greek only began "providential" history when he had succeeded, paradoxically, in escaping it. He could discern meaning in his historical life, as did the Stoics, only when he had removed himself from history and affirmed his detachment and disengagement from it. But to be detached from history, to become as an object of nature, is to become unaware of time. Without the apprehension of time there can be no meaning in history. The Hebrew on the contrary could not escape time—every event that mediated divinity in time was sanctified and preserved in the historical memory.

History does not occur until selective judgments are pronounced upon the discrete events of the past. There is no history other than to him who remembers it. In some sense, therefore, history is a myth of memory. The history of historians, no less than the history of metaphysicians of history, is a myth—the former more reticulated by evidence, proofs, and confirmation, the latter more dangerously patterned by ideologies and theses. The history of historians, quite as profoundly as the history of metaphysicans of history, attempts to do more than recount faithfully the phenomenal display of connected events. Both wish to elicit their own meaning, to explain why this particular past invades their present. The contemporary historian cannot prevent himself from relating the past to our present, for he is of our present and addresses us—and not as did a slightly mad German scholar of this century, who preferred to discourse to the busts of Roman emperors who ringed his study rather than to his students. The historian is always locating in the past his own fixities, his own truths, and his own eternity, for as R. G. Collingwood observed, the historian, even the historian without metaphysical interests, is only interested in self–understanding. The metaphysician of history is but a more bizarre and unavoidably pretentious synthesis of the working historian; for where the scientific historian wishes to identify a portion of the whole, to describe the hazy limits of a single moment within the flow of history, the metaphysicians of history—Augustine, Hegel, Marx—wish to locate nothing less than the meaning of all history.

The philosophy of history is, therefore, the greatest myth–making. It stands in the great tradition which begins in early Christian times with the sacramental transformation of late Jewish and Apostolic eschatology and proceeds through a neutralization and finally, in the nineteenth century, a secularization of the doctrine of the end of history. The philosophy of history is as well an asking of the most crucial of human questions: What is that whole which comprehends time and eternity, death and life, being and the perfection of being? To be preoccupied with history as such is to confront an essentially religious problem: the relation of history to God and the meaning of God in history.

Man is not a bystander of history who records the weathering of the past and observes the maturation of the future. If such be a view of history, it is one which cannot help but destroy all that is meaningful in it. Indeed, it is possible to speak of ages and times in which man was so serenely integrated into nature that time and history vanished, that history became a distortion of purity, and contemplation the most significant form of human activity. Inescapably our own concentration upon historical reality—that the past is our own past and the future our own future and memory the eternal link which defines the substance of history—is the consequence of disquiet. What the Greek called *hybris*, the sin of excessive and arrogant pride, can be read as little more than the presumption of some men that they were capable of effecting their destiny rather than submitting to their fate. Such presumption was not a sin to the Hebrew, but a requirement. It was a requirement because the Hebrew believed himself, his community, and his universe to have a beginning and a consummation.

Man can only have a destiny if he has a beginning which originates outside of time and an end which will transcend it. Time, we believe, is but an epoch in eternity. The false infinity of time, as Hegel describes a history without origin and fulfillment, is never broken unless time is construed as an outcropping of eternity. So viewed, history is not a succession of events in time and historical knowledge is not simply the recognition of pattern or the delight in novelty. Historical reality becomes an occasion for the spirit and the historical memory enacts the drama of eternity. In our view—and we acknowledge much in it which is painfully obscure and difficult to explain—the essential nature of God is freedom. The freedom of God is not to be understood as being the unruly and capricious option of the tyrant. The unlimited freedom of God is what gives meaning to the Biblical understanding of divine pathos and divine potency. The completeness of God is to be understood as the completeness of potency—all is possible to God, but all is not actualized. Indeed, there could be *nothing* but potency in the divine nature were eternity God's only habitation. The outpouring of God into time—in creation, revelation, and redemption—is the process of actualization. This is not to say that man is the actualization of divinity; it is only to say that man is that creature through whose life the endless richness and variety of divine possibility is realized. Time is the medium and history the substance of divine actualization.

We can only suggest—as Lurianic mysticism has done, as Jacob Boehme has done, as Nicholas Berdyaev has done—what we understand to be the incredible drama of God's life. Process within God is providence for man; unceasing actualization in God is destiny for man. We can do little more, at this moment in our thinking, than propose that our age and our aeon are but moments in eternity; that what we know as history is but an epoch in God's "history"; that our beginning and our end mean not the beginning and end of the only revelation and the only truth, but the beginning and end of the only truth which has been vouchsafed to us. Our history may not have been the first and our history may not be the last, but it is *our* history and therefore the only one with which we can be concerned.

It is foolish to speak of human destiny unless we speak of creation and consummation. This is the religious postulate of any metaphysics of history. Destiny "can exist," Berdyaev has written, "only if man is the child of God and not of the world."[5] Freedom of potency in the divine nature is freedom to good and evil in history. Only as potency is life, and eternal potency is eternal life, can we speak of God as good. Only the advent of death and corruption possesses the reality of evil. It is unimportant that the realized nature of God is as self–evident as his potency. What counts is that we *believe* the fixities of his eternal nature, but *live* in the face of his potency; that we are committed to his perfection, but pass our life in the shadow of *his* passion to consummation. We can know little or nothing of what God is in himself; we can only know what it is that God has made us and to what destiny we are appointed in the service of his freedom.

In the image of God's freedom we were created; but from God's realized perfection we are departed. This is the schism in our nature which is not present in

God's. There could be no movement in our world if the freedom of God and the goodness of God were allowed to determine us. The interval which separates the beginning from the end is the interval of history in which faith makes the dead live, in which memory redeems the past and trust invests the future with novelty and hope.

Were history perfection it would be impossible to speak of incompletion, meaninglessness, waste, or distortion. History would contain its own fulfillment, its ends would be immanent in its unfolding; its process would be essentially good, even if it were obliged to press on through inadequacy to greater adequacy, through partial truth to consummate truth. Whether or not one's view of history is that of Vico or Condorcet (making reason the arbiter of progress) or Comte and Saint–Simon (viewing science and technology as the instruments of a continually self–perfecting man), the result is the same: history becomes a unity encompassing its own ends. For optimistic interpreters of history, history passes through evil to good. Good overwhelms evil as surely as reason overcomes superstition, science improves society, and technology enhances the comfort of man. In such views evil is not the foundation but the impediment of history.

It is our contention, however, that *within* history there is no meaning other than the self–illumination which the historian derives from the discernment of pattern and rhythm. Grand meaning does not exist, because grand meaning presupposes purpose and an end which uncreated and eternal history cannot allow. History becomes meaningful only when it is seen to commence and to conclude; and even though its commencement may be remote and unavailable to confirmation and its end but an image of an indefinite future, what passes between both points must be the inconclusive struggle of man to overcome the demonic. To consider the reality of evil as the foundation of history is never to say that history is evil *as such*; it is only to say that evil makes history significant, for in the evil which is possible to man our freedom and our finitude, our community with God and our estrangement from him are authenticated. We are not God's myth, but his creation; he created good and evil, said Isaiah, and we are both.

A metaphysics of history depends, therefore, for its significance upon the freedom to do evil—indeed, the reality of evil is the foundation of history.

It is in the presence of evil that we address ourselves again to the vocation and destiny of the Jews. Exile—that long and unbridged chasm which separates the Jew from his fulfillment—is a spiritual reality. To be sure, it is also a reality well founded upon the history and conduct of the nations. It is a spiritual reality of enormous importance, because it accords perfectly with that particular "freedom to evil" which is appropriate to the Jew. What the sin of Adam was to every man, the Exile of the Holy Spirit, the Exile of the community of Israel, the Exile of the faithful remnant of Zion, is to the Jew. The special destiny of the Jew is to witness to the evil which man does, not alone to the individual, but to providence. The election of Israel—that remarkable instance of God's unceasing pursuit of consummation—is degraded by the Exile of Israel; the good action of God is offset by the freedom to do evil which is at the root of history.

The Exile of Israel is, in the order of spiritual history, the first moment and the advent of the true Messiah is the last. God creates, man falls; God elects, the community sins; God disperses, the nations ravish. There is no center to history, no mid–point. There are innumerable centers, partial adumbrations; but the final word is indeed a final word. There can be no penultimate finalities, such as Jesus Christ. In the order of history Jesus is one among many centers, but if he be called Christ, the Messiah, he can be called such only by those who knew not the nature of history and discovered it through him. Jesus may be Christ for the Greek, but not for the Jew. Through Him the pagan discovered what had been known to the Jews: that God is present in history, that providence riddles time with possibility, and that no moment is ever the last until the final moment has come.

The rediscovery of sacred history is the first stage in the rejuvenescence of the Jewish theology. It was known to Scripture, known to the rabbis, known throughout the Middle Ages, known indeed until the dawn of modern history; but it was lost when history was disconnected from faith and the consummation of history was abandoned through the withering of trust.

Theology as the Science of Sacred History

Theology need not be a pretentious discipline; it need not usurp the sciences, dismiss natural philosophy, nor overturn logic. It is a modest discipline founded, to be sure, upon an immodest history. Once theologians ruled the sciences and held court in universities, whereas presently they are hidden away in drafty seminaries and muster disciples from the thin readership of lugubrious journals. The unhappy condition of theology has undoubtedly made theologians snappish and defensive, but we can ill afford to forget that whereas theologians are human their object of concern remains God.

Theology is not concerned with any God. This is only to say that there is no general theology (leaving aside, for purposes of this discussion, the special history of natural theology or theology founded upon the decretals of unaided reason). There is only a theology which works upon the materials of faith. Again, not any and all faiths; but rather one's own true and chosen faith. There is Moslem theology and Christian theology; there is Jewish theology.

Jewish theology is directed to the explication of the matter of Jewish faith. As we have indicated in the discussion just concluded, the matter of Jewish faith emerges from the juncture of God and history. The knowledge of God which we possess is knowledge consequent upon his action, whether it be his oblique conversations with the Patriarchs; his precise and disciplined discomfiting of Pharaoh; his marvelous manifestation in the flight from Egypt; his formal self–proclamation at Sinai; his innumerable rehearsals with the prophets of destiny and disaster; his alternately technical and passionate counsel to the sages. In all this history, in the transmitted word, in the myths of memory, in the written legacy, God is manifested. He is never manifest in generality. He is always a specific, concrete, and immediate presence to the Jew. He may be transcendent and distant, separated from us by the thin thread of eternity and the inadequacy of human words, but he is always a God of history, who is present in history to those who seek him.

The Jewish theologian must deal with a God of history; moreover he must deal with a God whose relation to history is not indefinite and uncertain, for the history through which God is disclosed is the theologian's *own* history—in seeking to understand God, the Jewish theologian, of necessity, seeks to understand himself. Insofar as the matter of Jewish theology is the history of God's presence to the Jew, theology becomes not a discipline of obscurity and abstraction, a spinning–out of formal answers to questions which nobody bothers any longer to ask, but a living discipline.

To the extent that theology is directed toward the God of history it becomes the link of the Jew to *all* history. The temptation of some Jewish theologians is to preserve the history of the Jews from contact and involvement with general history. The interpretation of Jewish history as sacred history, operating within its own time, its own logic of events, its own meaning, is deceptive. There is either real history or no history at all. The notion of Jewish history as independent of world history is a chimera. Its relation to general history may be paradigmatic—a distillate and pure exemplification of possibilities implicit in general history, but it is nevertheless real history, authentically united with the course of all history. The radical independence of Jewish history is an intellectual construction, a device whereby it is thought Judaism is rendered safe and protected from the challenge of alien doctrine; but, there can be no mistake: such construction is but a suspension of understanding, a refusal to acknowledge the inescapable fact of connection.

Secular history exists only in the absence of the transforming canon of faith. It is neutral and indifferent to providence, as long as the reality of providence is not interpolated into the action of events. Providence does not destroy normal causality or compromise scientific historiography—it merely adds to them the metaphysical optimism of which Joseph spoke when he addressed his malevolent and contrite brothers in the Land of the Pharaohs: "You meant evil against me, but God meant it for good" (Gen. 50:20; also 45:1–8). Joseph, the first Jewish metaphysician of history, understood that the fortunes of the Jews and the nations were bound together, that the neutral event shaped by the devisings of natural passions and interests could not compass the innumerable possibilities and perspectives with it contained. The single event—like all events—overwhelms the perspective of partial views. No man can perceive all the possibilities of an event. Its innumerable facets cannot be incorporated into the attitude either of the participant or of the historian who comes later. Faith assumes, however, that these possibilities are present to God, that his viewpoint is total and comprehensive, that his historical perspective is the perfect colligation of possibility and the understanding of what has actually come to pass.

There are those who will complain that this version of theology is vastly insufficient, that we have made the metaphysics of history into the sufficient subject matter of theology. Perhaps this is a legitimate criticism, but it should be noted in our favor that what we have foregone in rational theology—an inquiry into the nature of God and his formal relations to the universe—we have made up in revealed theology.[6] Otherwise spoken, we have declined to view theology either as a formal inquiry into the nature of God—which is too broad and uncompromisingly abstract— or as the narrow inquiry into the foundation of Jewish law and practice. Theology is neither the effort to apply the techniques of the sciences to the demonstration of God's existence (a hopeless enterprise) nor the attempt to apply findings of ethics, anthropology, or psychology to the rationalization of the commandments. Theology is rather the science of sacred history. It sets itself but one task: to apprehend and interpret the presence of God in time and history.

It is particularly appropriate that Jewish theology be understood as the knowledge (*scientia*) of sacred history. The disappearance of the theological center divests Judaism of both its special particularity and its catholic claim. Jewish history, removed from the antiphon of God and Israel, is little more than secular national history. The "theology" of the secular history of the Jews is sociology. Severed from the destiny and election of the Jews, Jewish history is but the consequence of the Jewish "problem." As the science of sacred history, however, theology is founded upon an immediate reality—the community—and its consensual agreement upon doctrine (the tradition, *masorah*). The past and future interactions of community and doctrine are the sacred (spiritual) history of the Jews; but the definition of the grammar and the speech by which sacred history is apprehended and transmitted are the tasks of theology.

Theology need not become system; what counts is not that theology should complete its deliberations and build its own monument, but that it should leave open to sacred history the possibility of new creation and new revelation. Since the God of theology is the God of revealed history, there can be no final determinations: there can be at best the models of the past which adumbrate the future, but God's freedom to disclose himself is not limited by what he has already disclosed. A theology which would concern itself merely with conserving the past destroys what is most precious in the theological enterprise—namely, that the already spoken Word of God contains within it the insinuations of the yet unspoken Word, that the past is really the portent of the future. The promise is given but the promise is not yet fulfilled; unless the fulfillment of the promise be possible, no promise was given; unless there be redemption, there was no creation.

Finally, Jewish theology may be seen as the sieve and winnower of history. It cannot hope to become the master of all history, since its perspective is not God's. At best it must operate within the compass set by its limitations: that it is the theological thinking of a given faith, committed to the riches and the incompleteness of its own experience; moreover that it surveys the expanse of its inherited past from the narrow catwalk of its present moment. It is in this sense that theology is both the product of culture and the illuminator of culture.

If Judaism is to realize its catholic nature it must rediscover its relation to culture—not merely Jewish culture, but the culture of any time and any society of which it is both creature and creator.

Messianism and the Consummation of Culture

Actually there can be no constructive thinking respecting history apart from culture. Since history is always the history of a people, it is reasonable that the historical event—a political movement, a style of are, a technological innovation, a scientific discovery—should be prepared by the ambience of culture. It is only possible to speak, therefore, with generality of the contours of culture, but not to fix them with finality, for culture is the latency of history, the actuality given and the possibilities implicit but unrealized.

The relation of Judaism and the Jewish people to the realities of culture has always been intimate and intense. Judaism was not matured independently of the formative and tributary cultures of the West. Judaism lived in profound and unbroken connection with the world that surrounded it, whether Near Eastern paganism, Hellenistic syncretism, Roman internationalism, pan–Islamism, or European Christianity. The Jewish people could not be sufficient to itself; its natural life was founded upon reaction and intermingling with the nations of the world. Were this condition *fact* alone it would only enable us to develop an argument based upon the historical involvement of Judaism with the West, and to define natural imperatives for the renewal of Jewish participation in the culture of the West. However, it is possible—as we have done throughout this study—to do more than adduce the compulsions of history as justification. It is not simply that Judaism can do no other than relate itself—for reasons of historical necessity, the urgencies of survival, or the requirements of ethnic pride—to the cultural life of the nations; it is rather that Judaism, theologically understood, cannot properly stand aloof from the world.

The vitality of Jewish culture is to be measured by the intensity with which it undertakes *galut* (Exile) as a cultural demand; indeed, as the living of its messianic vocation.

God witnesses the suffering of Israel, yet it is only to the natural eye of man that this suffering is suffering without purpose. The suffering is not ordained, nor, we believe, does God will our destruction. But if we are set among the nations who see themselves redeemed—whether through a God–Man or, as in the East, from the shambles of time—we are to them a mystery and a reproof. The role of Judaism, therefore, is not to create culture *as such*, but to be the critic of culture—to make culture the partial consummation of history and the anticipation of the Kingdom of God.

Culture is, we are increasingly aware, a precarious and indefinable phenomenon. As often as not culture is not discerned until it is past, until the new culture is born and the past may be accounted good or evil, productive or wasteful. The intellectual may call the culture of the moment popular and vulgar (and therefore inauthentic) and the historian who succeeds him in time may call it authentic (however popular and vulgar). The popular culture of Florence in the days of the Medicis was possibly no more exalted than the popular culture of contemporary American or England, but it is rather hard at this moment to set the prodigies and achievements of contemporary culture side by side with the culture of fifteenth–century Italy. It is our impatience to historicize that makes so many of our ventures into cultural appraisal risky; and yet such impatience is justified by the fact that our time and our history are not leisurely, that our age is covered with the veil of apocalypse and finality, and that many people—the best people of the West—are trying to locate the source of conservation and endurance.

The role of Judaism in the cultural enterprise is not different in kind from that of any other religion, although its role may be somewhat less precise and somewhat more oblique and tendentious. Any high culture—one that involves the amalgamation and fusion of well–articulated spheres of independent life and authority—results from the synthesis of different cultural traditions. It is not, as in primitive societies, the articulation of a unified whole, reflecting the penetration of primary myth into every aspect of life. In primitive society, the myth is so overwhelming as to transmute all activity into the bearer and fulfillment of the myth. The economy, the social organization, the family are all specific extrusions of myth, every aspect of life testifying to the psychic and spiritual claims of the regnant mythology. In the evolution of civilizations multiple cultural traditions are blended—not without pain to both the victor and the captive culture—independent spheres of authority are evolved, and individual and self–contained worlds of thought are refined and sustained. Where the culture succeeds, containing its diversity, the historic function of religion has been to conserve the vision toward which that unity is directed. Such societies are few and they have all declined, for the price of unity fashioned from the synthesis of discrete and individual centers of authority is that the vision is conventionalized by its conserving institutions and the rebellion of the diverse principalities of the mind and society which it once contained. The Kingdom of God on earth is always shattered when the vision is institutionalized; for the finite cannot routinize the infinite without tricking those whom it subjects, and the subjected finally rebel against the pretension of the conserving authority. It was the destiny of the medieval Church to pass and of the Holy Roman Empire to dissolve; it was the destiny of medieval Islam to decline in the face of the routinization of prophecy.

In our day the task of religion in culture is not to conserve the vision but to dislocate those who pretend to institutionalize *less* than the vision. In a disintegrating culture the task of religion is prophetic.

The paradox of God in time is always witnessed most acutely in the cultural consequences of the religious vision, for religion corrupts God when it would commit him now and forever to a single institution in time and yet it loses God when there is no institution at all through whom he speaks. This paradox drives us again to the unique vocation of Israel—neither committed nor aloof, neither rooted nor alien, neither of this world nor of any other. The Jew may stand astride time and eternity. Of needs he must! In the age of synthesis the cultural obligation of the Jew is to learn from culture that it may strengthen his prophecy, and in an age of prophecy to recapture tradition that the false prophet may not arise. So said, Judaism is the bearer of true prophets in ages of idolatrous self–sufficiency and the destroyer of false prophets in ages of dislocation.

The present obligation of religion to culture differs somewhat from its past, for the alternatives are no longer that religion either reigns or disintegrates. There is no religion; there is only religious sentiment. The real powers of our time are beyond the appeal of religion. This is, as Rosenzweig has said, the age of the Johannine gospel, which is beyond church and nation. There is no culture, as we have previously defined it; there are but the diverse authorities of society and the mind. There is profession; there is family; there are neighborhood and community; there are state, nation, and world—but there is little connection or communication between them. The spheres of authority are mute and inarticulate and, in the neutrality of the "between–sphere," the emptiness may be seen. There is neither vision nor the loss of vision; there is only ambiguity and the abyss.

The present task of the religious is neither to sustain nor to prophesy, but to begin again, to make new. It is here that Judaism is once more of the greatest importance, for Judaism has been committed neither to sustaining this world not to prophesying the immanency of the next. Ours is the position of the "between" because we do not believe that redemption has come.

If Israel is "chosen," it is chosen for a distinguished task—to outlast the world and its temporizing solutions, to be borne up to the end of time as His alone, to strain and winnow the pride of the world, to demonstrate that the burden of this incomplete time and this imperfect history is indeed insupportable, whereas all the ideologies of this world would render them bearable, indeed good and sufficient. This is unavoidably an aristocratic mission.

The messianic view of culture is not as the Rabbi of Prague said at the moment of the coming of the pretender savior, Sabbatai Zevi: We do not believe, for the world is not yet changed. The Rabbi of Prague was an insufficient messianist and a too committed mystic. But messianism is not mysticism; it is rather historical realism. It is the urging of undespairing realism toward this world. The transformation of the world is not demonstrated by the righting of wrongs, the justification of injustice; it is only partially this, for the transformation of the world consists in more than that the wolf and the lamb shall lie down together or that war shall cease from the world. This is the social image of salvation which is true enough as far as it goes. The change in the world that comes in the wake of the Messiah is not only social change, for social change requires but the restructuring of relations, the reordering of patterns. Social change assumes that the ultimate structure of the world, its being, is essentially perfect, but that its accidental historical arrangements are awry.

God does not work social change, attend diplomatic conferences, listen to political invocations, or bother with grace at charity banquets. He does not improve good will; rather he works on a universe in which society and man participate. Society does not reject God. The individual must first turn Him out of his life. It is the insufficiency of man that he should be unable to follow after God. A man may follow after his beloved, or seek after beauty, but to follow after God is a task of infinite difficulty. This is a condition of our world—and to such a world the Messiah comes not as reformer.[7] The Jew is the "between–man," between time and eternity, between the sadness of the world and the joy of redemption. He neither believes that in this time and history has the Kingdom of God been foretasted nor does he know when it is that God appoints this time and history for redemption.[8] For this reason the Jew is not bound to the stabilities of the world: he can create in ages when others would destroy and destroy in ages where others create—for he is the leaven of history. And this, we would think, is the messianic relation of the Jew to culture.

Epilogue: The Renewal of the Jewish Vocation

A natural history of the Jewish mind is impossible. The Jewish mind, as a natural and empirical phenomenon, is an absurdity. It consists in but the pale images of theological models—prophetism and messianism transformed into social and political ideologies, Exile recast as social alienation, the loneliness and spiritual discomfort of Biblical man translated into the self–estrangement of modern man. For the natural Jew all that remains of the supernatural community is a treasury of inspiriting maxims and heroic legends, divested not only of their mythological content but of their divinity as well. Judaism has been quietly and unconsciously demythologizing its tradition for centuries; but the purgation of myth has not been accompanied by a sharper, more compelling awareness of the personal truth and meaning of its history (much demythologizing, but little kerygma).

The Jewish mind is demythologized, but the natural Jew has lost, in the process, all contact with and approach to his supernatural life. For centuries the supernatural Jew struggled to survive, and though he perished in the flesh, he did survive. Faith in the promise of the past and trust in the consummating action of God enabled him to survive the assaults of Christendom and Islam. The loss in our time of that supernatural pride which is called the "stubbornness" of the Jew is partially responsible for the loss of contact with the legacy of tradition and the passion to give witness to the incomplete sanctity of the natural order; moreover, the immolation of European Jewry in this century has exploded the last vestige of Jewish mythology—an eschatological trust which was indifferent to the course of world history and culture.

The supernatural Jew, defined as he is by those concerns and preoccupations which form the historic consensus of the Jewish mind, is the last of the eschatologists, for the Jew, more than any other man, lives on the recollection of first things and the anticipation of the last. Each moment comes to the supernatural Jew full of unrealized meaning, for each moment is abundant with the unrealized possibility of God in history. Every moment is potentially an eschatological moment; every moment collects the history of the past and portends the unfulfilled future. There is no such thing for the supernatural Jew as the denial of history, the repudiation of its meaning, the despair of its justification. Where the natural Jew may know despair, the supernatural Jew knows only trust.

But the natural and the supernatural Jew are joined in every Jew. The supernatural Jew may occasionally forget that he is also flesh and blood; he may detach himself from the world and disengage himself from history that he may pursue a path of self–denial and private illumination. Such a Jew is as much in error as is the natural Jew who forgets what links him to eternity. The natural Jew enmeshed in the historical, cannot help but despair; destiny disappears for him and only the hard and implacable fatality of his life remains. The despair of the historical is but the consequence of fate obliterating destiny; while the ecstasy of the mystic, no less an example of fate, is centered exclusively upon the actuality of God, indifferent to his involvement in the contingent and dangerous war of history.

The religious dilemma which makes the unity of the natural and the supernatural so imperative for the Jewish mind is that the representation of God in history is not pure actuality but actuality committed to the unfulfilled possibility of history. The eschatological consummation toward which Judaism turns its face in history with God, the actual God realizing new creation, and new concreteness. As such, each moment of the present may become a redemptive moment, a moment in which the new possibility of God and the renewed sensibility of the Jew may meet and sanctify.

The renewal of the historical, the reunion of the Jew with general culture, the reassertion of the catholic claim of Judaism depend upon the rediscovery of the implicit polarity and dialectic of the Jewish nature—that it is natural, participating in all the forms and events of history and culture, and supernatural, transforming those forms and events into bearers of ultimate and consummate meaning. God is not an eschatologist nor is God a messianist. God does what can be done—this is indeed part of the tragedy which we may sense when we speak of God, for God cannot compel history to fulfillment; he can but enrich the moment with those possibilities which become the bearers of meaning. It is man who victimizes God. God maintains freedom and the free destiny; it is human obduracy and folly which refuses such terrifying freedom and finds consolation in the refusal of destiny and the comforting delusion of fate.

The historic moment that bears ultimate meaning is always at hand. But when the argument is done and the historic precedents of the Jewish mind have been adduced and displayed and the consensus of Judaism has been recapitulated, the same question recurs: Can the testimony of all truth compel human decision? Is it possible that the sense of supernatural vocation—lost as it is in the abyss of natural fate—may be renewed? This question still remains, and only Jews can answer it.

Notes

[1]Actually Schechter was born in 1849 in the small Rumanian town of Foscani, but his arrival in England in 1882, where he was to make his home until he came to the United States to become president of the Jewish Theological Seminary of America in 1902, justifies the propriety of describing him as an Anglo–American Jewish theologian. See Norman Bentwich, *Solomon Schechter* (Philadelphia, Jewish Publication Society of American, 1938).

[2]Solomon Schechter, *Studies in Judaism*, First Series (Philadelphia, Jewish Publication Society of America, 1945) xi–xxv; particularly xix. See also *Studies in Judaism*, Third Series (Philadelphia, Jewish Publication Society of America, 1924) 19; *Some Aspects of Rabbinic Theology* (New York, The Macmillan Company, 1909) viii. It should be noted that Schechter's notion of Catholic Israel has its origin in medieval doctrine—Christian, Moslem, and Jewish. The Jewish notion of *haskamat haklal* (general agreement) is Schechter's immediate precedent.

[3]Schechter, *Studies in Judaism*, First Series, xviii.

[4]Clearly this is a partial statement of the Greek view of history. If we were to undertake a more thorough treatment many refinements would emerge. It is true, however, that for Greek philosophy history was but an instructor of the natural fatality of events. History demonstrated only the limits of human power. It set the limit to expectation. It could not open the prospect of a transcendence acceptable to the gods, because man, nature, and the gods were all in competition and the gods invariably won. The Stoics were wise to counsel calm, serenity, and indifference.

[5]Nicholas Berdyaev, *The Meaning of History*, trans. George Reavey (London, Geoffrey Bles, 1936) 77.

[6]We would be inclined to argue that Maimonides' *Sefer Ha–Mada* or the first two parts of his *Guide for the Perplexed* fall within the provenance of rational theology. Maimonides did not need the revelation of Scripture to define the nature of God. Reason, working upon the foundations of natural philosophy, might adduce sufficient proofs of God's existence and adequate interpretation of his nature. Only when Maimonides decided in favor of *creatio ex nihilo* (rather than the Aristotelian eternity of matter) was Scripture favored. All this on Maimonides' own statement, that where reason is not contradicted by Scripture, the formal elaborations of reason are to be preferred. Maimonides becomes, in our view, a proper Jewish theologian when he turns to the nature of prophecy, for here he is confronting a phenomenon of history in which the God who is beyond reason is present.

[7]Indeed, the acute and critical disease from which Jewish messianic thinking suffers is that it has not perceived the enormous relevance which Rudolf Bultmann's demythologizing of Christianity has for Judaism. Jewish messianic thinking is beclouded by ethnic mythologies—the national restoration of Zion, the political rejuvenation of Israel, the punishing of the persecutors of the Jews, the miraculous return of all Jews to the Holy Land. Only if these limiting mythological conceptions are abandoned is it possible to discern what prophetic and rabbinic messianism really stands for— namely, the completion of one order of time and history and the inauguration of another. The regnancy of Israel is but a mythological symbol of a metaphysical transformation; for if the spiritual kingdom of the world is built again, that kingdom shall be the kingdom of the Jewish spirit.

[8]See a variety of the author's essays dealing with various aspects of the problem of messianism and the Jewish attitude toward Christian affirmation: "The Encounter of Judaism and Christendom," *Cross Currents*, 1/3 (Spring, 1951): 91–95; "Messianism and the Jew," *Commonweal*, 62/15 (1955): 367–69; "Moses, Mystery, and Jesus," *The Jewish Frontier*, 23/6 (June, 1956): 24–28; "Three We Have Lost: The Problem of Conversion," *Conservative Judaism*, 11/4 (1957): 7–19; "Semite According to the Flesh," *The Christian Century*, 74/38, 18 Sept. 1957, 1097–89; "The Jewish– Christian Contradiction," *Worldview*, 1/2 (1958): 3–5; "The Natural and the Supernatural Jew," in *American Catholics: A Protestant–Jewish View*, ed. Philip Scharper (New York, Sheed & Ward, 1959) 127–57.

Chapter 9

Jewish Theology in North America
Notes on Two Decades

Arnold Eisen

From the onlookers who also participate in the events they describe, we conclude with a theological statement in the guise of an essay that claims merely to present a simple description of the theological work accomplished in American Judaism from Viet Nam to the end of the Cold War, that is, from ca. 1970 to ca. 1990. In fact we see a kind of theology that is otherwise not represented in these volumes, which is, a theology that appeals not to the Torah but to immediate experience in the present minute. Eisen sets forth through his description of what has happened what is, in fact, a theology lacking in encounter with the Torah. He seems to claim that theology of Judaism can be accomplished essentially within the ethnic framework of various Jews' personal religious experience, rather than within the religious framework of eternal Israel's encounter with God recorded in the Torah. For Eisen, capable of anthologizing sayings on a given subject but himself hardly renowned for mastery of the classics of the Torah, the theology of Judaism derives not from eternal Israel but from this morning's religious experience of individual Jews. The starting point of this essay will puzzle readers of these five volumes. Eisen claims "not much creative work has been forthcoming over the last two decades." But the rich and dense writings anthologized here contradict his opinion. The key word is "creative," for by "creative" Eisen apparently understands, making things up as we go along. He asks a question, then, that the writings anthologized here render inane: "why no theology?" But formidable theology has been done, and Eisen knows some of it. For he devotes his attention to these names, inclusive of those selected in these volumes: Borowitz, Irving Greenberg, Michael Wyschogrod, David Hartman, Richard Rubenstein; Fackenheim; Cohen; Green; and Judity Plaskow. He shows not that there has been no theology, but the very opposite. Still, what he does show is two things. First, theology outside of the received revelation and rigorous intellectual discipline governing in the writings we have read is ephemeral and un-Judaic. It is ephemeral because in the end nothing secures stable truth; it is un-Judaic because, as we have seen, characteristic of all Judaic theology worthy of the name is a serious encounter with revealed truth, the Torah. Celebrating what in Judaic parlance is called am haratzut, that is, ignorance, indifference to the disciplines of the Torah, Eisen appeals to contemporary experience instead of to the Torah. In what way he resolves what should endure as the creative tension: the negotiable space between Torah and today.

*Originally appeared in *American Jewish Yearbook*, 1991. Used by permission.

His language is significant: "There is reason to believe that Jewish theologians in the coming decades . . . will . . . move away from personalist conceptions of God in favor of new–mystical formulations that ring true to contemporary experience of the transcendent." Eisen's prediction will be tested over the next half–century. Then, someone else will produce five volumes of writings on the theology of Judaism in response to the age that is coming.

***

If there is one point of agreement among students and practitioners of Jewish theology in North America, it is that not much creative work has been forthcoming over the last two decades. Eugene Borowitz, reflecting on "the Form of a Jewish Theology" at the start of the period under review here, wondered whether systematic Jewish thought could even be attempted in our time. "Holism" was essential, he argued, but it was perhaps unavailable.[1] Neil Gillman, for that very reason, titled his book, issued in 1990, *Sacred Fragments: Recovering Theology for the Modern Jew*. Fragments were all we had at this point in the history of Judaism, he maintained. As a result, theology could not simply by written, it had to be "recovered."[2] This sentiment is widespread. Few would disagree with Emil Fackenheim's pointed lament in 1982 that "in the realm of purely theoretical Jewish thought, and despite claims in this or that quarter to having 'gone beyond' Buber and Rosenzweig, the main characteristic of more recent Jewish thought is, by comparison, its low level. . . . The consequence is that the pioneering work then accomplished still waits for adequate successors."[3]

Our first task in this overview of the Jewish theology produced in America since Lou Silberman's *Year Book survey* in 1969,[4] then, will be to join practitioners of the craft in wondering why their number and productivity have remained so limited. To be sure, there has been a prodigious amount of Jewish religious reflection in America. Homilies, topical essays, halakhic opinions, guides for laymen, ideological statements, and prayerbook revisions abound.[5] But the theological forms known to us from past eras in the history of Judaism have largely been absent in the United States, particularly in recent decades. Understanding why that is so provides invaluable insight into the theological literature that has been produced—and tells us a great deal about the religious community that has produced it.

Our second task will be an interpretive sketch of the existing literature, focusing on the major figures and trends. Two issues clearly occupy center stage: the attempt to refine the "covenant theology" characteristic of much twentieth–century Jewish thought;[6] and the confrontation with the Holocaust that, as Silberman predicted, has received far more attention in the period than any other subject. This review completed, there will be an opportunity to consider the trends emerging in the 1990s and to reflect on what they portend for the decades to come. The outlook is not entirely bleak, but no responsible observer could possibly call it bright.

Theology and Its Practitioners

A word of definition is in order at the outset. As used here, the term "theology" refers to thought (1) of a relatively systematic character that (2) is informed by serious philosophical competence and (3) evinces real grounding in Jewish history and tradition. Most articles published in most Jewish journals by most scholars and rabbis in the past two decades are beyond the purview of this essay because they tend, in the nature of the case, to be occasional pieces, often homiletic, generally topical, and aimed at a fairly wide readership. Theology, by contrast, is an elitist pursuit directed at a limited audience, even if its impact on the mass of believers is far from inconsequential. In America today—by far the most egalitarian society in which Jews have lived—concern with theology is perhaps rarer than ever before.

Several thinkers, seeking to understand why this is the case, have pointed to the Christian connotations of "theology."[7] Most normative Jewish thought, after all, has shunned the question of God's nature, believing it inaccessible to human understanding. All but the kabbalists have preferred to examine God's interaction with and intentions for Israel and the world. Modern Jewish thinkers, for somewhat different reasons, have paid relatively little attention to God's role as creator, and only slightly more to the divine activity of redemption.[8] The focus has instead been on revelation—what God wants Jews to do, and how we know what God wants.[9]

There is also a widespread sense that the term "theology" bespeaks a systematic form rarely adopted in Judaism even when—as with biblical and rabbinic thought—one finds a wide range of issues addressed in more or less coherent fashion. If "theology" means form rather than content, Jews have rarely engaged in the enterprise, preferring other genres such as commentary, legal code, or responsa, or—in the modern period—the essay. Still, the form is amply represented in the history of Judaism, and the presence of systematic presentations of content in every period is striking. Jews have engaged in theology in the past, and indeed they continue to do so. The question is why it has not been more evident on the American Jewish scene in recent decades.

Why No Theology?

One is tempted to ascribe the lacuna to an alleged American proclivity toward praxis rather than theory.[10] American Protestantism, after all, has also not generated the outpouring of theology produced in German. But neither has Protestant theology been utterly absent here. From the Puritan divines through Jonathan Edwards to Horace

Bushnell to Paul Tillich and the Niebuhrs, America has developed a rich theological library.[11] One gets closer to the mark with the observation that this library has not grown significantly in the past twenty years, anymore than American Judaism has found successors to Abraham Heschel and Joseph Soloveitchik. The suspicion arises that something in the social and intellectual context of America in this half–century, rather than America per se, has militated against the creation of theology. Three possible components of that something come immediately to mind.

First, theology is inherently particularistic.[12] It primarily concerns a single faith community and its unique relationship to God. Theology arises when belief and practice are challenged from outside, the challenge being so serious, and internalized to such a degree, that it cannot be ignored. It proceeds by elaborating upon the distinctiveness of the inside path, and usually involves reaffirmation of the insiders' special claim to truth. American Jews, seeking integration in America denied them elsewhere, have tended to emphasize what could readily be projected outwards. They have sought to be a part rather than apart, and so have downplayed or reinterpreted key theological ideas, such as chosenness, which might have proven offensive to others. In this they have not been alone.[13] In short, pluralism and egalitarianism have exacted their toll in terms of the articulation of difference. One cannot imagine a Rosenzweig writing in America that Judaism is the fire which burns at the core of the Star of Redemption, Christianity its rays; that we stand at the goal, while they are ever on the way.[14] At most one finds a Soloveitchik averring that no individual and no community is in a position to judge the God–relationship of any other. We regard our faith as true; about the others, within certain bounds of acceptability, we cannot judge.[15] More than this probably cannot be said in America. Yet, saying less is generally not productive of theology.

A second factor militating against Jewish theology on these shores has been the lack of Jews qualified to practice the discipline or to appreciate its products. Note the apparent prerequisites for the craft: (1) firm grounding in Jewish sources of various periods—halakhic and aggadic, philosophical and mystical, from the Bible to the present (meaning, increasingly, competence in the secondary literature devoted to the texts and their contexts); (2) serious acquaintance with modern philosophy (Kant, Hegel, and Heidegger seem basic, if we accept as normative the knowledge base assumed by the twentieth–century Jewish corpus from Cohen to Fackenheim); and (3) some sense of how Christian thinkers in the modern period have responded to very similar challenges (recall Heschel's use of Barth or Soloveitchik's of Kierkegaard). As we approach century's end, some understanding of social and literary theory has probably also become essential. This combination of talents is indeed a formidable demand.

Even if a given individual possesses it, however, he or she may well lack a fourth apparent prerequisite for the production of theology—a faith community on which to meditate. Theology in Judaism has meant both Halakhah—"life lived," as Jacob

Neusner has put it—and Aggadah—life reflected upon.[16] If American Jews have rarely done theology, it is perhaps because they by and large lack both Halakhah and Aggadah in this sense. Outside of Orthodoxy there is no defined faith community within which a distinct life is lived, and which may be reflected upon. Christian thinkers, too, suffer from the absence of such communities, but the problem is if anything more troubling for Jews, precisely because Jewish theology has tended not to inquire into the nature of God but rather to probe the way Jews are meant to behave collectively, in God's presence. Without a visible community in which covenantal commitments are enacted, the meaning of the covenant becomes more difficult to articulate.

Theologians also suffer from an acute shortage of potential readers. Previous generations of theologians wrote either for each other (a problem today, when the number of active practitioners is so small) or for congregational rabbis (probably still the primary consumers of Jewish theology) or for colleagues at the university (who today are less and less inclined to take religious belief seriously) or for educated lay people (the number of whom has declined precipitously of late). Judaism is a leisure–time activity for most American Jews, and even the most committed religiously are far less concerned with systematic belief or observance than with appropriating selected elements of the tradition in their lives. They are better served by the sort of occasional (or introductory) literature produced in abundance than they would be by systematic work which they could not read and could not easily apply. The seminaries meanwhile—and most theologians and potential theologians are still employed by them—often focus on denominational needs: new editions of the *siddur*, revised statements of principles, reflection on the altered status of Halakhah, and so on. In this realm American Judaism has been absolutely prolific, never more so than in the past two decades.[17] Explanations of what differentiates the several movements are a far cry from theology, particularly when, as is often the case, they bear all the marks of authorship by committee.

The final obstacle in the path of Jewish theology in the United States is the doubly problematic character of contemporary Jewish belief. Van Harvey, writing about American Protestant theology at the same time that Silberman did his survey, gave eloquent expression to the dilemmas of what he called "the alienated theologian." Harvey described a Christian thinker "concerned with the articulation of the faith of the Christian community" but "himself as much a doubter as a believer." The doubt had been evident in Protestant thought throughout the modern period. Harvey argued, but it had emerged with particular force in the 1960s, posing "fundamental questions for the church concerning the future of theology itself."[18] In this respect Jews have perhaps had a certain advantage. The Protestant, losing faith, may well leave the Church. The Jew may nonetheless retain a primordial commitment to the Jewish people. Still, the parallel with Christianity is rather exact. Modern Judaism is beleaguered by the same forces as modern Christianity (and often influenced by the latter in its modes of defense);[19] it is also under siege of late from a new source of doubt, which has come to be known in theological shorthand as "Auschwitz." Religious *ideology*—partial in character, relying more heavily on images than concepts—can perhaps survive the twin doubts posed by modernity and the Holocaust far better than theology, which in the nature of the case must strive for system.

Still, some Jews continue to require theology. Hence the literature which we are about to survey. Borowitz, while all too aware of the dilemmas just recounted, has concluded that "it is difficult to see how one can escape the holistic question altogether."[20] Fackenheim, writing eloquently on the impossibility of "systems" in our time, has nonetheless sought—relatively systematically—to lay the "foundations of future Jewish thought."[21] Gillman has given us "fragments" artfully combined into a fairly systematic whole.[22] All, in short, have proclaimed that a "new Jewish theology" is imperative, and have reached for syntheses which have eluded their grasp and that of their generation as a whole. We turn now to their imperfect, but nonetheless substantial, achievement.

Covenant: The Commanding Presence

A sizable portion of American Jewish theological literature of the last two decades has been focused on redefinition of the covenant relationship binding the Jewish people with God. In this respect American Jewish thinkers have carried on the line of inquiry that has preoccupied their predecessors throughout the modern period. The attractions of the covenant model for modern thinkers, and its pitfalls, are equally apparent. On the one hand, Jews seek ultimate purpose for their identity, ultimate authority for their observances, and personal relation to their Creator, and the covenant promises all three. On the other hand, the "suzerainty" paradigm of covenant (in which the sovereign binds his vassals to a set of obligations that he defines, in return promising his protection) has run afoul of the Kantian concern with autonomy and the related reluctance by many modern Jews to bear any "yoke of obligation" imposed by their religion. Commandments from on high, according to liberal thinkers, compromise human dignity and insult human reason. In short, the authority of the King of Kings has to emerged unscathed from the assault on all earthly monarchies.

The "parity treaty" model of covenant (which stipulates reciprocal obligations) has proven somewhat more attractive to modern Jews because it stresses mutuality of obligation and emphasizes partnership and relation rather than subordination and command. But the modern period has seen a lessening of personal religious experience among Jews, and a falling away from religious observance. Moreover, even before the Holocaust, Jews displayed an increasing disinclination to view history as the arena in which God rewards or punishes them for covenantal fidelity or betrayal. The fabric of the putative partnership has, as it were, frayed at both ends, and even been torn right down the middle. Jewish thinkers have found themselves drawn more and more to a theological concept which—given what they do and do not believe about revelation, commandment, and the historicity of the biblical narrative—has become less and less theologically defensible.

American Jewish theologians in recent decades have had to wrestle with all these problems, plus others. Thus, they have come to recognize that Jewish religious knowledge, practice, and experience can no longer be assumed. The leading thinkers of the previous generation (*e.g.*, Heschel and Soloveitchik) grew up in European settings of traditional practice and belief. Neither the current generation of thinkers nor their readers can call upon such experience. Much of the effort by current thinkers, in fact—one thinks especially of Borowitz's *New Jewish Theology in the Making* (1968), *How Can a Jew Speak of Faith Today* (1969), and *The Mask Jews Wear* (1973)—has been devoted to the question of whether American Jews can be brought to any degree of Jewishly authentic faith or observance. Borowitz, more than any other contemporary theologian, has been intimately involved with lay believers, through his work in the Reform movement.[23] It is telling that he has consistently articulated the alienation of the theologian from his or her fellow Jews most clearly, even as he has relied more heavily than any other thinker on the concept of Israel's covenant with God. Giving meaning to the covenant in the American setting is never without pathos.

Eugene Borowitz

Borowitz's systematic exposition of *Liberal Judaism* (1984), addressed explicitly to the lay audience, is a case in point. The title conveys fidelity to the German liberal tradition rather than to the far more radical bent of American Reform. The organization of the book follows the traditional triad of Israel, God, and Torah. Borowitz in uncompromising in his insistence that God is real and is involved with our world. God's age–old covenant with Israel is still binding. In fact, a good Jew is defined as one who has "a living relationship with God as part of the people of Israel and therefore lives a life of Torah." Prescribed duties—both ethical and ritual—flow from this relationship. So does involvement in the life of the Jewish people as a whole and with the State of Israel: "The Covenant, being a collective endeavor, can best be lived as part of a self–governing Jewish community on the Land of Israel. A good Jew will seriously consider the possibility of *aliyah*."[24]

Borowitz knows, however, that the vast majority of Reform readers will not give that option serious consideration, any more than they will assume their covenantal duties in more than rudimentary fashion. What is more, he himself cannot accept the Torah (written or oral) as divine revelation, and is unwilling to compromise his commitment to the autonomy of each individual believer. The author emphasizes that he makes "no special claims to 'authority,' " hoping only to persuade. He can suggest appropriate behavior but he cannot guide, let alone command. If each Jew decides how to live the covenant out of the depth of knowledge and in terms of his/her own deepest commitment, Borowitz avers, "whatever we choose from the past or create for the present should rest upon us with the full force of commandment."[25]

One notes that ethics remains the heart of *mitzvah* in Borowitz's liberal Judaism, although ritual is highlighted to a degree still unusual in American Reform. But the force of both sets of obligations is not clear. Halakhah is rejected on principle, and normative communities—in practice nonexistent—would be objectionable if they did exist because of their infringement on individual autonomy. What authority remains? Borowitz seems to rely (as did Kant and Buber, in differing ways) on the inborn sense of duty or conscience that summons each and every human being. He relies, too, on his Jewish readers' unwillingness to sever the ties linking them to their parents, grandparents, and the Jewish past more generally, however much they might strain these ties to the breaking point. Conservative colleagues wrestling with the same issues—and appealing to "*mitzvah*" and "tradition" rather than "covenant" and "ethics"—find themselves in a similar sociological situation, with similar theological results.[26]

Irving Greenberg

One sees these same dynamics at work in the notion of "the voluntary covenant" developed by Orthodox thinker Irving Greenberg. Once more the appeal of the idea is clear: just as the rabbis had reassumed and reinterpreted the covenant with God following the destruction of the Temple, so today's Jews must undertake the more radical reinterpretation and reassumption of covenantal responsibilities mandated by the more radical destruction accomplished by the Nazis. Prophecy was gone even by the rabbis' day. Their focus on study of God's word shifted the weight of the Jewish role from passive reception of commands given on high to active partnership, often initiated from below. In another favored rabbinic metaphor, Jews enjoyed a marriage bond with God and carried it on with full devotion.[27] The word "voluntary" is crucial to Greenberg. It emphasizes that the initiative—now, more than ever—is on the human side rather than on God's. It suggests that *we* will be faithful, *we* will uphold the covenant, even if God in the Holocaust did not—precisely the reverse of what the prophets said to Israel in the wake of Jerusalem's fall in 586 B.C.E. Issues of heteronomy and sovereignty fall away. Activism, freedom, the rescue of dignity from degradation are pronounced. "By every right, Jews should have questioned or rejected the covenant" after Auschwitz, Greenberg writes. Instead,

> the bulk of Jews, observant and non–observant alike, acted to recreate the greatest Biblical symbol validating the covenant, the State of Israel. . . . [I]n the ultimate test of the Jews' faithfulness to the covenant, the Jewish people,

regardless of ritual observance level, responded with a reacceptance of the covenant, out of free will and love. For some, it was love of God; for others, love of the covenant and the goal; for others, love of the people or of the memories of the covenantal way. In truth, it hardly matters because the three are inseparable in walking the covenantal way.[28]

Greenberg builds daringly on Soloveitchik's idea of the twofold covenant of fate and destiny, the former involuntary and symbolized by Pharaoh (or Hitler), the latter involving free acceptance of the yoke of the commandments, and symbolized by Sinai. The "voluntary covenant" also extends Soloveitchik's teaching that the Jewish people, committing itself to the covenant of destiny at Sinai, "had committed their very being . . . the covenant turned out to be a covenant of being, not doing."[29] In Greenberg's reading, the commitment to "being" after the Holocaust is virtually equivalent to the "doing" of commandments. One wonders, however, whether he means it to include existence a hair's breadth away from assimilation. Is it really true that "it does not matter," that any Jewish commitment inevitably carries with it all the others? Greenberg exaggerates, I believe, to make the important points that in our generation any and all Jewish commitment is remarkable, and that such commitment often takes the form of caring for the Jewish people (Israel, Ethiopian Jews Operation Exodus) rather than *shul*-going or observance of the commandments. But a price is paid for this exaggeration: the concept of covenant is strained to the breaking point.

Michael Wyschogrod

In *The Body of Faith* (1983), Orthodox thinker Michael Wyschogrod challenges the reigning theological paradigm of voluntarism and its accommodation to the realities of American Judaism. Where Jewish thought since Mendelssohn has stressed human adequacy and brought religion before reason's stern bar of judgment, Wyschogrod pictures a humanity largely in the dark, its reason blocked at every crucial turn. Only a few shafts of light guide our way—and Torah is the brightest.[30] Where most modern Jewish thinkers, particularly in America, have apologized for the idea of Jewish chosenness, universalizing it to include all righteous Gentiles and interpreting it to stress fulfillment of covenantal obligation, Wyschogrod writes that "the election of the people of Israel as the people of God constitutes the sanctification of a natural family." God did not choose according to a spiritual criterion. "He chose the seed of Abraham, Isaac and Jacob. . . . The election of Israel is therefore a corporeal election."[31] Finally, where thinkers such as Borowitz have affirmed autonomy, Wyschogrod argues that "the ethical is not autonomous in Judaism. It is rooted in the being and command of God, without which no obligation is conceivable."[32]

Most recent Jewish thought in America has skirted the issue of God, preferring when it does speak of God to employ the rationalist discourse of "spirit" or "intelligence." Wyschogrod (with brilliant use of both the Bible and Heidegger) argues the necessity of a personal God whom he calls by His personal name—"Hashem," literally, "The Name." The argument, briefly,[33] is that Heidegger was correct in claiming that beyond Being there can be only Non–Being. Identification of God with being, in the manner of Spinoza, cannot avoid the threat posed to the meaning of all human endeavor by the encompassing power of non–being. Only a God beyond both being and non–being can satisfy our demand for ultimate meaning and ultimate grounding. Only Hashem can conquer death and create life: "On the one side there is being and thought, the enterprise of Heidegger. On the other side is Hashem and faith, the enterprise of Judaism. And then there is man, who attempts to understand himself in the setting provided by these concepts and in light of the tensions generated by them." Where rational language must fall silent in its search for description of the Lord of Being, unable to transcend the limits of our world, "the power of Hashem acts through the language of revelation," the Bible, and gives us the power of speech. "Hope conquers the despair of silence," Wyschogrod asserts.[34]

Wyschogrod's argument is Jewishly and philosophically learned, captivating in its break with the conventional givens of American Jewish theology—and, of course, not without serious problems. For one, the magnificent interpretive freedom derived from Wyschogrod's refusal to demythologize the Bible's descriptions of God depends on the belief that the text is somehow divine. That belief is never argued in the book, let alone justified. Unless Moses really did write the text in accord with divine instruction, it is hard to see how we can resist reason's demand for reinterpretation of the text's descriptions of God.

Second, and no less important, the conviction that Israel's is a "corporeal election" transmitted from generation to generation by the organs of generation rather than a "spiritual election" dependent upon observance of the covenant raises obvious empirical and moral dilemmas. Are Jews really one race? Are non–Jews so utterly beyond the covenant? Wyschogrod observes: "What, now, of those not elected? Those not elected cannot be expected not to be hurt by not being of the seed of Abraham, whom God loves above all others. The Bible depicts clearly the suffering of Esau. . . . The consolation of the gentiles is the knowledge that God also stands in relationship with them in the recognition and affirmation of their uniqueness."[35] Wyschogrod has preferred the minority view of election in Judaism—associated with Yehudah Halevi, the Maharal of Prague, and the Kabbalah—over the predominant stream represented by Maimonides and Mendelsson. It is as if he wants to shout to the Jews described (and accommodated) by Borowitz: You are bound, like it or not, to an eternal covenant. Its mark is imprinted on your flesh. You cannot escape it. There is no meaning to your life—or being itself—outside the reach of Hashem. Embrace your destiny! Any other option—all the options preferred by reason and recommended on grounds of social acceptability—means suicide.

David Hartman

The polar opposite to Wyschogrod's book in virtually every respect except the shared centrality of covenant is David Hartman's *A Living Covenant: The Innovative Spirit in Traditional Judaism* (1985). Hartman, now an Israeli, writes that his attempt to articulate a "covenantal anthropology" stressing human freedom and adequacy grew out of his experience of American pluralism, his graduate work among the Jesuits at Fordham, and his conviction that secularism can be the framework for meaningful life and rigorous ethical commitment. It also emerged from the reality of Israeli society—a feature that separates him from all the other theologians considered in the present article.[36] Hartman has "Halakhah" and "Aggadah" in the sense discussed earlier: a communal reality in which to live and on which to reflect. That reality has affected his thinking decisively.

One should note, before considering his views, that the subject of Israel is virtually absent from American Jewish theology.[37] That is not to say that the state does not matter, and matter deeply, to American Jews, including the theologians. Israel's existence, however, has had no major impact on Jewish religious life here. Some synagogues celebrate Israel Independence Day, and many recite a prayer for the state; sermons, now as before, are full of Israel's troubles and achievements. But Israel has not seriously altered religious observance and is not a topic for American Jewish thought except (as we will see below) in the context of the Holocaust. The sacredness of space—a prominent theme in current Israeli thought—is an alien notion to American thinkers content with Heschel's dictum that Judaism sanctifies time and not space. The possibility that our time is witnessing the first footsteps of the Messiah—as some in Israel forcefully contend—tends to frighten American Jewish thinkers rather than to receive serious consideration.

Hartman sets out to counter both the excessive zealotry of the Israeli messianists and the ethereal quality of much Diaspora thought with a call to collective covenantal responsibility. Sinai, not Exodus, is his paradigmatic event, and Sinai is interpreted as a divine "invitation" to partnership and intimacy rather than as an act of dictatorial command. Hartman's favored metaphor, in fact, is neither the suzerainty covenant nor the parity treaty but the marriage vow. God and Israel need each other. Only their partnership can bring *mitzvot* into the world. The covenant, far from precluding human initiative, creativity, and freedom, presumes it at every turn. Tradition does not merely allow innovation, it demands it. God counts on Israel's participation in the building of His kingdom. Jews freely accept this invitation because they love God and appreciate the meaningfulness of the life shaped by God's commandments.[38]

Hartman's thrust is twofold. First, he is carrying forward a theological agenda begun in our era by Soloveitchik and the Israeli thinker Yeshayahu Leibowitz, both of them inspired by Hartman's principal teacher: Maimonides. The stress falls on human activism, the centrality of human reason, the role of human initiative and creativity, the dignity of halakhic observance—all this in contrast to Christian (and classical Reform Jewish) depictions of the Halakhah as rote behavior under a burdensome yoke. Hartman rejects Soloveitchik's call for a degree of submissiveness and resignation in the face of divine decrees. Covenantal activism, he writes, enabled the rabbis (and enables us) to counter and contain the experience of life's tragedy and terror.[39] Similarly, Hartman adopts Leibowitz's call for halakhic creativity while rejecting his restriction of the covenant to halakhic observance. The total human being is required, Hartman writes—precisely as he or she is required in a marriage.[40] Nothing less will do. Eloquently and with characteristic passion, Hartman argues the case for human adequacy, human reason, and Jewish openness to the wider world.

This points to the second task undertaken in the book: the attempt to redirect the religious understanding of Israeli society. On the one hand, Hartman seeks to break down the dichotomy between *dati* (religious) and *lo dati* (secular), not by the creation of a middle ground but by the encouragement of mutual respect. Secular readers are brought to see a halakhic life which insists upon innovation and open–mindedness. Religious readers are challenged in their assumption that faith and it alone can provide a foundation for ethics or a life ultimate meaning. Hartman offers *a* covenant, not *the* covenant. He urges his readers, religious and secular alike, to see their shared history not as Exodus, i.e., divine manipulation, but as Sinai: an opportunity to actualize the covenant in an entire community. Borowitz, in the American context, can speak of ethics and ritual; Orthodox colleagues in America can call for greater halakhic observance; Hartman, as an Israeli, can discuss a Jewish society and culture. A thinker who does "not wish to divide my world into two separate realms, one of which is characterized by autonomous action based upon human understanding of the divine norm and the other by anticipation of and dependence upon divine intervention" requires an arena in which human beings can "unite the two realms and exercise autonomous action."[41] Israeli is that realm.

One wonders whether the split between *dati* and *lo dati* can be overcome in this manner, even on the level of theory. If God really is present in our world, how ignore that presence with impunity? If God really did command Israel at Sinai, how can disobedience to His commands be taken as morally neutral? And if both these claims are in fact delusions, their consequences pernicious, how could one possibly remain placid or indifferent? Hartman's generosity, like his equanimity, seems difficult to maintain. He purchases them by robbing both secularism and faith of potent energies, and not a little profundity.

There is a related problem with Hartman's model that seems even more intractable. As we have seen, he rejects the division of his world into one realm "characterized by autonomous action based upon human understanding of the divine norm" and a second realm in which human beings await, in dependence, the "divine intervention." Hartman rather "prefers to see God's will...as channeled exclusively through the efforts of the Jewish community to achieve the aims of the Torah given at Sinai."[42] But what happens when the awesome realities of God's presence intrude uninvited upon personal and collective life? What are we to do with the human failure and self–destructiveness which so often preclude fulfillment of covenantal responsibility? The effort to keep fear and trembling outside the bounds of covenant may be futile; moreover, it may rob the life of *mitzvah* of much pathos and passion. Hartman's model of covenant is adequate to some portion of human and Jewish experience, but not to the rest, in which darkness is pervasive and human adequacy far from unquestioned.

Each model of covenant proposed in the past two decades has the disadvantages of its own virtues. All attest to the difficulties which modernity has cast up before traditional belief. No less, they demonstrate the continuing resiliency of the covenant idea, despite and because of the fact that most Jews no longer feel bound by its traditional stipulations, the commandments. It seems likely that autonomy will remain precious to Jewish believers, and commandment fundamental. Covenant will therefore continue to feature prominently in Jewish theology, even as it continues to risk degeneration into cant—a traditional trope deprived of all traditional content. Like the bodily wounding which most symbolizes it, covenant will hold Jews, in large part, through the power of their own ambivalence.

God's Saving Presence—and Its Absence

American Jewish theology concerning the Holocaust falls broadly into two categories. Either the Holocaust was a unique event in human history which makes all the difference in the world to Jewish reflection—or it was not, and does not. The former claim can likewise be of two sorts: that of Richard Rubenstein, who holds that "after Auschwitz" the God of history, the God of the covenant, can no longer be affirmed, that Jewish existence is an absurd given, no more and no less meaningful than the existence of any other group of mortals in a senseless universe;[43] or one can hold, with Irving Greenberg, Emil Fackenheim, and Arthur Cohen,[44] that theological business as usual cannot continue, that existing models have been ruptured, that a "caesura" has opened in human thought and history dividing before from after Auschwitz—but that Judaism can and must go on, somehow. This latter version of the claim that the Holocaust makes all the difference borders so closely on the claim that it does not make all the difference as to make the two, to my mind at least, virtually indistinguishable. The two views are separated by a process of thought rather than its end–point; or, rather, one group insists on making the process explicit and devising new language to describe it, while the other regards the process as highly traditional and, therefore, not worthy of extended discussion. Eliezer Berkovits argues that the Holocaust is not unique, places it against the background of millennial persecution, cites the bewilderment of Job and the anger of Psalm 44—and claims that nothing has changed.[45] Fackenheim, Greenberg, and Cohen argue that everything has changed and devote many pages to explaining how, but end, like Berkovits, with the affirmation that Jewish life, Jewish obligation, the study of Torah, the service of God, must continue.

Not surprisingly, then, theological concentration on the subject has diminished of late. The point, after all, is *"To Mend the World"* (Fackenheim), not just to document its rupture; to "build a bridge over the abyss" (Cohen), not just to face up to *"The Tremendum."* As Rosenzweig, the crucial mentor of both Cohen and Fackenheim, put it at the close of *The Star of Redemption:* "into life."[46]

Richard Rubenstein

Rubenstein, in an eloquent critique of Cohen's book, summarized his own point of view most concisely. "The Holocaust renders faith in either the God of classical theism or the God of classical covenant theology exceedingly difficult," if not impossible. "Judaism makes the fundamental claim that God is uniquely concerned with the history and destiny of Israel," meaning that "the classical and logically inescapable mode of interpreting a monumental national catastrophe such as the Holocaust is that of divine punishment of a sinful people." This view of the Holocaust, Rubenstein writes, is unacceptable. Covenantal affirmation is thus precluded, and Jewish movements which strive to get around the problem are all of them unsatisfactory. Reconstructionism, proposing what Rubenstein calls "ethnic religion," fails to offer "a compelling rationale for maintaining Jewish religious identity." Zionism fails to attract most Diaspora Jews. All attempts to detach Judaism from belief in the Lord of History inevitably involve departure from the "Jewish religious mainstream." In short, Jews must choose between a God who is absent from history, "functionally irrelevant," or regard Hitler as "the instrument of an all–powerful and righteous God of history. I wish there were a credible way out of the dilemma. In the thirty years that I have spent reflecting on the Holocaust, I have yet to find it."[47]

One should note that for Rubenstein the Holocaust is not unique—far from it; its importance lies in the quandaries that it makes unavoidable in our time. In fact, Rubenstein argues, terms such as "the tremendum" are attempts to "mystify a phenomenon that can be fully comprehended in terms of the normal categories of history, social science, demography, political theory, and economics."[48] Rubenstein does not move from the Holocaust to an altered theology, therefore. He leaves God behind altogether and focuses the inquiry on the human decisions which led one group of people to persecute and then murder another. In this respect, ironically, Rubenstein is closer to Berkovits—who likewise denies the Holocaust's uniqueness, and likewise places the blame squarely on human evil rather than divine indifference—than to the theologians for whom, as for him, the Holocaust mandates a radical response.

Emil Fackenheim

Fackenheim is perhaps the best example of the latter. His earliest essays, collected in *Quest for Past and Future* (1968) and *Encounters Between Judaims and Modern Philosophy* (1973), sought to establish that the tenets of traditional faith, revelation first of all, were still philosophically respectable options. One expected, on the basis of these works, that he would proceed to a species of covenant theology more traditional than Borowitz's but, unlike Hartman's, non–halakhic. (It has in fact recently appeared, in popular form: *What Is Judaism?* [1987]). Instead, there came a break—presaging the claim that such a break is inevitable in contemporary Jewish faith as such. *God's Presence in History* (1970) laid the groundwork for Fackenheim's new direction by setting forth the two categories of "root experiences": historical events in which Jewish faith originated and "epoch–making events" that make a "new claim upon Jewish faith," testing it in light of historical experience. Exodus and Sinai are examples—probably the only ones—of the former; the destruction of the Temples, the Maccabean revolt, the expulsion from Spain, and now the Holocaust, are examples of the latter. Jewish faith had to remain open to the incursions of history if it were to remain vital, alive, true. Yet what faith could emerge from Auschwitz?[49]

In this book Fackenheim had only one reply: the "614th commandment." Jews were forbidden to hand Hitler posthumous victories. For secular Jews to abandon their people, or religious Jews their faith, would be to aid and abet the Nazis. Secular Israelis knew well what Fackenheim wished to teach: that "after the death camps, we are left only one supreme value: existence."[50] Fackenheim carried this lesson forward —particularly regarding the importance of the Jewish state—in *The Jewish Return into History* (1978). His most coherent statement, however—and his finest work of theology to date—came in *To Mend the World* (1982). The book is striking on two counts. First, it perceptively situates itself in the history of modern Jewish theology, so as to lay the "foundations for future Jewish Thought." Recognizing that one cannot do everything, Fackenheim focuses on key thinkers (Spinoza, Buber, and Rosenzweig) and confronts them with philosophical (Hegel, Heidegger) and historical (modernity, Holocaust, Israel) challenges. As Fackenheim puts it, "It is clearly necessary for Jewish thought (and not for it alone) to go to school with life."[51] Theology had to catch up with what history had wrought, and item number one in the curriculum was of course the Holocaust.

The second striking feature of the book is indeed Fackenheim's treatment of the Holocaust. Unrelentingly, and always thoughtfully, Fackenheim looks at the awful face of the facts and in that context asks "the central question of our whole inquiry . . . how Jewish (and also Christian and philosophical) thought can both expose itself to the Holocaust and survive." The ability to survive should not, he insists, be taken for granted. Fackenheim concedes that his previous, Kantian, confidence that "we can do what we ought to do" was a lapse into "unconscious glibness."[52]

Some 200 pages later, after situating Rosenzweig opposite Spinoza and Hegel, after confronting the challenge of Heidegger's philosophy and the conundrum of his support for the Nazis, and (less satisfactorily) after a highly judgmental survey of "Unauthentic Thought After the Holocaust," Fackenheim arrives at the effort of repair or *tikkun*. Resistance to Auschwitz, repair of Auschwitz, is possible now because it occurred then. German philosophers in the name of their philosophical convictions opposed the Nazis, on pain of death. Christian martyrs opposed Hitler in the name of Christianity. Jews defied him in Warsaw and elsewhere—and out of the ashes of the Holocaust created the single most important *tikkun* in the world today, the State of Israel. "The Tikkun which for the post–Holocaust Jew is a moral necessity is a possibility because during the Holocaust itself a Jewish Tikkun was already actual. This simple but enormous, nay, world–historical truth is the rock on which rests any authentic Jewish future, and any authentic future Jewish identity." Israel, the Jews' emergence from powerlessness, "has been and continues to be a moral achievement of world–historical import."[53]

The principal problem with the work, as Cohen noted in a review, is that the depiction of rupture is so convincing that the promise of repair lacks all credibility. The book, he wrote, "utterly collapses" this side of the Holocaust.[54] It is not so much that one can do what one ought to do, as that one ends up doing what one must do, what one knew all along one would do. *Tikkun* must be possible or there is no foundation of future Jewish thought, and Rubenstein's answer to Auschwitz is decisive. Fackenheim had to cross the abyss—or violate the 614th commandment. The question was never whether, but only how, he could cross. But if that is the case, if the circle of covenant must remain unbroken, how is Fackenheim different from Berkovits?

It seems that in *To Mend the World* Fackenheim has backed off somewhat from earlier unequivocal claims about the Holocaust's uniqueness. After devoting a page to a brief statement of five arguments for that uniqueness—"a complex subject that will require much space in the present work"—Fackenheim writes that "all this is by no means to deny the existence of other catastrophes equally unprecedented, and endowed with unique characteristics of their own."[55] Still, fackenheim does not proceed from the repair of one rupture to the depiction and repair of the others. Auschwitz matters in a way Hiroshima does not because Fackenheim believes in the Hegelian notion that some peoples and events are of "world–historical" significance while others are not. In the Holocaust fully one–third of the people most associated with the God of the Bible were destroyed by the people most associated in the modern period with the project of philosophy, the crowning achievement of the human spirit.[56] That claim, outside the Hegelian framework, is difficult to defend.

Even inside it, however, Cohen's charge that the rupture cannot be so speedily repaired requires an answer which Fackenheim does not provide.

Irving Greenberg

Greenberg's argument, very similar to Fackenheim's, is best expressed in an essay entitled "Cloud of Smoke, Pillar of Fire: Judaism, Christianity and Modernity After the Holocaust" (1977). He convincingly lays out the damage done to traditional notions of covenant and redemption, argues that "the Holocaust challenges the claims of all the standards that compete for modern man's loyalties" and allows no "simple, clear or definitive solutions," and then propounds one definitive principle. "No statement, theological or otherwise, should be made that would not be credible in the presence of the burning children." Greenberg proposes a "dialectical faith" which holds fast to the disbelief in divine redemption occasioned by Auschwitz but is also open to "moments when the reality of Exodus is reenacted and present." The Holocaust challenges prevailing secular conceptions no less than it does religious faith; it teaches us to recognize the dangers of powerlessness as well as of power. "The cloud of smoke of the bodies by day and the pillar of fire of the crematoria by night"—powerful relocations to Auschwitz of the biblical marks of God's presence in the wilderness—"may yet guide humanity to a goal and a day when human beings are attached to each other; and have so much shared each other's pain, and have so purified and criticized themselves, that never again will a Holocaust be possible."[57] In the meantime, Greenberg counsels return to *The Jewish Way* (1988) entailed by the covenant—apparently finding it not only credible but necessary in the face of "burning children."

Arthur Cohen

Cohen's premise is more radical; he assumes in effect, that nothing whatsoever is credible by that criterion. The question must be refocused, moved from religious observance to the classical ground of theology: the nature of God.

> My interest—first, last and always—is about the God who created the world, not the God who provided the occasion for religion. What Jews do about their religious life . . . of the conferred and optional requirements of living as Jews I can hardly speak. . . . I might almost assert as a first principle of any modern Jewish theology that it should begin by thinking without Jews in mind.

Cohen finds it necessary to undertake this effort—to engage in theology despite the fact that "there is virtually no modern Jewish theology"—because the Holocaust marked a novum, "the election of the Chosen People to be the first people in human history to be systematically annihilated. . . . Such a theological novum entails theological response."[58]

Cohen's response is as follows.[59] One must not deny either God's presence in the world or the reality of evil. God must be seen as related to every aspect of creation. God confronts us then, first of all, not as Father or King but (borrowing Rudolph Otto's classic term) as the Tremendum—a Power both awesome and mysterious. We cannot return after Auschwitz to the classic categories of Western philosophical theism. There has been a rupture, a "caesura." To repair or at least cross it, Cohen turns from the rabbis to the Kabbalah, which penetrated Western philosophy, reaching Rosenzweig and then Cohen, through the person of Schelling. "The human affect," Schelling taught,

> is toward the overflowing, the loving in God; his containment, however, the abyss of his nature, is as crucial as is his abundance and plentitude. These are the fundamental antitheses of the divine essence . . . the quiet God is as indispensable as the revealing God, the abyss as much as the plentitude, the constrained self–contained, deep divinity as the plenteous and generous.[60]

God had made room in the divine plenitude for human beings endowed with freedom and speech. The space in which we abide, in which God gives us leave to abide, is therefore full to overflowing with our "enduring strife and tension, enlarged and made threatening by our finitude," enhanced and made more dangerous by our freedom.[61]

Cohen is not seeking language adequate to God's nature. We do not have it, he believes, for reasons that his theology helps to clarify. He seeks only to be adequate to the caesura, and this he may well have achieved—at the cost of belief in the covenant as traditionally (that is, nonmystically) understood. Like the rabbis, and without explanation, Cohen affirms the unique connection between the being of the Jewish people and the being of God. There can be no explanation of that connection, he avers. We will understand the nature of "Jewish being, Jewish history, and the meaning of God's self–narration" only "when it is done and past or else completed in the last minute of redemption."[62] As Rosenzweig put it, "not yet"; the meaning is present, but not yet apparent. "Redemption" is, significantly, the final word of the book. The covenant may be broken theologically, but its observance continues despite and because of the caesura.

Silberman, concluding his survey of American Jewish theology two decades ago, wrote that confrontation with *hurban* (destruction) was the inescapable task of Jewish theology. Jewish thought could ignore Auschwitz only at its own peril.[63] Two decades later one can say that the task of confronting Auschwitz has probably been undertaken as thoroughly as possible at this juncture, and that the refusal to make the move of repair linking Cohen, Fackenheim, and Greenberg to Berkovits is to present no less a peril than the other to future Jewish thought. Survival, the 614th commandment, demands an answer to the question: survival for what, in what faith, with what obligation? Survival, if it is to be continuous with the Jewish past, entails some relationship to the 613 commandments which, according to the 614th, Jews are forbidden to abandon. The next generation of Jewish thinkers, while not entirely ignoring the Holocaust, will likely move on to efforts—dialectical or otherwise—to make sense of Jewish life, the previous generation having focused, perhaps necessarily, on the threat posed to Judaism by unprecedented Jewish death. That effort, in fact, is already under way, informed by recent currents in American society and undertaken by a new generation of theologians. We turn now to two of its most noteworthy exemplars.

Experience, Tradition, Community

It is doubtful that either of the two themes that have preoccupied American Jewish theology for the past 20 years will continue to hold center stage in the next 20. A new generation of theologians is now at work, and it has announced its intention (as did the previous generation) to reorient theological discourse rather substantially. Two reasons for that reorientation have already been noted: the problems besetting covenant theology in the absence of either a satisfactory notion of revelation or a community intent on covenantal observance; and the need—articulated even by those for whom the Holocaust has been central—to move from (or through) confrontation with the "rupture" or "caesura" of Auschwitz to *tikkun:* renewed Jewish commitment. The question becomes what sort of commitment, grounded in what authority, inside what sort of community? The answers emerging from a variety of quarters comes in terms which have not loomed large in recent decades but which have a venerable theological history in Judaism as in other faiths: experience, tradition, and community. I will illustrate this emerging trend with the work of two thinkers who will, I expect, assume increasing importance as the decade unfolds.

Arthur Green

The first is Arthur Green, president of the Reconstructionist Rabbinical College and as such the intellectual leader of Reconstructionism. Green is trying to take his movement, and American Judaism as a whole, in a new theological direction centered on the renewed religious experience of the individual believer. Green's approach was adumbrated in a 1976 address before Conservative rabbis[64] and further elaborated (albeit implicitly) in his masterly biography of Nachman of Bratslav, *Tormented Master* (1979). It has received its fullest expression to date in a programmatic essay entitled "Rethinking Theology: Language, Experience and Reality" (1988), the subtitle of which offers a précis of Green's argument.

First the matter of religious language. Green begins with "one of the great tragedies of Judaism in modern times"—the widespread perception that Judaism is "empty of, or even opposed to, the depths of individual religious experience." In fact, Green argues, Kabbalah and Hassidism have bequeathed "a rich vocabulary . . . for discussion of religious states"; the problem is that the vocabulary (as we have seen in the present essay) rarely figures in contemporary Jewish discourse. Green aims to reintroduce it, thereby helping to create "a religious language that will speak both profoundly and honestly to Jews in our time."[65] Honestly, to Green, demands that Jews admit their distance from traditional symbols and beliefs. We are necessarily both insiders and outsiders to our inheritance. Profundity connotes the effort to penetrate to the wellspring of faith deep inside every human being. We should, like Hassidism, seek "spiritual wakefulness and awareness . . . cultivation of the inner life." Judaism does not so much demand leaps of faith as intensity of vision. The path does not lie in more adequate theories of revelation, but more penetrating searchings of the soul.[66]

The key, in other words, is experience. All human beings know transcendence at some moments of their lives. Religion exists to "make constant, or at least regular, [the] level of insight that has already existed in moments of spontaneous flash," and to design ways of life appropriate to the illuminations that transcendence provides.[67] Like his teacher Abraham Heschel (albeit in language more attuned to the counterculture of the 1960s), Green begins with wonder, awe, transcendence—"we praise before we prove," as Heschel put it—and only then moves to God, whom Heschel regarded as the only satisfactory "answer" to the "questions" made imperative by our wonder. Green's understanding of God, however, diverges from Heschel considerably and—ironically enough, given the Hassidic language in which it is couched—brings Green remarkably close to the teaching of Mordecai Kaplan. "YHWH is, in short, all of being, but so unified and concentrated as to become Being." God is "the universe . . . so utterly transformed by integration and unity as to appear to us as indeed 'other,' a mirror of the universe's self that becomes Universal Self." God is "none 'other' than we ourselves and the world in which we live, transformed as part of the transcendent vision."[68] Kaplan, I think, could have assented to all of these formulations, and certainly to Green's caveat that "the figure of God imaged by most religion is a human projection."[69]

Where the two thinkers would differ, perhaps, is on Green's belief that human beings need to pray to God, that psychology should not be employed to explain away "supernaturalism" but rather to underline its importance as a mode of expression. In his words, "'God' is in that sense a symbol, a human creation that we need to use in order to illuminate for ourselves, however inadequately, some tiny portion of the infinite mystery." And, besides, "our imagination, we should always remember, is itself a figment of divinity."[70]

It is clear from the quotations just cited that Green's God is far from the real personal God encountered by Heschel or Buber. Green's notion of *mitzvot* must therefore be different as well; the idea of divine covenant is utterly inapplicable. *Mitzvot* enter Green's Judaism from two directions. "The religious life is a life lived in constant striving for this awareness [of relation to the transcendent] and in response to the demands made by it." And we turn to Judaism for the pattern of that striving and response, "not because it is the superior religion, and certainly not because it is God's single will, but because it is our own...our spiritual home." Green prefers the "tradition in its most whole and authentic form" because "traditions work best when they are least diluted. . . . Serious Judaism means serious engagement with *mitzvot*."[71]

This statement of the Jewish religious situation is, I would suggest, remarkable in more ways than one—not least in its adaptation of Kaplan to the very different cultural milieu of the 1990s. "Such a religious viewpoint" is indeed, as Green claims, "that of mystic and naturalist at once."[72] Moreover, Green may well articulate the assumptions of a large number of contemporary American Jews (particularly intellectuals), just as Kaplan did for the generation of the 1930s. Note that the vision starts and ends with self: the experience of transcendence, the search for God leading "through our deepest and most pained emotional selves,"[73] the turn to tradition because it fulfills that quest in a "whole" and "authentic" form. This is not to accuse Green of narcissism. Quite the opposite. He has simply worked with, and for, the prevailing reality of Jewish life which Kaplan urged upon his readers over half a century ago: namely, that Judaism will either be a palpable source of meaning, enriching life in tangible ways, or Jews will not choose to accord it a central place in their lives. Moreover, like Kaplan, Green has sought to encourage that move to Judaism by couching it in language which does not challenge prevailing conceptions of reality and by deemphasizing claims of guilt or obligation. *Mitzvot* deepen life, heighten awareness, proffer the authenticity available only (or most readily) in one's natural "spiritual home"—and necessitate community. One discovers the self, and so God, when one joins with other searchers who share one's language, one's "spiritual home," one's life. "Our 'liberal' views should not serve as a cloak for cavalier desertion or disdain of our traditions," Green writes.[74] The force of that "should not" bears attention: not because God has willed it, nor even because our ancestors have covenanted with God in a way which binds us, but because what we seek in and for ourselves is achievable through no other route than "serious engagement with *mitzvot*."

Judith Plaskow

A similar appeal to experience, grounded still more powerfully in the life of a particular community of Jews, underlies Judith Plaskow's groundbreaking effort to formulate a feminist Jewish theology. If the history of Judaism written to date largely ignores the role played by women; if the tradition's classical texts were written by and for men, according little space to female characters and evincing little interest in female consciousness; if the founding moment of the Jewish people, the covenant at Sinai described in Exodus 19, excluded women entirely (the injunction "do not go near a woman" seems to indicate that "Moses addresses the community only as men")—then, asks Plaskow, where is a woman to find entrée to this tradition? How is she to appropriate it, carry it forward? Jewish women can either "choose to accept our absence from Sinai, in which case we allow the male text to define us and our relationship to the tradition," or they can "stand on the ground of our experience, on the certainty of our membership in our own people."[75]

Note that the authority invoked to correct and supplement the "partial record of the 'God wrestling' of part of the Jewish people"—Plaskow's understanding of Torah[76]—is experience: Plaskow's, her community's, and that of the readers to whom she appeals. Accepting that authority, one can "begin the journey toward the creation of a feminist Judaism." All interpretation relies upon experience to some degree, of course. One reads the text into and out of the world as one has come to know it. One adapts tradition to reality and reality to tradition. In Plaskow's work, however, the role of experience is necessarily greater—because of the perceived lack of female consciousness and presence in the tradition that she wishes to adapt.

Plaskow's book *Standing at Sinai* (1990) draws upon efforts by Jewish feminists over the past two decades to create new midrash, design new rituals, and explore areas of Jewish history previously untouched, weaving them into the first systematic effort at feminist Jewish theology. After a quite sophisticated methodological introduction, Plaskow proceeds to take up each of the three topics in the classic triad—Torah, Israel, and God, adding a fourth discussion (sexuality), which is apparently central to feminist theology but which seems far less accomplished than the others. We shall focus here on several points which seem to presage the emergence of a new orientation for American Jewish theology.

First, already noted, the appeal to experience—here, in the feminist context, an experience neither purely personal nor purely human but rather gender–specific and communal. Plaskow is sophisticated enough methodologically to avoid the trap of appeal to a putative feminine mind or sensibility unified in itself and easily distinct from the masculine. She relies instead on the reasonable claim that women's experiences, however diverse they may be, have found little expression in Judaism thus far. The few women present in classical texts are either condemned outright or given short shrift; this has given rise in recent decades to a widespread feminist experience of exclusion from the tradition, suspicion of it, disenchantment with it. Plaskow also can point, however, to powerful experiences of transcendence—her own and those of others—which have engendered deep connection to the tradition. The community of feminists in which those experiences occurred becomes, for Plaskow, a point of reference in deciding the direction of feminist Judaism; it becomes, in a word, her authority.

> To say that this community is my central source of authority is not to deny the range of ideas or disagreements within it, or the other communities of which I am part. It is simply to say that I have been formed in important ways by Jewish feminism; without it I could not see the things that I see. It is to say that my most important experiences of God have come through this community, and that it has given me the language with which to express them. To name this community my authority is to call it the primary community to which I am accountable.[77]

Buber said that one carries forward that part of the tradition which speaks to one with "inner power." Kaplan stressed the role of the Jewish people in constantly redefining Judaism in accord with their highest ideals. Plaskow is less subjective than Buber, less universal than Kaplan, but like them she has dispensed with the need for revealed authority, in the belief that it is nowhere to be found. Community is all one has. It is, in fact, all one needs. "The experience of God in community is both the measure of the adequacy of traditional language and the norm in terms of which new images must be fashioned."[78]

Plaskow realizes that "to locate authority in particular communities of interpreters is admittedly to make a circular appeal."[79] Group X of Jews defines Torah as it does, on the grounds that—Group X has experienced it this way. Yet this circularity "has always been the case. . . . When the rabbis said that rabbinic modes of interpretation were given at Sinai, they were claiming authority for their own community—just as other groups had before them, just as feminists do today."[80] This claim of similarity to the rabbis, the second to which I wish to draw attention, features prominently throughout the book. It links Plaskow's work to a principal current both in recent Jewish theology and in philosophy more generally, namely: the argument that quests for objective authority will always be futile; that there is no ultimate foundation for any worldview or ethical system; that the most one can hope for is a community committed to certain norms and the view of reality that undergirds them; that one must define and fashion tradition as one goes. Time and again Plaskow argues that no other authority than one's community is available—and never was.

Hence her use of the rabbis as a role model, horrified as they might have been by the comparison. They too, after all, "expanded Scripture to make it relevant to their own times," they too "brought to the Bible their own questions and found answers that showed the eternal relevance of biblical truth."[81] The issue of revelation, which has so bedeviled Jewish theology in the modern period is sidestepped entirely here. One need not ask what is true, but only what authentically carries on the tradition. One leaves the answer to the decision of Jewish communities.

The thrust here, as one would expect in a feminist theology, is radically egalitarian. Plaskow expresses even more discomfort with the idea of the chosen people than Kaplan had and no inclination whatever to sneak the doctrine in with euphemisms such as mission or vocation. Plaskow utterly rejects "Judaism's long history of conceptualizing difference in terms of hierarchical separations,"[82] and her suspicion of hierarchy extends not only horizontally (Israel's relation to the nations) but vertically (its relation to God). She rejects the "image of God as dominating Other," criticizing a "relationship [that] is never balanced," in which "the intimacy of the 'you' addressed to a listening other is overshadowed by the image of the lord and king of the universe who is absolute ruler on a cosmic plane." Plaskow goes so far as to claim that "such images of God's dominance give rise to the terribly irony that the symbols Jews have used to talk about God as ultimate good have helped generate and justify the evils from which we hope God will save us." She prefers feminine or gender–neutral images of bountiful nature, of community, of "God as lover and friend."[83] The chapter on God concludes as follows: "In speaking of the moving, changing ground and source, our companion and our lover, we name toward the God known in community that cherishes diversity within and without, even as that diversity has its warrant in the God of myriad names."[84]

It would appear that more than feminist antagonism to "patriarchalism" is at work here. Plaskow is carrying forward the democratization of "God talk" evident throughout the modern period, never more so than in America in recent decades. The redefinitions of covenant surveyed earlier represent an attempt to reconcile traditional belief in the "master of the universe" with the growing self–importance of humanity in the age of science. Soloveitchik, in his famous essay "The Lonely Man of Faith" (1965), correctly saw the Adam I of majesty and honor standing in tension with the Adam II of covenantal relationship,[85] Borowitz only testified further to the tension with his reinterpretation of the covenant so as to make ample room for autonomy, and Hartman provided still more evidence with his reconception of the covenant as an egalitarian marriage bond (not at all like the marriage bonds pictured in, say, Hosea!). Recent Jewish theology, in short, seems content to imagine God as all of Being (Green), and is eager to reconnect alienated modern selves with that Being within and without them. But there is growing evidence of a disinclination to accept a God who has mastery over individual or collective life, who stands over against us as a real, personal deity demanding obedience—and having the right to it, because God is God, and we are not. Only Wyschogrod in the 1980s ventured the claim. One suspects that it will find few exponents in the 1990s, barring an Orthodox successor to the theological mantle of Soloveitchik.

Conclusion

There is reason to believe that Jewish theologians in the coming decades—whatever their denominational affiliation—will be more likely to engage in a combination of the strategies evinced by Green and Plaskow. They will probably move away from personalist conceptions of God in favor of neo–mystical formulations that ring true to contemporary experience of the transcendent. Cohen's turn to Kabbalah is a case in point. Efforts to demonstrate God's presence in history will continue unavailing; convincing answers to why "bad things happen to good people"[86] now, as ever, will continue unavailable. Revelation will not be easily reconceived. The authority for covenant, more and more, will probably be the experience of meaning which the covenant provides. "Voluntarism" and "creativity" will be paramount concerns. Authority will reside within the subcommunity of Jews with which one identifies, rather than in any given, objective set of norms binding the Jewish people, ever and always, as a whole.[87]

If the experience of personal transcendence within such subcommunities is powerful enough to resist dismissal as illusion, higher authority than this may well prove unnecessary, at least in the short run. Jews will likely continue in their present tendency of seeking tradition rather than faith—"sacred fragments" of meaning rather than entire systems of truth. If theologians find meaning in engagement with texts no matter whether they are divinely authored or even inspired, and find transcendence in rituals no matter how literal their status as divine commandment, they are unlikely to devote serious effort to proving the authority of text or ritual. It will be enough to demonstrate their profundity, their groundedness in what Gillman would call Jewish myth, their centrality to what Green would call Jews' spiritual home, their place in the lived experience of a community such as Plaskow's. It will be enough to postulate some reality underlying the various images we have of God, some link between the life we lead as Jews and the nature of ultimate reality. More than this may not be required, and so it will not be forthcoming.

The extent of this tendency should not be exaggerated. Theologians may reject Green's theology as they did Kaplan's, preferring to work with more traditional terms even if they cannot assent to them entirely. They may prove suspicious of the appeal to experience, particularly when religious experience among the highly rationalist, upper–middle–class American Jewish community is if anything even rarer than belief. There is no doubt, however, that appeal to "tradition" (rather than, say, "ethics" or "Halakhah") is now widespread, from moderate Reform on the "left" to modern Orthodoxy on the "right," and no doubt either than the entrance of women into the center of Jewish religious activity—ordained as rabbis, fashioning new rituals, composing new liturgy, and now writing new theology—presages a major shift in the character of American Jewish thought. Given the waning of focus on the Holocaust and the problems besetting covenant theology, the sheer energy underlying feminist theology and the existence of a substantial readership for that theology mean that its role in American Jewish theology as a whole will only increase in coming decades, and will probably increase dramatically.

If in conclusion we were to pose for the next two decades the question that Borowitz asked 20 years ago—the "problem of the form of a Jewish theology"—the answer would seem to be that American thinkers are likely to follow the example of Irving Greenberg's *The Jewish Way* or the acclaimed collection of essays *Back to the Sources* (1986), edited by Barry Holtz. They are likely, that is, to prefer exposition of the meaning to be found in the cycle of the Jewish year over systematic statement of the truth or essence of Judaism; they will turn to modern midrash, examples of how to read traditional texts, with no reading claiming exclusive truth or correctness, rather than to interpretations that claim to give the authoritative account of "Judaism for the modern Jew." The advantage of the former approaches is apparent. One circumvents the problems of revelation that no theologian in the modern period has yet managed to solve, at the same time as one provides what readers, lay and theologically sophisticated both seem to want. One does not argue for Jewish commitment, at least openly, but rather presumes it—and then suggests content for that commitment. The work of theology takes its place alongside literary criticism, anthropology, psychology, and so forth, much as Rashi greets us on a page of *Midra'to Gedolot* alongside Ramban and Ibn Ezra.[88]

The project of going "beyond Buber and Rosenzweig," then, may well lead American Jewish thinkers to explicit embrace—without apology—of the fragmentary forms which their immediate predecessors had seemed to adopt of necessity: responsa and commentary, essay and homily; fragments of Halakhah—Jewish "life lived," and of Aggadah—Jewish life reflected upon. They will offer *divrei torah*, words of Torah, along with designs for communities in which these words can be heard. And they will hope, somehow, that it will be enough to carry Jews forward to a time when acts of faith once again come more wholly and more easily.

Notes

[1]Eugene Borowitz, "The Problem of the Form of a Jewish Theology," *Hebrew Union College Annual*, 40–41 (1969–1970): 391.

[2]Neil Gillman, *Sacred Fragments: Recovering Theology for the Modern Jew* (Philadelphia, 1990) xv–xxvii. For a brief review of Gillman's work, and of others which figure in the present essay, see David Ellsenson, "The Continued Renewal of North American Jewish Theology: Some Recent Works," *Journal of Reform Judaism* (Winter 1991): 1–16.

[3]Emil Fackenheim, *To Mend the World: Foundations of Future Jewish Thought* (New York, 1982) 7.

[4]Lou H. Silberman, "Concerning Jewish Theology: Some Notes on a Decade," AJYB, 70 (1969): 37–58.

⁵For accounts of this outpouring in recent years, see Jack Wertheimer, "Recent Trends in American Judaism," AJYB, 89 (1989): 63–162; and Arnold Eisen, "American Judaism: Changing Patterns in Denominational Self–Definition," *Studies in Contemporary Jewry*, 8 (1991). For more general overviews of American Jewish thought in recent decades, see Arnold Eisen, *The Chosen People in America* (Bloomington, 1983); and Robert G. Goldy, *The Emergence of Jewish Theology in America* (Bloomington, 1990).

⁶See Arnold Eisen, "Covenant," in *Contemporary Jewish Religious Thought*. ed. Arthur A. Cohen and Paul Mendes–Flohr (New York, 1987) 107–12. An accessible account of how the idea of covenant figures in seminal modern thinkers is Eugene Borowitz, *Choices in Modern Jewish Thought: A Partisan Guide* (New York, 1983).

⁷Cf. the definition of theology as "the study of God and the relation between God and the universe." *Webster's New World Dictionary of the American Language*, College ed. (Cleveland, 1958) 1511.

⁸The principal exception to this generalization is Franz Rosenzweig's *The Star of Redemption*, trans. William Hallo (Boston, 1985)—but even Rosenzweig has far more to say about revelation and redemption than creation.

⁹Cf. Gillman, *Sacred Fragments*, xx, and Michael Wyschogrod, *The Body of Faith: Judaism as Corporeal Election* (New York, 1983) xiii.

¹⁰The argument is made, for example, by Robert Gordis, long an intellectual leader of the Conservative movement, who writes that "in its pragmatic approach and its distrust of abstract theory, [Conservative Judaism] is characteristically American in spirit." See Robert Gordis, *Conservative Judaism: An American Philosophy* (New York, 1945) 11.

¹¹For two surveys of these developments, see Sidney Ahlstrom, *A Religious History of the American People* (New Haven, 1972), particularly chaps. 18–19, 37–38, 55–56; and William G. McLoughlin and Robert N. Bellah, eds., *Religion in America* (Boston, 1968).

¹²Here I expand upon the analysis in Arnold Eisen, "Theology, Sociology, Ideology," *Modern Judaism*, vol. 2, (1982) 98–102.

¹³See John Murray Cuddihy, *No Offense: Civil Religion and Protestant Taste* (New York, 1978); and Arthur Hertzberg, "America Is Different," in Arthur Hertzberg, Martin E. Marty, and Joseph N. Moody, *The Outbursts That Await Us* (New York, 1963) 121–81; and Arthur Hertzberg, *The Jews in America* (New York, 1989) 350–88.

¹⁴Rosenzweig, *Star of Redemption*, 298–379.

¹⁵Joseph Soloveitchik, "Confrontation," *Tradition* (Winter 1964): 18–23.

¹⁶Jacob Neusner, "The Tasks of Theology in Judaism: A Humanistic Program," *Journal of Religion*, 59/1 (Jan. 1979): 72–82.

¹⁷That is not to say, of course, that American Jews have not engaged in religious reflection of very high quality. They have. But this reflection has taken shape within genres—essays, legal responsa, homilies, and historical research—which demand analyses of a different sort. For one such analysis, see Eisen, "American Judaism" (cited in note 5). *Tradition* (published by the organization of modern Orthodox rabbis) often features sophisticated legal responsa and philosophical reflection on the nature and validity of Jewish law, while *Conservative Judaism* and the *Journal of Reform Judaism* tend to favor aggadic essays, debates on topical issues such as feminism or homosexuality, and analyses of Judaism in terms of disciplines such as anthropology and literary criticism. The Conservative movement has also given rise to impressive reflection on the nature (and legitimate revision) of Halakhah. See, for example, Elliot Dorff and Arthur Rosett, *A Living Tree: The Roots and Growth of Jewish Law* (Albany, 1988); Joel Roth, *The Halakhic Process: A Systemic Analysis*

(New York, 1986); and David Novak, *Law and Theology in Judaism* (New York, 1974). For a comparable work by a leading modern Orthodox thinker, see Eliezer Berkovits, *Not in Heaven: The Nature and Function of Halakha* (New York, 1983). I would call attention, finally, to Simon Greenberg's collection of essays, *A Jewish Philosophy and Pattern of Life* (New York, 1981), which—along with two volumes published previously, *Foundations of a Faith* (1967) and *The Ethical in the Jewish and American Heritage* (1977)—constitutes and most sustained attempt by an American rabbi since Mordecai Kaplan to provide a philosophy of Jewish living in America. Efforts such as these are probably far more influential on American Jewish belief and observance than the theological works analyzed in the present essay—but they will not be treated here, for reasons which I hope I have made clear.

[18]Van a. Harvey, "The Alienated Theologian," *McCormick Quarterly*, 23 (May 1970): 234–65.

[19]On this issue, see Arnold Eisen, "Secularization, 'Spirit,' and the Strategies of Modern Jewish Faith," in *Jewish Spirituality: From the Sixteenth–Century Revival to the Present*, ed. Arthur Green (New York, 1987) 283–316; and Peter Berger, *The Heretical Imperative* (Garden City, 1980).

[20]Borowitz, "Problem of Form," 391.

[21]Fackenheim, *To Mend the World*, chap. 1.

[22]Gillman, *Sacred Fragments*.

[23]He is, for example, the author of the movement's most recent statement of principles and of an accompanying text of explanation. See Eugene Borowitz, *Reform Judaism Today* (New York, 1978). Lawrence Hoffman calls Borowitz the principal theological influence upon the new Reform *siddur*, *Gates of Prayer* (New York, 1975). See Lawrence Hoffman, ed., *Gates of Understanding* (New York, 1977) 6.

[24]Eugene Borowitz, *Liberal Judaism* (New York, 1984) 129–36.

[25]Ibid., 125

[26]On the Conservative dilemmas, see Eisen, "American Judaism," as well as the classic treatment by Marshall Sklare in *Conservative Judaism: An American Religious Movement* (New York, 1972).

[27]Irving Greenberg, *The Voluntary Covenant* (New York, 1982).

[28]Ibid., 16–28.

[29]Ibid., 17.

[30]Wyschogrod, *Body of Faith*, chap. 1.

[31]Ibid., xv.

[32]Ibid.

[33]Ibid., chaps. 4–5.

[34]Ibid., 144, 172.

[35]Ibid., 64.

[36]David Hartman, *A Living Covenant: The Innovative Spirit in Traditional Judaism* (New York, 1985) 12.

[37]On this matter, see Arnold Eisen, *Galut: Modern Jewish Reflection on Homelessness and Homecoming* (Bloomington, 1986) 156–74.

[38]Hartman, *Living Covenant* 1–8, 22–59.

[39]Ibid., chaps. 3–4.

[40]Ibid., chap. 5.

[41]Ibid., 232–33. See also 148.

[42]Ibid., 232–33.

[43]Richard Rubenstein, *After Auschwitz: Radical Theology and Contemporary Judaism* (Indianapolis, 1966).

[44]Irving Greenberg, "Cloud of Smoke, Pillar of Fire: Judaism, Christianity, and Modernity After the Holocaust," in *Auschwitz: Beginning of a New Era?* ed. Eva Fleischner (New York, 1977) 7–55; Emil Fackenheim, *God's Presence in History* (New York 1970) and *To Mend the World*; Arthur A. Cohen, *The Tremendum: A Theological Interpretation of the Holocaust* (New York, 1981).

[45]Eliezer Berkovits, *Faith After the Holocaust* (New York, 1973) and *With God in Hell* (New York, 1979).

[46]Rosenzweig, *Star of Redemption*, 424.

[47]Richard Rubenstein, "Naming the Unnameable; Thinking the Unthinkable (A Review Essay of Arthur Cohen's *The Tremendum*)," *Journal of Reform Judaism* 31 (Spring, 1984): 43–49.

[48]Ibid., 51–54.

[49]Fackenheim, *God's Presence*, 3–31.

[50]Ibid., 79–98.

[51]Fackenheim, *To Mend the World*, p. 15.

[52]Ibid., 24, 200.

[53]Ibid., 300–304.

[54]Arthur A. Cohen, "On Emil Fackenheims' *To Mend the World:* A Review Essay," *Modern Judaism*, 3 (May 1983): 231–35.

[55]Fackenheim, *To Mend the World*, 12–13.

[56]I own this insight to Michael Morgan—but bear full responsibility for its formulation.

[57]Greenberg, "Cloud of Smoke." The quotation is found on 55.

[58]Arthur A. Cohen, "On Theological Method: A Response on Behalf of *The Tremendum,"* *Journal of Reform Judaism*, 31 (Spring 1984): 56–63.

[59]Cohen, *The Tremendum*. See especially chaps. 3–4.

[60]Ibid., 90.

[61]Ibid., 92–94.

[62]Ibid., 110.

[63]Silberman, "Jewish Theology," 58.

[64]Arthur Green, "The Role of Jewish Mysticism in a Contemporary Theology of Judaism," *Conservative Judaism*, Summer 1976, 10–23.

[65]Arthur Green, "Rethinking Theology: Language, Experience and Reality," *The Reconstructionist* (Sept. 1988): 8–9.

[66]Ibid., 9–10.

[67]Ibid.

[68]Ibid., 10–11. For Heschel's view, see particularly *Man Is Not Alone* (New York, 1951) chaps. 1–9; for Kaplan's, see *The Meaning of God in Modern Jewish Religion* (New York, 1962) and Eisen, *Chosen People in America*, chap. 4.

[69]Green, "Rethinking Theology," 11.

[70]Ibid., 12.

[71]Ibid., 10, 13.

[72]Ibid., 11.

[73]Ibid., 12.

[74]Ibid., 13.

[75]Judith Plaskow, "Standing Again at Sinai: Jewish Memory from a Feminist Perspective," *Tikkun*, 1/2 (1986): 28.

[76]Ibid., 29.

[77]Judith Plaskow, *Standing Again at Sinai: Judaism from a Feminist Perspective* (San Francisco, 1990) 19–21.

[78]Ibid., 122.

[79]Ibid., 21.

[80]Ibid.

[81]Ibid., 35, 53.

[82]Ibid., 96.

[83]Ibid., 128–69.

[84]Ibid., 169.

[85]Joseph Soloveitchik, "The Lonely Man of Faith," *Tradition* (Summer 1965): 5–67.

[86]Harold S. Kushner, *When Bad Things Happen to Good People* (New York, 1983).

[87]For a Conservative statement of this position, see Elliot Dorff, *Conservative Judaism: Our Ancestors to Our Descendants* (New York, 1977), and "Towards a Legal Theory of Conservative Judaism," *Conservative Judaism* (Summer 1973): 76–77.

[88]These features of the "market" for Jewish thought in America probably account for the prevalence of introductory volumes such as Emil Fackenheim's *What Is Judaism?* (New York, 1988), Borowitz's *Choices in Modern Jewish Thought*, or even Gillman's *Sacred Fragments*—which concludes with a chapter entitled "Doing Your Own Theology." That is possible for the average reader, of course, only given an understanding of the enterprise radically at variance with the one assumed in the present essay.

Part Four
A Closing Affirmation

Chapter 10

Judaism in the Secular Age

Jacob Neusner

Professor Harvey Cox defines secularization as "the movement of man's primary interest and attention from other worlds beyond or above this one and to this world. This includes the loosing of this world from its dependency on mythical, meta-physical, or religious dualism of any sort. It means, therefore taking this earthly realm, with all its health and hope, with all its sickness and sin, in utter seriousness."[1] What is the meaning of the new age for Jews, for Judaism's relationships to the world, and to Christianity?

Secularization and the Jews

No religion may be adequately compared to another. Each has its particularities which render comparison a distortion. Judaism cannot be compared to Christianity, for example, as if each component of the one had its functional or structural equivalent in the other. Christians understand by "religion" a rather different phenomenon, for it seems to Jews, perhaps wrongly, that Christians lay far greater stress upon theology and matters of belief as normative and probative than does Judaism. A Christian is such by baptism or conversion, by being called out into a new and sacred vocation of faith. A Jew is never *not* a Jew according to Jewish law. He is *born* into the Jewish situation. There was never a time that he was a man but not a Jew. There can be no time when he will cease to be a Jew, for, as the Talmud says, though he sin, he remains "Israel." The Jewish ethnic group is never perceived by Jewish theology to be a secular entity, therefore, and therein lies the root of much misunderstanding. Christians speak of "secular Jews," by which they mean Jews divorced from the profession of Jewish faith and the practice of the *mitzvot*. But Judaism does not, and cannot, regard such Jews as "secular," for they are all children of Abraham, Isaac and

*Previously published in *Judaism in the Secular Age: Essays on Fellowship, Community, and Freedom.* Copyright 1970, KTAV Publishing House, Inc. Used by permission.

Jacob. Their forefathers stood at Sinai and bound them for all time by the terms of a contract to do and hear the word of God. That contract has never been abrogated, and though individuals may forget it, its Maker can never forget them. A Jew who does not keep the Covenant still has its imprint engraved in his flesh. His children do not require conversion if they choose to assume its responsibilities. The world, moreover, has understood the indelibility of the covenant, for it has persisted in regarding as Jews many who regard themselves as anything but Jewish; and it has murdered the seed of Abraham into the third generation.

These remarks by no means represent the universal judgement of the Jewish community, which has mostly lost a theological understanding of itself. The larger part of Jewry regards being Jewish—"Jewishness"—as mostly an ethnic affiliation, and prefers to understand that affiliation in a this–worldly and secular way. Judaism, that is, the corpus of Jewish tradition from Biblical and Talmudic times onward, has a very different view, one more familiar to educated Christians from their studies of religious history, but less familiar from contemporary observation. It should be clear that I understand Jewish existence within the norm of classical Jewish theology. We are a people called forth to constitute a kingdom of priests and a holy nation, to serve as God's suffering servant and to bear upon ourselves the burden of humanity. Our collective vocation began with the call to Abraham, Isaac, and Jacob, carried us to Sinai, and will at the end of days reach fulfillment. "Secular" Jews do not see things this way, but however they see themselves this is, I believe, how Judaism sees *them*.

It is a fact, moreover, that Jews quite alien to the Torah retain a very vivid sense of being part of a historical, if not of a supernatural, community. They yearn to see their children marry other Jews, though this may represent no more, in the eyes of the world, than an ethnic loyalty. They insist that their children associate with other Jews, even though association may have what Christians will regard as a wholly secular setting. But Judaism cannot regard the Jewish group as a secular enterprise, as I said, for it advances a very different view of what it means to be a Jew. It lays great stress upon community, upon the chain of the generations, upon birth within the covenant. As Professor Monford Harris writes: "The secularized Gentile is precisely that: a secularized Gentile. But the secularized Jew is still a Jew. The Jew that sins is still a Jew, still a member of the covenantal Israel, even when he denies that covenant."[2] One cannot stress that fact too much: *there can be no Judaism without Jewishness*, that is, without ethnic identification. Judaism cannot be reduced to its "essence," whether that be construed as ethical, theological, or even behavioral. We know full well that there can be Jewishness without Judaism, and against this many of us struggle within the Jewish community. In our effort to keep the issues of Judaism to the fore, we may criticize the ethnic emphasis of the community as it is. But we struggle within that community precisely because it is what it is: all that is left of the remnant of Israel in this world. Its worldliness is a challenge. But the ethnic–Jews are right, and we are wrong, when they see as quite legitimate, *Jewish* welfare activities of no particular Jewish relevance, and when they stress the value of association with other Jews for its own sake. They want thereby to preserve the group. Our regret is that they seem to have forgotten why. But the instinct is fully sound, and we critics must never forget it.

And who are these Jews, who cannot despite themselves achieve secularization? They are the bearers of an unbroken myth, a this–worldly group affirming the world and joining in its activities with religious fervor, yet regarding themselves, whether they be religious in the Christian sense or not, in terms the objective observer can regard only as other–worldly and religious. Jews see themselves as a group, though their group should have ceased to hold them when the faith lost its hold upon them, and that is a paradox. They see themselves as bound to others, in other lands and other ages, whom they have never seen, and with whom they have practically nothing in common but common forefathers. This, too, is a paradox. They see themselves as one people, their history as *one* history, though they are not everywhere involved in it. They reflect upon the apocalyptic events of the day as intimately and personally important to them. They died in Auschwitz. They rose again in the State of Israel. They passionately respond, no matter how remote they are from Judaism, to the appeal of the flesh, of Israel *after the flesh*. They view themselves in a way that no religious Jew can call secular, however secular they themselves would claim to be. This, too, is a paradox. They bear fears on account of the past, though that past is nothing to them except that it is the Jews'. They have nightmares that belong to other men, but are not within their personal experience at all, except that they are Jews. They see themselves as brands plucked from the burning, though they never stood near the fire. The classical faith demands that each man see himself as redeemed at Sinai from bondage to Pharaoh. The modern Jew, secure in America or Canada or Australia or the State of Israel, persists within the pattern of the classical faith, but in a far more relevant form of it. He was saved from Auschwitz and rebuilt the land. The ties that bind other groups of immigrants within the open societies in the West have long since attenuated. Despite the decline of faith, the ties that bind the Jews are stronger than ever, into the third and fourth and fifth generation and beyond. Nor can one ignore the mystery of Soviet Jewry, of whom we know so little and understand nothing. They persist. They ought not. All we know is that almost fifty years after the Bolshevik revolution, young people, raised in isolation from their tradition and from the Jewish world, trained to despise religion and, above all, Judaism, profess to be Jews, though they need not, and accept the disabilities of Jewishness, though these are by no means slight. Before this fact of contemporary Jewish history we must stand in silence. We cannot understand it. No worldly or naturalist explanation suffices to explain it completely. In my view, it is not a secular phenomenon at all, though it can be explained in a worldly way to the satisfaction of the world.

This is the paradox of the secular age. The Jews have said for almost two centuries that they are a religious group, and have accepted, by and large, the Christian world's criteria for religion. They have told the world they are different by virtue of religion, though they claimed that religion for them means what it means to others. And yet the secular world sees Jews who are not different from itself, for they have no professed religion. By their own word, such Jews, and they are very many, should have ceased to exist. Yet they are here, and they are Jews, and "Jewishness" is important to them in terms that the Christian and secular worlds alike find not at all "religious."

A second paradox is that the Jews have allied themselves with secularizing forces from the very beginning. Claiming to be merely Britons, Germans, French, Canadians, or Americans of the Jewish faith, they have chosen for themselves a place among those who struggled for the secularization of culture, politics, art, and society. The reason is, alas, that they had no choice. The forces of religion, meaning Christianity wherever it was established, invariably allied themselves to those of reaction, in opposing the emancipation of the Jews. Rarely do we find an exception to the rule: the more he was a Christian, the more he hated Jews. It is therefore no paradox at all that Jews have favored the secularization of institutions and of men, for if they hoped for a decent life, it was only upon a secular foundation that emancipation was possible. Even today, moreover, Christians would still prefer to use the institutions of the common society to propagate their faith. The public schools are still supposed to celebrate the great events of Christian sacred history, and Jewish children must still confront, and deny, the Christian message once or twice a year.

Christian opposition to secularization is by no means a mere vestige of earlier days. It is rather, I think, a fear of the need to believe *despite* the world, a fear of faith itself. For many centuries it has been natural to be a Christian. The world was mostly Christian, and where it was not, it was the realm of the devil and the Jews. Christians could aspire, therefore, to the creation of a metaphysic and a natural theology which, from the bare artifacts of the world, would rise, in easy stages, to the heights of Calvary. Metaphysics, religious philosophy, natural theology—these are naturally Christian enterprises, for only a Christian could conceive so benign and friendly a vision of the world that he might ask the world to strengthen, even to provide reasonable foundations within experienced reality for, his Gospel. It is no accident that Judaism has produced only a highly parochial metaphysic, very little natural theology, and a religious philosophy whose main task was to mediate between Judaism and the world.

Judaism has had to stress revelation, and not a worldly apprehension of faith, because the world for two thousand and more years has offered little solace. Judaism has had to say *no* to many worlds, though it is not therefore a habitually negating tradition. It has had to say to pagans that God is not in nature; to mighty empires that the King of Kings alone is king; to Christians that redemption is not yet; to

Bolshevism that Israel lives despite the "laws" of history. It has had to say no because of its first and single affirmation: We shall do and we shall hear. The result is that Judaism has looked, as I said, for very little help from the world. It has not presumed that the artifacts of creation would lead to Sinai; that a natural theology would explain why a Jew should keep the Sabbath or refrain from eating pork; that a communicable, non–mythological metaphysic would show Israel in a rational situation.

In its early centuries, Christianity comprehended the Jewish situation. The apostle Paul offered not a reasonable faith, beginning with worldly realities and ending at the foot of the cross. He offered a scandal to the Jews and foolishness to the Greeks, and said it was faith, and faith alone, which was demanded of the Christian. It was by virtue of that faith, for it was a very difficult thing, that the Christian would be saved. From the fourth century onward, to be a Jew was a scandal to the Christians and foolishness, later on, to Islam. It was faith despite the world, and not because of it, that Judaism required, and received. This is the kind of faith with which Christianity begins, and, I believe, which is demanded once again. The Christian today is called upon to choose between Christ and the world, for the world is no longer his. I do not say it is a better world on that account, but it *is* a different world. I do not, however, think that Judaism has suffered for its recognition and acceptance of the situation of *Golah*, of exile not only from the earthly land, but also from the ways of the world. Although Christianity is entering a time of exile, it need not greatly fear, if Christians are prepared to affirm their faith through faith, not merely through a reasoned apprehension of reality, which is not *faith* at all. As Christianity enters the Jewish situation, it need not, therefore, fear for its future. *Golah* is not a situation to be chosen, but to be accepted at the hand of God as a test of faith and an opportunity for regeneration and purification. We did not choose to go into exile, any more than the Christians would choose to abandon the world. Having gone into exile, having lost the world, Jew and Christian alike may uncover new resources of conviction, new potentialities for sanctity, than they knew they had. We who witnessed the destruction of an ancient temple learned of new means of service to the creator, that God wants mercy and not sacrifice, in Hosea's terms—deeds of loving kindness in those of Rabban Yohanan ben Zakkai. It is the world, and not the temple, that became the arena for God's work. Having lost the world, or wisely given it up, Christians, too, may recall that "the whole earth is full of His holiness," and that every day and everywhere the world provides a splendid opportunity for witness.

Finally, the advent of secularization offers still another welcome challenge to both Judaism and Christianity. In the recent past exponents of both traditions have accepted the world's criteria for the truth or value of religion, both Judaism and Christianity. In its grosser form, this acceptance has led to such arguments for religion as those that claim religion is good for one's mental health, or is important as a foundation for ethical behavior, and valuable as a basis for a group's persistence, or a nation's. In all instances religion has been evaluated for its service to something else, to health, to decency, to group solidarity. In its more refined form, the worldly argument on behalf of religion has stressed man's need of religion in the face of the absurd; or his dependence upon religion as a source of cogent and unified world–views. We have been told that religion is an answer to human needs. We are supposed to conclude that we ought therefore to foster it. These arguments represent the final blasphemy, the affirmation of faith for worldly purposes. Though Cox does not necessarily suggest it, secularization represents an inquisitorial judgment: the world does not *need* religion. It can provide a sound basis for mental health, a reasonable, though tentative, foundation for ethical action, even—as the Jewish community seems to prove—an adequate basis for group life, without faith in any form. Man does not need religion to overcome the absurd, for he can accept the absurd with the same enthusiasm and life–affirming vitality that he accepts the other artifacts of reality. He can meet his needs elsewhere than at the holy war.

We who affirm that God made the world need not claim on his behalf that he needs to have done so. We who hold that God acted freely and out of love need not deny that love and that freedom in the name of worldly rationality. Mankind does not need religion. The worldly uses of religion have far more acceptable, secular surrogates. Man does not need to believe in God to avoid insanity, or absurdity, or social disintegration. He does not need to accept revelation in terms that render revelation the result of worldly ratiocination. Mankind is challenged by the world's own power to accept or reject revelation, to affirm or deny God, upon judgment of the real issues. These issues are: Did God make the world? Does Providence govern history? Is Torah, meaning truth, from Heaven? The world cannot resolve them for us, and in the joyful acceptance of its perquisites, Jews and Christians alike are much enriched. They regain the opportunity to believe, as I said, and to assent with rejoicing to the imperative of Sinai, to accept in submission the yoke of heaven, to love God with all our heart. These have been the classical paradigms of Jewish existence. This world once more renders them vivid.

Secularization and Judaism

Judaism is both admirably equipped for, and completely unprepared for, secularization.

It is well equipped to confront an uncomprehending world, as I have said, because of the exigencies of its history. It is, moreover, able to face this world with something more constructive than ungenerous disdain. It has always regarded the world as the stage upon which the Divine drama may be enacted. The world presents Judaism with it highest challenge, to achieve sanctity within the profane, to hallow the given. For this task, Judaism comes equipped with Torah and *mitzvot*, Torah which reveals God's will for the secular world, *mitzvot* which tell us how to carry out that will. Through *mitzvah*, we sanctify the secular, not in a metaphysical sense, nor through theologizing intractable givens. One sees the setting sun and lights a candle, the one a natural perception of the course of the earth upon its axis, the other a perfectly commonplace action. But he adds, "Who has commanded us to light the Sabbath light," and the course of nature becomes transformed, and a commonplace action transforms it. We don a piece of cloth with fringes, and say, "Who has commanded us concerning fringes." That cloth is no longer like any other. It serves as a means of worshipping our Creator. We build a frail hut of branches and flowers at the autumn season, an act of quite natural celebration of the harvest. But we say, "Who has commanded us to sit in the Sukkah," and those branches become a scared shelter. Our table becomes an altar, and the commonplace and profane action of eating food becomes the occasion to acknowledge the gifts of Him who gave it. We speak of our people's humble happenings, of their going forward from slavery to freedom, but doing so is rendered by the commandments into a sacred action, a moment of communication. We open our minds to the wonders of the world, and this, too, is Torah and requires a benediction. A man takes a wife, and we proclaim the blessings of Eden, the memories of besieged Jerusalem, and the hope for future redemption. Our tradition leads us not away from the world, but rather into it, and demands that we sanctify the given, and see it as received, commanded from Heaven. All things inspire a sense of awe and call forth a benediction. Nothing is profane by nature, nor is anything intrinsically sacred, but that we make it so. The heavens tell the glory of God. The world reveals his holiness. Through *mitzvot* we respond to what the heavens say; through Torah we apprehend the revelations of the world. Judaism rejoices, therefore, at the invitation of the secular city. It has never truly known another world; and it therefore knows what its imperatives require.

Judaism has always, moreover, understood history, or social change, to be in some measure exemplifications of Divine sovereignty. It has understood daily affairs to reveal more than commonplace truths. The destruction of a worldly city was understood from prophetic times onward to be a call for penitence and *teshuvah*, return to God. The sorrows of the age were seen as the occasion for renewed inwardness, prayer, repentance, and deeds of compassion, so that men might make themselves worthy of the compassion of God. It has at the same time recognized a tension between event and Divine will. Judaism has never merely accepted history, any more than it accepted nature, but sought rather to elevate and sanctify the profane in both. History does not speak God's will in unequivocal terms, for history is to be interpreted, not merely accepted, by means of the Torah. We have seen in revelation a guide to understanding events, and have never uncritically accepted events as themselves bearing unexamined meaning. All things are seen under the aspect of Sinai, and all events must be measured by the event of revelation. We are not, therefore, at a loss to evaluate the changes of an inconstant world. We have, moreover, demanded that God, like ourselves, abide by the covenant. In times of stress, we have called Him to account, as much as ourselves. To offer a most recent example: the journal of Chaim Kaplan contains the following passage:

> There is a rumor that in one of the congregations the prayer leader came and dressed himself in a *kittel* [shroud] and prepared to lead his poor and impoverished people in the *Neilah* [closing prayers for the Day of Atonement] service, when a boy from his congregation broke in with the news about the ghetto. At once the Jew dispensed with Neilah, took off his *kittel*, and went back to his seat. There is no point in praying when the gates of mercy were locked.[3]

We have taken events so seriously that we are prepared to call God to account, and even to remind Him, as did Ezekiel, that His good name and ours are one and the same. What happens to us happens to Him; the covenant measures the loyalty of both its signatories.

Judaism has offered a worldly understanding of man's part in the achievement of God's kingdom. Man is the partner in the building of the kingdom. He is needed to perfect the world under the sovereignty of God. Just as the commonplace may be profane or sacred, but the *mitzvot* consecrate, so too the world, society, may be sanctified. That sanctification is a most practical sort. We are told to heal the sick, free the captives, loosen the bonds that enslave men. A starving world is an affront to God. All the technical skills of men possess the potentiality to achieve holiness, therefore, and all the vocations of man may serve to sanctify the world. The secular city, Professor Cox writes, requires the skill of men. The kingdom of God cannot do without men's abilities. The kingdom of God is meant to find a place in the history of this world, moreover, according to the eschatological theory of significant Jewish thinkers. The only difference between this world and the world to come, or the age to come, will be the end of subjugation to paganism, so said Samuel, the third–century Babylonian master. Israel is meant, furthermore, to live in this world, to bear witness to God in the streets of the city. For centuries, and most immediately in modern Judaism, Jews have seen themselves as bearers of the kingdom, as witnesses to the rule of God over the world. One need hardly stress, therefore, that Judaism is ready and eager for the worldly encounter.

That encounter, however, is by no means neutral. Judaism has seen itself under a very special vocation, as I said, to say *no* to the lesser claims to Divinity entertained by this world. It has told the world that sanctity inheres in it, but denied that the world as it is is holy. It has offered the world the promise of redemption, but denied that redemption is just yet. It has borne unflagging testimony to the unredemption of mankind, and insisted upon a radical criticism of the *status quo*. These are the vocations, too, of the secular city, which denies ultimacy even to religion, all the more so to lesser structures. Judaism has insisted that the world is ever secular, both so that it may be sanctified *and* so that it may not lose the hope for ultimate redemption.

And yet Judaism is utterly unready for secularization in the current sense. Professor Cox writes that secularization is "the loosing of the world from religious and quasi–religious understandings of itself, the dispelling of all closed world–views, the breaking of all supernatural myths and sacred symbols..." Nothing in my understanding of Judaism suggests that Judaism can accept, or even comprehend, "the loosing of the world from religious...understandings of itself." If from my perspective there can be no "secular Jew," then surely no "secularized Judaism" can develop, except as Judaic naturalism. But this we now have. Judaism begins with the affirmation of a religious apprehension of reality, however courageously we may try to formulate that consciousness in naturalistic or psychological or humanistic terms. It begins with the proclamation of the unity and sovereignty of God. It offers to the world the spectacle of a people bound to God's service and governed by His will. It tells the world that this people serves as the heart of humanity, the barometer of its health, and that its history becomes paradigmatic for the human condition. Judaism may cope with the world, may indeed affirm this age in the terms I have outlined; but it can never turn away from itself and its primary assent. Our prophets have offered the world the belief that at certain times God may hide his face from man. This may be such an age. We can never confuse, however, our own difficulties in belief with ontological or anthropological Godlessness. Sinai has happened. We may not have seen his face, but we have the record that His glory passed before us. Not every age has an equal apprehension of the glory. A handmaiden saw at the Red Sea what was not given to the prophets to see. We know through Torah, and can never, therefore, claim ignorance, only frail forgetfulness. We may, as Rabbi Abraham J. Heschel says, be messengers who have forgotten our message. But we can never forget that we once had a message. We may comprehend the hiddenness of God; indeed, we are those who have most suffered in His absence. We can never confuse that comprehension of *our* condition with the illusion of *His*. We have lived for a long time within the gates of the secular city. Our tradition has prepared us for, and our condition has taught us the imperatives of, its discipline. We have aspired to its liberties. But these imperatives we accept, these liberties we demand, *upon our own terms*. We are not secular within the secular city, but we are Jews, *yehudim*, upon whom the name of the Lord has been called. We cannot change our name, either to add to his discipline that of the world, or to win for ourselves the blessings of the world. In the city of this world, or in the world to come, we can only be ourselves, Jews. This is the final paradox of our current situation: we who have confronted the date of secularization long before our neighbors now rehearse our ancient response to these data. We who first told the world of its secularization now need remind it of its consecration.

Judaism and Christianity in the Secular Age

It is frequently said that we live in a post–Christian age, by which is meant that we live in an age no longer characterized by the normality of Christian vocation. How are the two traditions to cope with the new situation? What are its promises? Both faiths clearly meet parallel challenges. Indifference to religion, disbelief, a wholly worldly view of man—these are problems faced by all men who strive for religious faith. Jews and Christians have much more in common than they ever had. The world has given them a common struggle.

Jews need not, however, find the disestablishment of cultural–Christianity the occasion for rejoicing, nor quite obviously, for gloating. Christianity understood us as Jews, and gave us the privilege of martyrdom as Jews. When the new age sees us, it does not see us in the perspective of sacred history. To the Christian, our Scriptures are revealed truth. To the secularist, they are literature. The Christian finds us a question to his faith. The secularist sees us as curiosities. The Christian understands our professions. The secularist interprets them. The Christian sees in us a mystery. The secularist reduces the facts of our existence to an anomaly in the laws of sociology. Whether or not we were well off in a Christian age, we are not better off in a post–Christian age. Both are ages of unredemption, but we can say so to the Christian.

This is not, however, a time to forget the past so that we may work together in the future. It is a time to remember the past and reconsider its lessons. Christians must not ask us, or surely themselves, to gloss over the inhumanity of Christianity towards Judaism, and the indecency of Christians towards Jews. If we now turn a new page in history, it is not because we shall never review the pages already written. Jews preserve the memories of the past, because in them are enshrined consecrated hours of our loyalty to our tradition, even at the gates of death, of our capacity for piety, of our ability to love God. We can no more forget the destruction of European Jewry than we can erase from our Scriptures the destruction of Judea by the Babylonians. It is no exaggeration to say this: The Temple of our spirit that was razed at Auschwitz is no less sacred to us than the Temple of Jerusalem. It is nearer; it is a greater tragedy; and these we loved, our flesh and blood. If, however, Christians choose to take seriously the Hebrew Scriptures and the Jewish people, if they wish to achieve a reconciliation and a better way for the future, as it is clear they do, then they, too, need to remember. Their memory is not, however, meant as an act of guilt or penitence—for if it is, a Jew cannot say so—but rather, I think, an act of completion. If the anguish of Auschwitz is not a Christian anguish, as much as a Jewish anguish, then Christians by their indifference cut themselves off from the human lessons of Auschwitz, and retrospectively accept a measure of the burden of Auschwitz. More broadly phrased: if the Christian regards the Jewish people as the children of Abraham, Isaac, and Jacob, as he does, then he must want to know the story of his cousins. He must need to bear their pain, for the sake of a whole and complete apprehension of sacred history.

For their part, Jews must enlarge the dimensions of their memory. We know our own pain, but we too easily forget that we were not alone in bearing pain. At every stage of Jewish martyrdom under Christianity, many men suffered with us, Christian, Moslem, and pagan. We are all too easily enticed into the sin of judging Christianity by the deeds of Christians, and Christians by the actions of some Christians. It is not our task to lay blame for Auschwitz. The judge of all flesh will also have to come to judgement. It is not for us to say that Christianity is morally and spiritually bankrupt. It is not for us to accuse others of bearing "a criminal past." We believe, moreover, in man's capacity for atonement and regeneration. We affirm, not merely for ourselves, the call to repentance, and we believe that the children's children of Haman taught Torah in Israel. We do not believe that guilt inheres in blood. And we do not claim to have the right to apportion guilt. All men stand in need of God's mercy and forgiveness, and we are not the least of them.

We Jews cannot ignore, moreover, the varieties within Christianity as a religious tradition, and among Christians. If the record of German and Polish Christianity is unsavory, that of Danish, Dutch, and Italian Christianity is not. The same "Christianity" that produced so many centuries of antisemitism gave the world men of conscience and of charity as well. The same Scriptures which say, "His blood be upon our heads" say also "Forgive them, for they know not." Christians hold that the world, and they within it, are redeemed, and we, in our error, measure them by that claim. We Jews, however, hold that the world is unredeemed, but awaiting its redemption. Shall we therefore judge, or even understand, it according to others' counsels of perfection? If within the Churches men compromise the right because of political realities, ought we not to see it, with sadness, to be sure, as yet another testimony of worldly unredemption? It is part of our task to suffer the world, in the certain hope that we bear its sorrows. We cannot repudiate that task, though we may sorely regret the occasion for it, by a mere this–worldly response to our suffering.

Our task is quite different. We Jews have to come to a further understanding of Christianity's, and Islam's, place in sacred history. We need to ask ourselves the question: Are Christians merely "sons of Noah," or are they, as they claim to be, sons of Abraham, Isaac, and Jacob? Sons of Noah, that is, all mankind, are expected to keep the commandments not to murder, not to worship idols, not to blaspheme the name of God, not to commit adultery, not to rob; to establish courts of justice, and not to be inhumane to animals. Christians affirm these laws, but much else. It is through Christianity and Islam that the Name of God of Israel has come to vast parts of mankind. It is through Christianity and Islam that the Torah has reached distant places on earth. And the contrary needs to be said: it was *not* through Judaism. One can, of course, provide a historical explanation, that Judaism was prevented by Christianity and Islam from carrying out the sacred mission. But Judaism affirmed that prohibition, and abandoned its mission, or revised its concept of it so that, in effect, Christianity and Islam were regarded as preparing the way for monotheism among men. Medieval Jewish thinkers said exactly that. If so, one must reflect upon its implications.

In the new age, Jews are enabled to reflect upon the old. For long centuries Christians and Jews had no serious desire to talk together. Jews were held to be eternally cursed. Christians were seen as persecutors only. The task of dialogue was merely self–justification, denial of the other's claim to truth, and exchange of proof–texts to support one's own claim and destroy the other's. It now seems to some that another kind of conversation is possible. We seek not the disintegration of dogma, as H.J. Schoeps puts it,[4] but rather "real understanding . . . of spirit and truth." Two Jewish thinkers in the modern mode have come to grips with the reality of Christianity, Franz Rosenzweig and Martin Buber. Rosenzweig wrote:

> Our recognition of Christianity rests, in fact, upon Christianity, namely, upon the fact that Christianity recognizes us. It is the Torah...which is spread abroad by Bible societies. . . . What Christ and his Church mean within the world—on this point we are agreed. No one *comes* to the Father except through him. No one *comes* to the Father—but the situation is different when one need no longer come to the Father because he *is* already with him. That is the case with the nation of Israel. The nation of Israel, elected by its Father, keeps its gaze fixed beyond world and history towards that last, most distant, point where he, Israel's Father, will himself be the one and only . . . . At this point, where Christ ceases to be Lord, Israel ceases to be elect. On this day, God loses the name by which Israel alone may call upon him; God is then no longer Israel's God. But until this time it is Israel's life to anticipate this eternal day in confession of faith and action, to stand as a living symbol of this day, a nation of priests with the law, to hallow the name of God through its own holiness.[5]

Martin Buber wrote:

> If we want to express in a simple formula the difference between Jews and Christians, between Israel and the Church, we can say: The Church is grounded upon the belief that Christ has already come, redemption has been granted to man through God. We as Israel are unable to accept this belief. The Church views our position either as unwillingness to believe, a hardness of heart in a very dubious sense, or as a constraint, a fundamental limitation of ability to perceive *vis–à–vis* reality. . . . We as Israel understand our ability to accept this proclamation in another fashion. We understand the Christology of Christianity throughout as an important event which has taken place between the world above and the world below. We see Christianity as something the mystery of whose coming into the world we are unable to penetrate. But just as we know that there

is air which we breathe into our lungs, we know also that there is a space in which we move; more deeply, more genuinely, we know that the history of the world has not yet been shattered to its very core, that the world is not yet redeemed. We feel the unredemption of the world . . . for us the redemption of the world is indissolubly one with the perfecting of creation, with the establishment of a unity no longer limited in any respect, no longer suffering contradiction, realized in all the multiplicity of the world, one with the fulfilled kingdom of God.[6]

As Schoeps points out, what is important in Buber's statement for our problem is that he is prepared to say, Christianity must be understood as an "important event which has taken place between the world above and the world below." Buber speaks as "we as Israel."

Buber and Rosenzweig were attempting to formulate a *Jewish theology of Christianity*. I find it difficult to recognize how they have succeeded, although I can offer no better way. It is not enough to affirm that Christianity has brought important Jewish theological and moral teachings to the nations of the world though in a form we do not always approve. That is merely a sociological fact, which may or may not yield a theological affirmation. Rosenzweig does not help us when he says that "others" come to the Father through the Son, first, because he ignores the even more impressive role of Islam; second, because Judaism cannot be either relativized—as good only for the Jews, or ethnicized—as good for the Jews alone; and third, because Christians themselves could scarcely agree. So we have gained nothing. Buber does not explain adequately what he means by "an important event . . . between the world above and the world below." Buber seems in the end to have come to Rosenzweig's view, for he stated, "The gates of God stand open to all. The Christian need not go through Judaism, the Jew need not go through Christianity, in order to come to God." I find Schoeps' criticism wholly valid:

> Israel and Christianity *must* assert the exclusive and ultimate nature of
> the revelation granted to each on the grounds of the truth of revelation itself;
> for in fact God cannot transcend his own word, which is absolute truth, if he
> does not wish to make a mockery of human belief.[7]

A Jewish theology of Christianity must begin, therefore, with a recognition that Christianity has played a role in the history of human redemption. But the meaning of this role must remain a mystery for Jews. Schoeps points out that the two faiths come together in their eschatological expectation of God's rule on earth. In the meanwhile, they may agree to disagree. What is it that forms the Foundation for their common conversation, even for their disagreement? I think it clear that the *Tanakh* provides that foundation. Is it possible that Christians have a better understanding of its imperatives than Jews, or that the contrary is the case? Is it possible that we may illuminate the Scriptures for one another, out of the experience that each has had in history? These are not questions posed to scholarship, but posed to faith by faith.

At the same time, it is important for Jews to specify our expectations. We ask Christians to take our existence seriously, just as we must theirs. We ask that they learn about our faith, just as we must learn about theirs. Jews are afflicted with vast ignorance about Christianity. They speak of it, frequently, as if Marcionism and Manichaeism were normative and not heretical; as if the New Testament had not been studied for close to two centuries by critical and penetrating scholars; as if Jesus' claim were to be evaluated only by reference to parallel teachings in rabbinic literature. Jews must overcome much ignorance. Christians for their part, must abandon the well–worn contrast, in the words of Rabbi Robert Gordis,[8]

> between the "Old Testament Lord of Justice" and the God of Love of the New Testament. . . . Closely related to this unwarranted distinction is the widespread practice of contrasting the primitivism, tribalism, and formalism of the Old Testament with the spirituality, universalism, and freedom of the New, to the manifest disadvantage of the former. Another practice which should be surrendered is that of referring to Old Testament verses quoted in the New as original New Testament passages. . . . Finally, the dialogue between Judaism and Christianity can be mutually fruitful only if it always is kept in mind that Judaism is not the religion of the Old Testament, though obviously it is rooted in it.

Beyond the neo–Marcionism to which Rabbi Gordis raises objection lies the ancient presupposition that with the advent of Christianity, Judaism became a dead religion. I know of no facts adequate to refute such a theological opinion. It would be futile to point to the achievements of the Jewish spirit, achievements of Scriptural study, of Talmudic application of law to life, of theological inquiry. The only fact that should carry weight is this: The Jews today live to deny it, and they live as Jews. If we Jews need, as I said, to take seriously the whole record of Christianity, Christians similarly need to reckon with us, and to cease to look upon us ignorantly or malevolently, surely to cease ignoring our part of sacred history. I realize the difficulty is no less than what we face. It seems to me that the apostle Paul was first to face it, for to him are ascribed, in Romans, chapters 9 to 11, reflections upon Israel "after the flesh." Not competent in New Testament studies, I cannot, quite obviously, venture an exegesis of these passages. But I am struck by Paul's affirmation that God has not rejected his people, but rather

> Through their trespass salvation has come to the Gentiles, so as to make Israel jealous. Now if their trespass means riches for the world, and if their

failure means riches for the Gentiles, how much more will their full inclusion mean! . . . For if their rejection means the reconciliation of the world, what will their acceptance mean but life from the dead? . . . As regards the gospel they are enemies of God for your sake; but as regards election they are beloved for the sake of their forefathers. For the gifts and the call of God are irrevocable. Just as you were once disobedient to God but now have received mercy because of their disobedience, so they have now been disobedient in order that by the mercy shown to you they also may receive mercy. For God has consigned all men to disobedience, that he may have mercy upon all.

In the early generations, Jews and Christians, both weak before the power of pagan gods, spoke angrily to one another, but they spoke. The Jews reflected very little about Christianity. Rabbi Tarfon merely said, for instance, that the Jewish–Christians were to be despised because they knew God and then abandoned him. The Christians offered more thoughtful comment upon the Jews. In time, as we have seen, the two groups moved far away from one another. No longer did anger, and thus, deep concern, characterize their relationship. No longer did they see one another as erring brothers, surely not as mysteries to one another. The world has brought them back together, through the disestablishment of the daughter, and the untold suffering of the mother. It is this last, least expected event of the age of secularization which may prove, in time to come, the earliest event in the new redemptive drama.

We Jews have still another expectation. We ask not only to be taken seriously, we ask that our apocalyptic history be taken seriously. We have lived through our darkest and our brightest days. From 1933 to 1945, we suffered near–total destruction. At the portal of Auschwitz in 1945 the path did not lead to what was then Palestine. It seemed to lead nowhere. Yet within three years, the nations of the world voted, and the Jewish people created, the State of Israel. To non–Jews this is merely a political event. To Jews it is a miracle. It is no less the work of Providence than the cleansing of the Temple by the Maccabees, than the return to Zion under Joshua and Zerubbabel, indeed than the freeing of the slaves of Egypt. We see it as a mystery in the drama of redemption, and not merely—though in all honesty, it would have sufficed—as worldly balm for worldly suffering. If the exodus from Egypt is seen by Christians as a moment in sacred history, they ought to understand why we see the exodus from Auschwitz as another. If the one is sacred, so is the other. If the State of Israel is seen merely under the aspect of a secular world, then so is the entry into Canaan. We do not ourselves pretend to fathom the mystery, or to know the meaning of these days. We ask only that Christians remain open to the possibility that something of great importance has happened.

Is there no way forward? Are we to be left paralysed by the categories of traditional theology, understood in a fundamentalistic way? I think not, if we recognize, as I have implied, that Buber and Rosenzweig do not in the end provide very relevant guidelines. They make it clear that Judaism and Christianity are mutually contradictory when looked upon from the perspectives of the beginning, or the end, of time. But, as Rabbi Jacob Agus pointed out to me (in a letter, 22 August 1966), "In regard to what lies between beginning and end, that is, the actual course of history, Judaism, through Maimonides, accepted Christianity as a 'preparation for the days of the Messiah,' and Christianity, through St. Paul, accepted the existence of Israel as a providential act 'until the fullness of the Gentiles will be gathered in.' In detail, both Judaism and Christianity are complexes of ideas and judgement, which differ sometimes radically, sometimes only in nuance, and sometimes not at all."

Rabbi Agus rightly stresses the importance of focusing "upon the living people behind the official façades." He sees the error in the preceding paragraphs as "the attempt to continue a fundamentalist concept of history in a non–fundamentalist universe of discourse. The history of ancient Israel is used by us and by Christians as a *text* of religious instruction. It is an illustration of the way in which the values of faith spring out of events. This illustrative value is frankly homiletic, being independent of the objective truth of the historical event. It is our duty so to use the *text* of Scripture as to serve the ends of religious humanism. It can easily be used for opposite purposes. In the case of the New Testament, which contains in some places hostile polemics against Jews, it is the duty of Christians to interpret their text in the spirit of religious humanism. This result emerges almost inevitably from the confrontation of Christians with the kind of living Judaism that explicitly incorporates the thrust of religious humanism."

Rabbi Agus stresses that as non–fundamentalists, we need to see in history both the values of faith and its distortions. "History is placed under judgement in terms of the values of our faith," he says, adding, "So the history of the Christian conquest of the West provides illustrations aplenty of every kind of sin and of every type of heroic ardor. . . . We do regard the Christian faith as a great extension of 'ethical monotheism,' and we deplore its numerous failings, as being due in part to human nature and in part to the ambivalence of every religious heritage. Are Christians 'Israel of the spirit' as they claim to be? Yes and no, in the same way in which no Jew can claim by his descent alone to be part of 'the remnant of Israel.' For 'God looks to the heart,' and only He can tell who his saints are."

A measure of nominalism seems in order, invariably the counsel of one who, like myself, sees things mostly as an historian, and all too little as a theologian. So far as the world contains faithful Jews and faithful Christians, these today constitute "Judaism" or "Christianity," for *this* hour and in *this* place. Perhaps they represent a segment of an "eternal people" or "the Church," but surely only by their own temporal professions and measured only by their own partial witness. "Judaism" and "Christianity"—and other traditions must be seen in a similarly extreme–nominalistic way—are all too complex in their ordinary realities to be understood so cosmically and so one–dimensionally, as monolithic constructs facing one another. It is not these, but rather the faithful Jew and the faithful Christian who once again are meeting, each in the integrity of his tradition, each in his own uniqueness, but each also bearing in his soul and spirit and flesh the stigmata of a common humanity and also of uncommon faith. As people they meet to be sure, but as special kinds of people, who find each other different, for particular historical and theological reasons, from the rest of humanity, and reckon with one another differently on that account.

With these expectations met, and with the necessary theological enterprise undertaken both among Jewry and within Christendom, what do we seek? We seek an exchange of mutual respect, a respect which will be earned, and not bestowed by either upon the other. We seek to merit one another's esteem because of the intrinsic worth of each. Men of differing traditions seek to understand each other and, recognizing their differences, to live together in harmony. In these words I have paraphrased those of Moses Hadas, in his introduction to *Aristeas to Philocrates.*[9] Hadas thus describes the exchange between the "King of Egypt" and the High Priest of Jerusalem. When the Jews assemble at the table of the king—a table, incidentally, prepared according to the dietary laws of Judaism, but without great *éclat*—what is it that takes place? What is the result of mutual respect? They ate together, and discussed great questions. How might the king preserve his kingdom unimpaired to the end? What is the best course in all actions? How might the king keep his friends like–minded with himself? How might he obtain a good report even from those disappointed in their suits? How might he be invincible in warfare? What is the highest good for life? How could he endure whatever befell with equanimity? What is the goal of courage? One could go on at considerable length. It is clear from these questions—and I have not quoted the replies—that the purpose of the conversations was mutual illumination.

What are equivalent questions for today? I think it is obvious that the issues of secularization, confronted by both traditions, provide a meaningful agenda. What does it mean to affirm faith in a relativistic, pluralistic society? What does it mean "to take this earthly realm . . . in utter seriousness"? How may Israel and the Church alike carry out the task of bearing witness? of healing? of affirming the humanity of man? How, indeed, may we speak of God, separately or together, among men who cannot hear us? Just as the secular age has permitted us to come together, so it provides us with a purpose for our meeting.

But, I think, before a genuine meeting, let alone "dialogue" or "conversation" or "confrontation," can take place, Christians will have to face up to the antisemitism seemingly ingrained in their traditions and culture. Jews and Judaism are subjected now, just as before, to an uncomprehending hatred, to bigotry and prejudice. Jews are excluded from Christian, not only pagan, circles, and Judaism is still deliberately misinterpreted or discussed with an unbelievable arrogance, not to say ignorance, by Christian scholars, particularly of the New Testament. The exceptions are many, but they serve in the end to testify against the rule. In the name of Christianity Jews continue to suffer, to be judged, to be left out and ignored, to be treated in a manner Christian apologists regard as "un–Christian." How then is there place for meeting, for the inauguration of the discussion of questions and mutual interest, in the face not only of a bitter past, but an equally bitter present? When all is said and done, the time is not yet ripe for genuine theological confrontation, and I for one am not certain that we who now live will ever see that time.

Our respective traditions have much, much more to say than the secular world is able to comprehend. Can we resume the discussions cut off so tragically at the outset of the common era? What is the meaning of revelation? What is the purpose of man? What is the role of law in piety? Of faith? What is the nature of salvation? What does Scripture mean? And what does Scripture want of us? We are not limited to the agenda of today. We have a long agenda of our own, one which has been neglected far too long. If we come together once again in a neutral, secular city, which is equally indifferent to us both, we still hope together, praying each in the way he has been instructed, to see the kingdom of God, when the secular city will become His dominion, and may it come speedily and in our own time.

Notes

[1]"Secularization and the Secular Mentality: A New Challenge to Christian Education," *Religious Education* 61/2 (1966): 83. See above for another definition.

[2]"On Marrying Outside One's Existence," *Conservative Judaism* 20/2 (1966) 64.

[3]Quoted by J. A. Isaacson in *Conservative Judaism* 20/2 (1966): 87.

[4]*The Jewish Christian Argument* (New York, 1963) 126 f.

[5]Cited in Schoeps, 141.

[6]Cited in Schoeps, 150 f.

[7]Schoeps, 152–53.

[8]*The Jewish Frontier.*

[9](New York, 1951) 61.